THE COMPLETE BOOK OF
CHINESE
HOROSCOPES

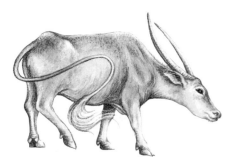

THE COMPLETE BOOK OF
CHINESE
HOROSCOPES

LORI REID

Shaftesbury, Dorset • Rockport, Massachusetts • Brisbane, Queensland

First published in Great Britain in 1997 by
ELEMENT BOOKS LIMITED
Shaftesbury, Dorset SP7 8BP

Published in the USA in 1997 by
ELEMENT BOOKS, INC.
PO Box 830, Rockport, MA 01966

Published in Australia in 1997 by
ELEMENT BOOKS LIMITED
For JACARANDA WILEY LIMITED
33 Park Road, Milton, Brisbane 4064

Designed and created with The Bridgewater Book Company

ELEMENT BOOKS LIMITED
Editorial Director: **Julia McCutchen**
Managing Editor: **Caro Ness**
Production Director: **Roger Lane**
Production Control: **Sarah Golden**

THE BRIDGEWATER BOOK COMPANY
Art Director: **Peter Bridgewater**
Designer: **Jane Lanaway**
Managing Editor: **Anne Townley**
Editor: **Margaret Crowther**
Page makeup: **Chris Lanaway**
Picture Research: **Vanessa Fletcher**
Illustrations: **Pauline Allen**

Printed and bound in Italy by Graphicom Srl

British Library Cataloguing in Publication data available

Library of Congress Cataloging in Publication
data available

ISBN 1 86204 063 X (hardback)
ISBN 1 85230 941 5 (paperback)

Acknowledgments

The publishers would like to thank the following for the use of pictures:
Bridgeman Art Library: pp. 8/9, 12/13, 20/21, 32, 50, 58, 66R, 67, 74, 80, 82, 83, 88,
89TR, 98/99, 106TR, 114/115, 118/119, 121, 122/123, 132/133. **e.t. archive**: pp. 10, 11T, 26,
26/27, 42/43, 43, 50/51, 58/59, 90/91, 99, 106/107, 114BL, 114/115. **Fine Art Photographic
Library**: pp. 25L, 39, 41, 49R, 51, 59, 61BL, 64, 73, 73T, 74/75, 79, 91, 95, 97T, 103, 105, 107,
111, 122, 123. **Hulton Getty Picture Collection**: pp. 29BL, 29C, 37BL, 37CB, 37TR, 37BR,
45TL, 45CT, 45BR, 53BL, 53TR, 53BR, 61TL, 61TL, 61BL, 69C, 69BR, 77BL, 77C, 77TR,
85TL, 85C, 85TR, 85BR, 93BL, 93TL, 93CT, 93CR, 101TL, 101TR, 109BL, 109CL, 109CR,
109BR, 117TL, 117CR. **Images/Horizon**: pp. 23, 49L, 65, 72, 96, 113. **Images Charles
Walker**: pp. 11B, 55. **Images Colour Library**: pp. 33, 40, 57, 81, 97B, 89TL. **Mirror
Syndication International**: pp. 29TL, 29TR, 29BR, 37CT, 45TR, 45CB, 53TL, 53CR, 61TL,
69BL, 69TR, 77TL, 77BR, 85BL, 93CB, 101BL, 101C, 101CL, 109TR, 117CL, 117TR, 117BL.
Zefa Picture Library: p. 56.

Contents

Introduction

Predating the Western Zodiac, Chinese horoscopes have been in use in the Orient for thousands of years and are still consulted by millions of people on a daily basis. Yet, despite its ancient history and widespread use throughout the Far East, Oriental astrology is only a recent newcomer to the West, having only begun to make its impact here some 30 years ago.

But such is the depth of wisdom contained within this fascinating and complex

subject that, even in this short space of time, Chinese horoscopes have captured the imagination of the Western mind. People are fast becoming familiar with its concepts, and many will declare that they are Monkeys or Dogs or Roosters just as easily as they might announce that they were born under the sign of Leo, Gemini, or Sagittarius.

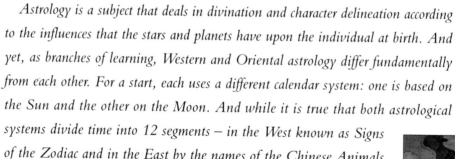

Astrology is a subject that deals in divination and character delineation according to the influences that the stars and planets have upon the individual at birth. And yet, as branches of learning, Western and Oriental astrology differ fundamentally from each other. For a start, each uses a different calendar system: one is based on the Sun and the other on the Moon. And while it is true that both astrological systems divide time into 12 segments — in the West known as Signs of the Zodiac and in the East by the names of the Chinese Animals — in the West the cycle around the Zodiac takes only 12 months to complete, while the astrological cycle of the Orient takes 12 years. Other discrepancies involve the elements, here four and there five. And then, of course, in China the principles of Yin and Yang, unfamiliar in the West, permeate all life and are quintessential to the Oriental philosophy of life.

Yet, notwithstanding the differences, there is much that each system can learn from the other. Each is a formidable analytical tool in its own right, with a valuable role to play in today's world. And each contains fundamental inner truths that are just as relevant now to you and me as they ever were to our ancestors in days gone by.

How to use this book

According to the philosophy of the Far East, luck has very little to do with the successes and failures we make of our personal lives. It is "the Animal that hides in our hearts" that explains our fortunes and characters and the way we respond to events. In the complex art of Chinese astrology there are twelve Animals organized in a 12-year cycle. Each year within the cycle has an Animal sign attributed to it, and that Animal influences both the events of the year and the character of people born within it.

PART ONE introduces the history and philosophy behind the system of Chinese horoscopes and explains how the theories of Yin and Yang and the 5 elements are applied to the astrological 12-year cycle.

The lunar year of birth is the first key to our characters. A year chart for the years from 1900 to 2007 shows which Animal and which element rules each year, and whether the year is Yin or Yang.

Each Chinese hour – a two-hour period by the Western clock – is governed by one of the 12 Animals, and this part of the book explains how the Animal hour of our birth affects our personalities.

PART TWO gives a general introduction to all the Animal characters. It then explains in detail the personality associated with each Animal in turn, and how it is modulated by each of the five elements. Health, home, career, money, likes and dislikes, friends, and behavior as parents, as lovers, and as children are all described in separate sections. A final section shows how each Animal sign is affected by the signs of the Zodiac.

PART THREE shows how the events of each year are influenced by the Animal governing that year, and gives the year-by-year Animal fortunes for each sign, covering the whole of the current cycle, from February 1996 to February 2008.

The text is illustrated throughout with pictures that aptly sum up the qualities of the Animals in the Chinese horoscope.

Key information is presented in boxed form for easy reference.

For each Animal a panel outlines how the person born under this sign is likely to get on with the others, and how the other signs are suited as love partners.

A key highlights the Animal sign under discussion for easy reference.

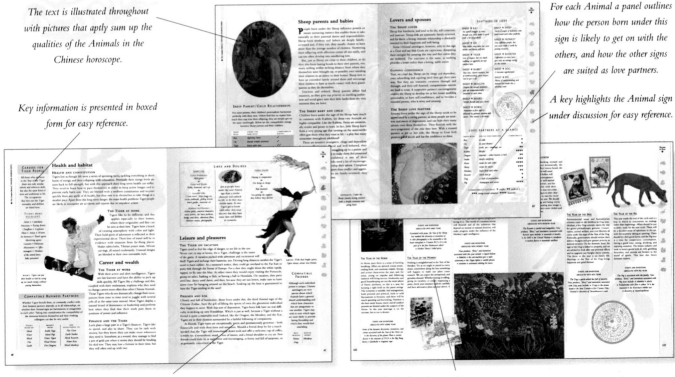

Each Animal in the horoscope is described in detail.

The final section contains a year-by-year guide to fortunes for each Animal sign in turn.

Part One

THE HISTORY
of
CHINESE HOROSCOPES

*A system of lunar months
and Animal years*

The system of Chinese astrology

The ancient Chinese calendar is a complex system, and for those used to calculating time on a solar basis, it can be difficult to grasp. Based on the phases of the Moon, each of its months lasts for either 29 or 30 days, and is divided into two two-week periods, or fortnights. Weeks consist of ten days, and each individual day is broken up into 12 2-hourly periods. Years are grouped, not into decades as in the Western world, but into cycles of 12.

In the West, the days and months have been given names to distinguish one from the other. The Chinese calendar, however, organizes the days into a complicated cycle of number combinations that are known as Heavenly Stems, of which there are 10 (denoted by the numbers 1 to 10), and Earthly Branches, of which there are 12 (written in Roman numerals I to XII). Combining these sequences of 10 and 12 time-cycle periods is a complicated affair, and, needless to say, the computations involved to reckon time according to this system would require a great deal of mathematical understanding and skill.

NAMING THE YEARS

Giving names to days, months, and years would certainly help to simplify this mathematical system, and although the exact origin is not known of when or how the exotic Animal names became substituted for the complex numbering method for the lunar years, legend has accorded this intervention to Buddha. The story goes that before the Buddha left this world he invited all the animals to join him around his table for a feast. Of all the creatures in the land, only 12 arrived. The steadfast Ox led the way, but, at the last moment, the Rat, opportunistic and fleet of foot, scampered over the Ox's back to arrive first at the Buddha's door. For their loyalty and faithfulness these animals were rewarded in perpetuity by having a year named after each one of them in order of their arrival.

So it is that each year of a 12-year cycle now has the sign of one of these 12 Animals, whose characteristics are said to influence worldly events for that year, as well as the personality and fate of each living thing that comes under its dominion. The 12 Animals run in sequence, beginning with the Rat and followed by the Ox, Tiger, Rabbit, Dragon, Snake, Horse, Sheep, Monkey, Rooster, Dog, and, last but not least, the Pig.

ABOVE *The cycle of the years imposes patterns on earthly affairs, deciphered long ago by Chinese sages. Understanding each year's influence can help us adapt to changing circumstances.*

The elements in Chinese philosophy

According to Chinese philosophy, everything and everyone is influenced by the five elements that make up all matter. These elements are Metal, Water, Wood, Fire, and Earth, and they are also known as agents or modifiers, for they have the power to subtly alter the quality or nature of whatever or whomever they represent.

MODIFYING POWERS

Metal adds fixity and strength of will to a person's character. Water encourages qualities of sensitivity and persuasiveness. Wood enhances creativity and powers of imagination. Fire produces dynamism, energy, and passion. And Earth instills stability, industry, and practicality.

A STATE OF BALANCE

Held in a state of equilibrium, the elements produce order and harmony in the universe. For this reason, a person is considered well-balanced if in life he or she is represented by all, or at least by as many as possible, of the five. These may be accounted for by the elements that rule the year in which the individual was born, the Animal sign, the season and even the day of birth. If there is a noticeable imbalance or deficiency of a particular element in a person's makeup, measures should be taken to compensate for it. For example, marrying someone who has a predominance of the element in question may be one such reparative strategy, or working in a profession where the lacking element is prevalent. For someone who has a dearth of Metal in his or her horoscope, becoming a silversmith, for instance, would go a long way toward balancing that person's personality.

ABOVE *The dualities of Yin and Yang are represented in the intertwined symbol. These forces govern the whole universe and every aspect of life.*

BELOW *The twelve Animal years follow each other in strict order, with Yin years coming after their paired Yang years, from Rat and Ox to Dog and Pig.*

YIN AND YANG

In Chinese philosophy, Yin and Yang are the terms given to the dynamic, complementary forces that keep the universe in balance at every level, from macrocosm to microcosm, and which are the central principles behind all forms of life. In a completely value-free way, Yin is seen as feminine and described as passive and negative, associated with water, night, and the Moon, while Yang is seen as masculine and described as positive, active, and associated with day, fire, and the Sun. But all Yin contains an element of Yang, and Yang likewise contains Yin, as represented by the central spots in the Yin-Yang symbol. The two forces interrelate, dominating and yielding to each other and waxing and waning like day and night, summer and winter, birth and death. Yin attracts Yang and Yang attracts Yin. Balance between the two is the key to harmony, and if you are aware of your Yin-Yang aspect in terms of your lunar year of birth, you can temper your responses and behavior to encourage a harmonious balance and avoid disastrous excesses or disharmony in your life.

The year of birth

Animal years, according to the Chinese calendar, are grouped into blocks of 12, with the years always following in the same order, beginning with the Year of the Rat and ending with the Year of the Pig.

YIN AND YANG YEARS

Additionally, as well as an Animal ruler, each year is also assigned a negative or positive polarity, with alternate years being known as either Yin or Yang years. Each Animal year is constantly linked to its own particular polarity, but is also traditionally governed by one of the five elements, which puts a subtle spin on the characteristics of that year.

Every Animal year is complementary to the one that follows it – in short, every Yin year follows a Yang year. The opportunistic Rat is always a Yang sign and is linked with the hard-working Ox, which is Yin in nature. The spirited Yang Tiger is coupled with the gentle, creative Yin Rabbit, and so on with the next four pairs of Animals. Thus, as the Moon is to the Sun or the Day to the Night, each sign in a pair is a mirror image of the other; each balances the other. Meanwhile, the five Chinese elements, each of which influences two years in turn, are overlaid on this cycle, each element following on from the one before in strict rotation.

THE SEQUENCE OF THE ELEMENTS

The full cycle begins with a Wood Rat Year, and looking at the sequence already in force in the year 1900, we can see that that Rat Year was Yang and was influenced by Metal. The succeeding Ox Year was Yin and was also influenced by Metal. But the following Tiger Year, again Yang, was governed by Water, like the next, Yin, year (the Rabbit), and so on, through Wood, Fire, and Earth, to end that sequence on Metal.

It can be seen that the next group of 12 years, again headed by the Yang Rat, was this time influenced by the Water element to begin with. The subsequent Rat year, 12 years later, was influenced by Wood, the next by Fire and the next by Earth, until we start the whole process afresh again in 1960 with the Yang Metal Rat, as in the year 1900.

Thus, the combination of Animal signs, elements and Yin-Yang polarity together forms a cycle that takes 60 years to complete. The present 60-year cycle began with the Wood Rat in 1984 and ends in 2044.

THE HOUR OF BIRTH

While your year of birth describes your fundamental character, the Animal governing the actual hour in which you were born describes your outer temperament – how people see you or the picture you present to the outside world. The traditional Chinese system of dividing the day into 12 equal portions results in 12 "double hours," with the mid-point, noon, occurring in the middle of the middle double hour. This is the system that is applied to the Chinese horoscope.

The significance of the birth hour in the horoscope reading dates back about 2,500 years, although the Animal names were not given to the hours themselves until more recently. The double hour 11am–12:59pm is now the "Horse hour," 11pm–12:59am the "Rat hour," and so on. Note that each Animal rules over two consecutive hours by the Western clock and that these are standard times, so that adjustments need to be made for people who were born during Summer or daylight saving time.

11PM – 12:59AM ✎ RAT

This hour is known as Tzu. The Tzu birth hour produces characters who are generally pleasant, sociable, and easy to get along with. The Rat-hour person comes across as being active, confident, busy, and successful – but can be a bit of a busybody to boot, and is inclined to be hot-tempered.

1AM – 2:59AM ✎ OX

This hour is known as Ch'ou. People born in the Ch'ou hour tend to be level-headed and down-to-earth. Other people find them to be knowledgeable and reliable – but sometimes a bit biased. They may seem to attract ill-fortune when young, but this is usually reversed later in life.

3AM – 4:59AM ✎ TIGER

This hour is known as Yin. People born in this hour are enthusiastic and self-assured. Others see them as having a strong and positive personality – which can at times be a little over-exuberant. For this reason, family relationships can be difficult for people born at this hour.

5AM – 6:59AM ⟣ RABBIT

This hour is known as Mao. Mao hour people are generally sensitive and shy and do not project their real selves to the world, always feeling they have to put on an act to please others. Their confidence and success in close relationships usually develops as they mature.

7AM – 8:59AM ⟣ DRAGON

This hour is known as Ch'en. The Dragon hour of birth conveys independence and makes for interesting people who also come across as colorful and unusual. People born at this time can have an over-supply of self-confidence, which other people may find irritating.

9AM – 10:59AM ⟣ SNAKE

This hour is known as Zu. The Zu hour conveys great talent, but it can also make people a bit difficult for others to fathom, because they appear so controlled. Other people either take to Snake-hour individuals instantly or do not like them at all, although to those who like them and whom they like, they make kind and thoughtful friends.

11AM – 12:59PM ⟣ HORSE

This hour is known as Wu. People born in the Wu hour always appear to others as open, cheerful, happy-go-lucky individuals. These people are extroverts, and it generally shows – on the go and clever, they can also be obstinate.

1PM – 2:59PM ⟣ SHEEP

This hour is known as Wei. Wei-hour people have an unassuming nature that doesn't allow them to foist themselves upon others, so that people see them as quiet and retiring, but eminently sensible. Sometimes over-reserved, they are family-orientated and feel better in company than alone.

3PM – 4:59PM ⟣ MONKEY

This hour is known as Shen. The monkey character produces people who are lively and talkative, with a twinkle in the eye that guarantees they make friends wherever they go. This birth hour can make people lively and active, but also easily bored.

5PM – 6:59PM ⟣ ROOSTER

This hour is known as Yu. Rooster-hour people usually have something rather stylish in their approach and create an impression of elegance and glamor. But they don't suffer fools gladly, and they often find it difficult to get along with others during their youth – perhaps because they always want to rule the roost.

7PM – 8:59PM ⟣ DOG

This hour is known as Hsü. To some, Dog-hour people seem steady and reliable; to others they are quiet and graceful, while to others still they may come across as dull and unimaginative. It all depends on the individual's point of view. Those born at this hour are hard-working and capable – sometimes to the point of doggedness – and are always ready to help anyone in need.

9PM – 10:59PM ⟣ PIG

This hour is known as Hai. People born at this time have a laid-back manner that conceals a depth of interest, cultivation, and intelligence that doesn't always come through at first. While they may have few close friends, they have great warmth and they never harbor grudges.

Year chart

In the Oriental calendar, which is based on the movement of the moon, New Year's Day does not fall on a fixed date, although it always occurs in January or February of the Western year. The following chart shows the first and last dates of each Chinese Year from 1900 to 2007. It also shows by which Animal sign each is ruled, whether the year is Yin or Yang, and which of the five elements modifies it.

Year	From – To	Animal sign	Element	Aspect	
1900	31 Jan 1900 – 18 Feb 1901	Rat	Metal	+	Yang
1901	19 Feb 1901 – 7 Feb 1902	Ox	Metal	–	Yin
1902	8 Feb 1902 – 28 Jan 1903	Tiger	Water	+	Yang
1903	29 Jan 1903 – 15 Feb 1904	Rabbit	Water	–	Yin
1904	16 Feb 1904 – 3 Feb 1905	Dragon	Wood	+	Yang
1905	4 Feb 1905 – 24 Jan 1906	Snake	Wood	–	Yin
1906	25 Jan 1906 – 12 Feb 1907	Horse	Fire	+	Yang
1907	13 Feb 1907 – 1 Feb 1908	Sheep	Fire	–	Yin
1908	2 Feb 1908 – 21 Jan 1909	Monkey	Earth	+	Yang
1909	22 Jan 1909 – 9 Feb 1910	Rooster	Earth	–	Yin
1910	10 Feb 1910 – 29 Jan 1911	Dog	Metal	+	Yang
1911	30 Jan 1911 – 17 Feb 1912	Pig	Metal	–	Yin
1912	18 Feb 1912 – 5 Feb 1913	Rat	Water	+	Yang
1913	6 Feb 1913 – 25 Jan 1914	Ox	Water	–	Yin
1914	26 Jan 1914 – 13 Feb 1915	Tiger	Wood	+	Yang
1915	14 Feb 1915 – 2 Feb 1916	Rabbit	Wood	–	Yin
1916	3 Feb 1916 – 22 Jan 1917	Dragon	Fire	+	Yang
1917	23 Jan 1917 – 10 Feb 1918	Snake	Fire	–	Yin
1918	11 Feb 1918 – 31 Jan 1919	Horse	Earth	+	Yang
1919	1 Feb 1919 – 19 Feb 1920	Sheep	Earth	–	Yin
1920	20 Feb 1920 – 7 Feb 1921	Monkey	Metal	+	Yang
1921	8 Feb 1921 – 27 Jan 1922	Rooster	Metal	–	Yin
1922	28 Jan 1922 – 15 Feb 1923	Dog	Water	+	Yang
1923	16 Feb 1923 – 4 Feb 1924	Pig	Water	–	Yin
1924	5 Feb 1924 – 24 Jan 1925	Rat	Wood	+	Yang
1925	25 Jan 1925 – 12 Feb 1926	Ox	Wood	–	Yin
1926	13 Feb 1926 – 1 Feb 1927	Tiger	Fire	+	Yang
1927	2 Feb 1927 – 22 Jan 1928	Rabbit	Fire	–	Yin
1928	23 Jan 1928 – 9 Feb 1929	Dragon	Earth	+	Yang
1929	10 Feb 1929 – 29 Jan 1930	Snake	Earth	–	Yin
1930	30 Jan 1930 – 16 Feb 1931	Horse	Metal	+	Yang
1931	17 Feb 1931 – 5 Feb 1932	Sheep	Metal	–	Yin
1932	6 Feb 1932 – 25 Jan 1933	Monkey	Water	+	Yang
1933	26 Jan 1933 – 13 Feb 1934	Rooster	Water	–	Yin
1934	14 Feb 1934 – 3 Feb 1935	Dog	Wood	+	Yang
1935	4 Feb 1935 – 23 Jan 1936	Pig	Wood	–	Yin
1936	24 Jan 1936 – 10 Feb 1937	Rat	Fire	+	Yang
1937	11 Feb 1937 – 30 Jan 1938	Ox	Fire	–	Yin
1938	31 Jan 1938 – 18 Feb 1939	Tiger	Earth	+	Yang
1939	19 Feb 1939 – 7 Feb 1940	Rabbit	Earth	–	Yin
1940	8 Feb 1940 – 26 Jan 1941	Dragon	Metal	+	Yang
1941	27 Jan 1941 – 14 Feb 1942	Snake	Metal	–	Yin
1942	15 Feb 1942 – 4 Feb 1943	Horse	Water	+	Yang
1943	5 Feb 1943 – 24 Jan 1944	Sheep	Water	–	Yin
1944	25 Jan 1944 – 12 Feb 1945	Monkey	Wood	+	Yang
1945	13 Feb 1945 – 1 Feb 1946	Rooster	Wood	–	Yin
1946	2 Feb 1946 – 21 Jan 1947	Dog	Fire	+	Yang
1947	22 Jan 1947 – 9 Feb 1948	Pig	Fire	–	Yin

ABOVE AND FAR RIGHT *The lunar year of birth dictates which Animal a person is ruled by and the dominant characteristics shared by all people born in that particular year.*

Year	From – To	Animal sign	Element	Aspect	
1948	10 Feb 1948 – 28 Jan 1949	Rat	Earth	+	Yang
1949	29 Jan 1949 – 16 Feb 1950	Ox	Earth	–	Yin
1950	17 Feb 1950 – 5 Feb 1951	Tiger	Metal	+	Yang
1951	6 Feb 1951 – 26 Jan 1952	Rabbit	Metal	–	Yin
1952	27 Jan 1952 – 13 Feb 1953	Dragon	Water	+	Yang
1953	14 Feb 1953 – 2 Feb 1954	Snake	Water	–	Yin
1954	3 Feb 1954 – 23 Jan 1955	Horse	Wood	+	Yang
1955	24 Jan 1955 – 11 Feb 1956	Sheep	Wood	–	Yin
1956	12 Feb 1956 – 30 Jan 1957	Monkey	Fire	+	Yang
1957	31 Jan 1957 – 17 Feb 1958	Rooster	Fire	–	Yin
1958	18 Feb 1958 – 7 Feb 1959	Dog	Earth	+	Yang
1959	8 Feb 1959 – 27 Jan 1960	Pig	Earth	–	Yin
1960	28 Jan 1960 – 14 Feb 1961	Rat	Metal	+	Yang
1961	15 Feb 1961 – 4 Feb 1962	Ox	Metal	–	Yin
1962	5 Feb 1962 – 24 Jan 1963	Tiger	Water	+	Yang
1963	25 Jan 1963 – 12 Feb 1964	Rabbit	Water	–	Yin
1964	13 Feb 1964 – 1 Feb 1965	Dragon	Wood	+	Yang
1965	2 Feb 1965 – 20 Jan 1966	Snake	Wood	–	Yin
1966	21 Jan 1966 – 8 Feb 1967	Horse	Fire	+	Yang
1967	9 Feb 1967 – 29 Jan 1968	Sheep	Fire	–	Yin
1968	30 Jan 1968 – 16 Feb 1969	Monkey	Earth	+	Yang
1969	17 Feb 1969 – 5 Feb 1970	Rooster	Earth	–	Yin
1970	6 Feb 1970 – 26 Jan 1971	Dog	Metal	+	Yang
1971	27 Jan 1971 – 15 Jan 1972	Pig	Metal	–	Yin
1972	16 Jan 1972 – 2 Feb 1973	Rat	Water	+	Yang
1973	3 Feb 1973 – 22 Jan 1974	Ox	Water	–	Yin
1974	23 Jan 1974 – 10 Feb 1975	Tiger	Wood	+	Yang
1975	11 Feb 1975 – 30 Jan 1976	Rabbit	Wood	–	Yin
1976	31 Jan 1976 – 17 Feb 1977	Dragon	Fire	+	Yang
1977	18 Feb 1977 – 6 Feb 1978	Snake	Fire	–	Yin
1978	7 Feb 1978 – 27 Jan 1979	Horse	Earth	+	Yang
1979	28 Jan 1979 – 15 Feb 1980	Sheep	Earth	–	Yin
1980	16 Feb 1980 – 4 Feb 1981	Monkey	Metal	+	Yang
1981	5 Feb 1981 – 24 Jan 1982	Rooster	Metal	–	Yin
1982	25 Jan 1982 – 12 Feb 1983	Dog	Water	+	Yang
1983	13 Feb 1983 – 1 Feb 1984	Pig	Water	–	Yin
1984	2 Feb 1984 – 19 Feb 1985	Rat	Wood	+	Yang
1985	20 Feb 1985 – 8 Feb 1986	Ox	Wood	–	Yin
1986	9 Feb 1986 – 28 Jan 1987	Tiger	Fire	+	Yang
1987	29 Jan 1987 – 16 Feb 1988	Rabbit	Fire	–	Yin
1988	17 Feb 1988 – 5 Feb 1989	Dragon	Earth	+	Yang
1989	6 Feb 1989 – 26 Jan 1990	Snake	Earth	–	Yin
1990	27 Jan 1990 – 14 Feb 1991	Horse	Metal	+	Yang
1991	15 Feb 1991 – 3 Feb 1992	Sheep	Metal	–	Yin
1992	4 Feb 1992 – 22 Jan 1993	Monkey	Water	+	Yang
1993	23 Jan 1993 – 9 Feb 1994	Rooster	Water	–	Yin
1994	10 Feb 1994 – 30 Jan 1995	Dog	Wood	+	Yang
1995	31 Jan 1995 – 18 Feb 1996	Pig	Wood	–	Yin
1996	19 Feb 1996 – 7 Feb 1997	Rat	Fire	+	Yang
1997	8 Feb 1997 – 27 Jan 1998	Ox	Fire	–	Yin
1998	28 Jan 1998 – 15 Feb 1999	Tiger	Earth	+	Yang
1999	16 Feb 1999 – 4 Feb 2000	Rabbit	Earth	–	Yin
2000	5 Feb 2000 – 23 Jan 2001	Dragon	Metal	+	Yang
2001	24 Jan 2001 – 11 Feb 2002	Snake	Metal	–	Yin
2002	12 Feb 2002 – 31 Jan 2003	Horse	Water	+	Yang
2003	1 Feb 2003 – 21 Jan 2004	Sheep	Water	–	Yin
2004	22 Jan 2004 – 8 Feb 2005	Monkey	Wood	+	Yang
2005	9 Feb 2005 – 28 Jan 2006	Rooster	Wood	–	Yin
2006	29 Jan 2006 – 17 Feb 2007	Dog	Fire	+	Yang
2007	18 Feb 2007 – 6 Feb 2008	Pig	Fire	–	Yin

Part Two

THE CHINESE
ANIMALS

Each year is governed by one of

the twelve Animals and has its

own particular character

Introducing the Animals

The Chinese believe that the events of the years are affected by cosmic influences in a cyclical 12-year pattern, which the ancient astrologers discovered was linked to Jupiter's orbit around the Sun. Over time, it was observed that people born in each particular year were similarly affected by these influences, and, moreover, that people born in the same year shared characteristics and personality traits that were significantly different to those of people born in other years. When the years of the twelve-year cycle were given their names, it was no accident, then, that the ancient sages chose the Animals they did to symbolize the years, for each was judged to embody most aptly the collective characteristics associated with the year it represented.

By understanding the Animal governing our year of birth we can gain powerful insights into our own personalities, our talents and abilities, our likes and dislikes, our relationships and preferred way of life. But in getting to know our "Animal nature" we must bear in mind that the Chinese have a very different attitude from ours to many of these Animals. In our journey through the Chinese horoscopes, we must remember, therefore, not to judge the Animals with our Western preconceptions, but to learn their true significance as seen through Oriental eyes.

RAT

Outwardly cool but charming and sociable, Rats are always at their ease in company and get on well in groups of people, both at work and socially. Endowed

with intelligence, observant, and imaginative, Rats are quick to grasp the situation, and can readily size up what is going on from everybody's point of view. This enables them to give good advice to others who are slower to catch on, though they may at times say more than others wish to hear. While Rats are normally very self-controlled, they can't resist the chance to take advantage of opportunities, and with their perspicacity, these can be many! This can send them scurrying about chasing too many tails at once. They make passionate lovers with a depth of feeling that others often do not recognize.

OX

The Ox shoulders the plow and sturdily and uncomplainingly plows his or her own – sometimes rather lonely – furrow through life. Ox people can be "loners" who have little time for society, but they are strong, dutiful, and reliable types who form firm bonds with home and family and cherish their private lives. Not usually very adventurous, they like staying at home and working in their backyards, which they do with method and application. Sometimes the Ox's strength comes out in great shows of obstinacy or determination, and the Ox will always stoutly defend what he or she thinks is right. This is not necessarily the most romantic of the signs, but Ox people make steadfast lovers and faithful, affectionate partners and spouses.

TIGER

Tigers have passion, strength, speed, and courage – and a restless love of freedom. They need independence and they also like to dominate. They need to occupy powerful positions and are not afraid of meeting a challenge head-on. Tiger people dislike routine and anything that seems to them petty. They can be restless, always on the prowl, and not settling to anything for long, but they will also be prepared to sniff out and stalk what they want and take a bold leap for it when the moment seems right. Tigers make honest, generous friends, and passionate and sensual lovers. Flirty when young, once committed they make stable partners who keep their sexual allure and become good parents.

RABBIT

Peace-loving rabbits (or Hares, or cats, as they are sometimes called) generally like to keep out of arguments, even if at times it means turning a blind eye and a deaf ear to the situation. As a result, they can be very diplomatic, and also good at negotiating. Gentle, emotional, and even sentimental, Rabbits can also be quite selfish in the pursuit of their own pleasure, although they would not deliberately hurt anyone else in the process. While their diplomatic skills usually prevent them showing it, Rabbits can be badly hurt by thoughtless treatment or criticism from others. They present a well-groomed appearance, and are well-mannered, but they also like to play and their love of fun can take people by surprise at times. The Rabbit's strength is in observing the game, assessing the situation, and coming up with a solution or innovation when the time is ripe. Rabbits make sensitive lovers. They are shrewd and seek a partner who offers the security they need in life.

DRAGON

Dragons are exceptional creatures, but they can be proud, over-assertive, and intolerant of other people. Whether breathing fire or generally causing a stir, the Dragon person often attracts, and enjoys, attention, and is also more at home in demanding situations that require assertive action than in routine, everyday business. Dragon folk are self-reliant and can throw a lot of energy into dealing with the demands of the moment – to the point where they can get carried away and make misjudgements through impulsiveness, tiredness, or lack of consultation. From partners they get as much stimulation through empathy as they do from sex. Consequently, a companion on the same wavelength is essential to the Dragon.

SNAKE

Wise and meditative, the Snake may lie in coils for hours and then effortlessly dart out his or her tongue. Snake people usually know what they want and go and get it in their own good time with apparent ease, and certainly without hurrying. At their own chosen time, they may also shed their skins and take up something completely new. This ties in with Snake people's secretive or mistrustful side: others may be put off by the way they are never let into the confidence of a Snake person. Snake people may like to show off their social side, but they have a strong need to be left alone, too, and they also need to rest quietly after periods of activity. Passionate and strongly sexed, Snakes are attracted to elegant, refined partners, but they are deeply jealous and can be dauntingly possessive.

HORSE

Horse-born people are usually lively and popular, mentally alert, good with words, and also straight and honest. They seek success and enjoy a challenge, but can suddenly shy away with a jump or a kick of their heels and canter off in search of freedom, especially if they feel that they are being subordinated or expected to do things that to them seem pointless. At the same time they are prepared to devote tireless energy to making a success of something they have chosen for themselves, or feel committed to, without counting their time. Horse people rarely worry about being settled and generally like to be traveling or on the move, which can lead to an erratic or changeful way of life. For Horse people, love is blind. In losing their hearts, they lose their heads and often make several mistakes before finding the right partner.

SHEEP

Sheep-born people (or Goats, as they are sometimes called) dislike being hurried or to be put under pressure. They can be very charming, but sometimes hold back and do not let their emotions speak, so that others do not fully appreciate their true natures. Although they can be adaptable and sure-footed when they need to be, they do like stability and prefer to live and work in the company of other people. Of mild manner, even perhaps a little shy, the Sheep person has ready sympathy for anyone down on their luck. Lovers of nature and the arts, Sheep people can be so timid that they can be very easily hurt and upset, especially by anything that appears to be a confrontation. Domesticated home-lovers, they are made for marriage and find emotional satisfaction with a partner who provides them with security in life.

MONKEY

Bright, clever, inventive, witty, sometimes a bit of a tease, and so crafty, Monkeys are capable of deceiving others if it suits them. These people are fast learners, quick on the draw, and are adaptable to many circumstances. They are generally gregarious and readily communicative, and often have a gift for languages or the gift of the gab. Some people find Monkeys' wit and originality irresistible, while others may find them a bit too smart, and mistrust them for their inquisitiveness, their ability to pull a fast one, and their restless ways. Monkey people have wide interests, which sometimes makes them dart from one thing to another at the drop of a hat. They are not cut out for the 9-to-5 routine, and need partners who will be able to keep them stimulated.

ABOVE *Despite the huge variety of human personalities we can still observe some very distinct types.*

ROOSTER

Rooster people are a little flamboyant, have good bearing, a sense of their own dignity, a love of forward planning, and no hesitation in raising their voices and speaking up when they feel like it. They are honest and reliable, if at times a little too outspoken for everybody's liking. Conscientious and hard-working, Rooster people are usually very efficient at their work, although they can sometimes get bogged down in details. They also enjoy taking part in social occasions, especially when getting dressed up in their finest feathers is involved, and they often find themselves the center of attention. Their stylish good looks guarantee that Roosters will attract many suitors, but, once committed, they make loyal, level-headed partners who take a rational approach to their relationships.

DOG

Most Dog people are cheerful and forthright, direct and honest, and, above all, loyal. They have a sense of justice and fair play, and like helping others. Always alert, Dog people are normally good at assessing the situation, yet when things go wrong, they are also prone to worrying. They are particularly good at rounding up problems and finding logical solutions to them. Good at conversation, Dog people make good companions and trustworthy friends, but when hurt will gnaw away at their grievances until they feel appeased. Even so, many Dogs will not forget in a hurry. Normally sensible, level-headed, and reliable in a crisis, Dog people can sometimes flare up into a temper, which is usually soon forgotten. A loving, stable relationship is an essential component in the lives of Dogs. Once they have found their mate, they remain faithful for life.

PIG

Pig – or Boar – people are kind, honest, generous, and good-humored, as well as having an excellent sense of fun and a talent for making jokes. They usually love their homes, and often these are far from being pig-pens – although some Pigs are quite cheerful about not being able to keep house. This may be because they also like indulging in their pleasures and would rather spend their time and money buying, preparing, and eating good food. Steady, patient, and enduring, good at organizing without being bossy, Pig people are very trusting and entirely trustworthy themselves. They generally love their homes, but when it comes to love they can also be sensual hedonists who enjoy making love between satin sheets, with caviar and champagne close by.

The Rat

YEARS OF THE RAT

First in the cycle, Rat Years begin the sequence and recur every twelfth year thereafter. Since the Chinese New Year starts on a different date each year, it is essential to check the calendar to find the exact day on which each Rat Year begins.

1900 ★ 1912 ★ 1924
1936 ★ 1948
1960 ★ 1972 ★ 1984
1996 ★ 2008

ABOVE *The resourceful Rat, first in the Chinese horoscope, is quick and clever.*

The Rat personality

Forget Western ideas of rats: from the point of view of the Chinese horoscope, being born a Rat is certainly nothing to be ashamed of. In China the rat is not despised, as in the West, but very much respected. Rats are not considered dirty or cowardly, but rather they are viewed as clever, resourceful, and brave, and it is considered an honor to be governed by their esteemed influence.

Rats are clever creatures. They know instinctively where to find the fat sacks of grain and flour upon which to feast in times of plenty. And when corn is scarce, they know where to forage for other rich pickings. They use their innate stealth and intelligence, as well as their astute powers of observation and their daring, to raid the best supplies available. Such resourcefulness ensures that these creatures are always among nature's great survivors.

THE SIGN OF THE RAT

The characteristics of the sign of the Rat are shown in the panel below. Being born under this sign confers many talents, as well as other, less admirable characteristics that have to be watched and kept in check or turned to good use. Rat people are very active and need a lot of stimulation. They can be cool and wise, but sometimes their active brains can produce in them a mental restlessness, and this can mean that they are tempted to take on too much, only to find in time that they are unable to meet all their commitments. That Rat people are clever is undeniable; they are blessed with one of the best intellects going. And to their quick intelligence, plus curiosity and considerable imagination, is added a penetrative insight that makes them seem as sharp as a new pin.

TAKING THE LEAD

The sign of the Rat being the first sign in the cycle imbues Rat people with leadership qualities; they actually like to be first and are good at taking the lead. Responsibility sits well on their shoulders and they have a strong presence that others respect. For those with the Rat nature, however, power and money are the greatest driving forces.

FACTS ABOUT RATS

People born in the Year of the Rat share specific characteristics that are common to all other Rats. To say that someone is a Rat is simply a shorthand way of describing that individual's personality. Here are the salient features associated with this sign.

RAT FACTS
*First in order ★ Chinese name – SHU, Sign of charm
Hour – 11pm–12:59am ★ Month – December
Western counterpart – Sagittarius*

CHARACTERISTICS
*Charisma ♥ Affability ♥ Intelligence ♥ Sociability
Quick-wittedness ♥ Popularity*

*Exploitation ✷ Deviousness ✷ Calculation ✷ Secretiveness
Greed ✷ Acquisitiveness*

IN YOUR ELEMENT

In addition to the Animal signs which recur once every 12 years, the 5 Chinese elements of Metal, Water, Wood, Fire, and Earth also play their part. This means that a 5-year cycle of characteristics is overlaid on the original 12-year cycle. The Rat birth year is the first guide to the personality as determined by the Chinese horoscope, but the characteristics of each generation of Rat are slightly modified by one of the elements, depending on the overlaying of the 5-year cycle.

THE METAL RAT 1900 AND 1960

Of all the elemental Rats, these are the strongest and most purposeful. They are also intensely idealistic and have a matching emotional intensity that can lead to strong feelings of anger, jealousy, or possessiveness. They like, and are good at, being in charge, and can act single-mindedly – even selfishly – to achieve what they want. In partnerships – whether business or personal – they can be stubborn or unyielding. It would help Metal Rats to bear in mind that aiming to meet their partner halfway would make their personal relationships considerably smoother. They usually feel very strongly about their homes and take great pleasure in decorating them in their impressively good taste.

THE WATER RAT 1912 AND 1972

Being governed by the Water element means that these Rats have the knack of influencing other people. With their strong intellectual powers and great mental acumen, they are also great puzzle and problem solvers. But they are quick to understand other people, as well as abstract problems, and are also innately practical people. They apply these talents to their everyday lives, making them accommodating, understanding, and sympathetic to other people. Amenable and flexible, they are generally liked and respected by everyone. Like all Rats, however, they can be keen to seek their own gain, and will not mind using these talents to achieve it – though generally without losing anyone's respect in doing so.

THE WOOD RAT 1924 AND 1984

Despite having an impressive façade of self-assurance, deep down, Wood Rats are probably the least confident of all the elemental Rats. However, they certainly wouldn't dream of showing this to all and sundry – only those close to a Wood Rat would ever suspect that he or she had such a thing as self-doubt. In fact they are often worried about failure, despite their aptitude for finding success. Popular, capable, and good leaders at work, Wood Rats nevertheless function best when they have the protective security of family around them. Friendly and sensitive, they are generally well-loved by family, friends, and colleagues.

THE FIRE RAT 1936 AND 1996

The Fire element adds a distinct touch of impulsiveness and great energy to the already lively Rat. These Rats have a love of change and travel and are always getting excited about new projects or setting off to see new places. Fire Rats are likely to change their jobs and addresses more often than most, and are definitely people unhappy with routine. They can be impatient as well as impulsive, but their enthusiasm for life is quite infectious, and they have the Rat's ability to get on smoothly with others. In comparison to other Rats, Fire Rats are likely to be more generous, independent, and dynamic – and the least self-disciplined.

THE EARTH RAT 1948 AND 2008

This affinity supplies a solid element to the Rat personality. An Earth Rat is conservative and a good achiever who likes to put down roots early on and then work toward a secure future for himself and his family. These Rats have the typical Rat cleverness and mental ability, but a strong sense of realism generally prevents them from chasing anything that could be fly-by-night. Earth Rats have great integrity and love of stability. A steady accumulation of wealth through life gives them peace of mind. Although not the most generous of the elemental groups, and capable of being downright stingy with money, they nevertheless have very warm relations with those close to them.

Health and habitat

HEALTH AND CONSTITUTION

The influence of the sign of the Rat is active, and conveys enough stamina to fight any illness that may arise. However, all Rats tend to be highly-strung, full of nervous energy, fretful, and prone to tension and stress. Also, Rats share an undercurrent of aggression, even if they generally manage to keep it well under control. This will find a beneficial release in active sports. Practicing yoga or meditation would also help Rats to calm their aggressive feelings and combat stress.

THE RAT AT HOME

A Rat person makes a good homemaker who is always willing to share the household chores. Rats are not usually very interested in keeping up with the Joneses, and to them it doesn't matter whether or not their furnishings are up-to-date. What does matter, though, is that their home is warm, comfortable, and in good taste. Light blue is likely to be prominent in their choice of décor. And because this is the sign of acquisition, the Rat person's house is probably bursting with many knick-nacks collected over the years. Most Rats are happy, domesticated individuals who find joy in their home and family.

Career and wealth

THE RAT AT WORK

The Chinese say that, as an advisor, the Rat should always be listened to. It is well recognized that with their quick intelligence and powers of observation, Rat people possess vision and foresight. They can see problems clearly, and are always able to take a broad view. They can home in on the issues in question and make objective and dispassionate judgements.

The same skills combined with their sense of ambition also make them shrewd operators. Power, money, position, and prestige are all important to the Rat, and Rat people have a sixth sense that alerts them to opportunities coming their way and which – if they listen to it – will warn them of potential problems in any business venture. The Rat makes a better boss than an underling and, although industrious, can be ground down by routine. Flexible hours and variety at work suit the Rat best.

FINANCE AND THE RAT

Clever and thrifty, Rats have a gift with money and are compelled to put some aside for a rainy day. In good times a Rat is a terrific saver, and, in lean times, knows how to turn something to his or her advantage. The Chinese say there are very few poor Rats. But they also have a proverb: they who pile up grain hoards have much to lose.

COMPATIBLE BUSINESS PARTNERS

Whether Rats benefit from, or constantly conflict with, their business partners, depends, as in all relationships, on whether their Animal signs are harmonious or antagonistic to each other. Taking into consideration the compatibility of the elements between themselves and their working colleagues can also be very useful.

RATS RULED BY	BENEFIT FROM	ARE ANTAGONISTIC TO
Metal	Earth Dragons	Fire Sheep
Water	Metal Rabbits	Earth Horses
Wood	Water Monkeys	Metal Snakes
Fire	Wood Oxen	Water Rats
Earth	Fire Pigs	Wood Roosters

LEFT *Yoga, meditation and Chinese exercises, practised regularly, have a calming effect that benefits Rat people.*

CAREERS FOR RAT PEOPLE

All those who are born in the Year of the Rat share not only similar talents and inherent skills but also the same kind of aims and ambitions in life. The occupations that best suit the Rat mentality and abilities are listed below.

RATS MAKE EXCELLENT

Writers ★ Broadcasters ★ Actors
Advisors ★ Counsellors
Lawyers ★ Politicians
Designers ★ Engineers
Managers ★ Directors
Administrators ★ Entrepreneurs
Musicians ★ Stand-up comedians ★ Researchers
Historians ★ Racing drivers

Leisure and pleasures

THE RAT ON VACATION

Rats like to keep moving, so travel will delight their hearts and stimulate their curiosity. Lying around on a sandy beach is not the way a Rat wants to spend his or her precious two weeks' vacation. People born under this, the leading sign of the Chinese Animals, are adventurers, so they will want to explore their environment, trace its history, examine the local ruins, visit the churches, the beauty spots and the bazaar, and, of course, take in the night life, too. Ruled by their senses, they will want to experience all the sights and sounds that are new and foreign to them, to experiment with the tastes and smells that are endemic to the area they have chosen to visit, and sample the culture of the region. And, of course, if they can come home with the odd memento or two to add to their collection – over which they will naturally have bargained robustly – their holiday will have been an even greater success.

FRIENDS AND FOE

On the whole warm-hearted and affable, the Rat is one of the extroverts of the Animal Zodiac. Generally cheerful and sociable, and with a special knack for putting people at their ease, it is not surprising that Rats are popular and have wide circles of friends. They are great talkers and interesting conversationalists, able to find something to say on almost any subject one cares to mention. And, of course, there is always that famous Rat allure that enables them to charm the birds out of the trees!

To the people they love and hold dear, Rats can be extraordinarily generous and supportive, even going to great lengths to ensure that their loved ones are comfortable and contented. On the other hand, those people that Rats do not like are considered fair game, to be manipulated for the Rat's own ends. When all is said and done, however, loyalty is a characteristic of the Rat, and Rats are renowned for sticking with their friends through thick and thin.

COMPATIBLE FRIENDS

Although each individual person is unique, Chinese astrologers are very precise about which Animals have a general shared understanding and which have characters that are antagonistic to one another. Rats may wish to note which signs are more likely to provide lasting friendship and which they would find unsettling.

BEST FRIENDS	MORTAL ENEMY
Dragons	*Horses*
Monkeys	

LIKES AND DISLIKES

RATS LIKE

Color Preference
light blue
❖

Gems and Stones
diamond, amethyst, garnet
❖

Suitable Gifts
construction kits, art books, maps, food hamper, a subscription to a gym, car accessories
❖

Hobbies and Pastimes
basketball, building things, interior design, handicrafts, painting, collecting

Just as people born under the same Animal sign share a similar character and outlook on life, so do they share similar tastes. As two Rats get to know each other, they soon discover that they have, many likes and dislikes in common.

RATS DISLIKE

Strict time-keeping
❖
Going without
❖
Routine
❖
Finding themselves at the end of the line

Rat parents and babies

Rat parents are devoted to their children. They surround their little ones with warmth and affection and laugh good-humoredly at all their offsprings' antics and funny little ways. When their children are tiny they fret a good deal over them. Rats worry if their babies do not develop as well or as fast as other youngsters. They agonize over whether they are doing the right thing for their young, bringing them up correctly, and sending them to the best schools available.

With the mental capacity to pick things up in a flash, Rats do tend to get impatient with people who are not quite as quick-witted as themselves. Little wonder, then, that this character trait could lead to a potential source of conflict between Rat parents and their young offspring, should any of them happen to be late developers or a little slow off the mark.

On the whole, though, Rats are generous and indulgent parents who cannot deny their little ones any of their heart's desires – and the Rat's children very quickly and successfully learn how to twist their parents around their chubby little baby fingers.

THE RAT BABY AND CHILD

Baby Rats love to be cuddled. Although in later life the Rat will develop natural qualities of leadership, when young these little creatures tend to cling to their parents and need to feel very secure and protected. During their baby years, Rats mature slowly, but as toddlers they soon gain momentum and begin to display active mentalities that keep them on the go. Consequently, in the early years, plenty of rest is required.

At school, the young Rat's lively mind and fertile imagination make him or her eager to learn. It is at this time, too, that Rats develop a taste for collecting things, and will happily fill their bedrooms with pebbles or shells, knickknacks and keepsakes of every description. In general, young Rats are intelligent creatures who do especially well in artistic and literary subjects. But they are actually good all-rounders, and many of them excel on the sports field, too. Being born in the first sign of the Chinese horoscope instills these youngsters with a pioneering spirit, but also with a need to be first in line.

ABOVE *Rats make affectionate parents, and Rat babies love to be cuddled.*

RAT PARENT/CHILD RELATIONSHIPS

For some parents, their children's personalities harmonize perfectly with their own. Others find that no matter how much they may love their offspring, they are simply not on the same wavelength. Below are the compatibility ratings between Rat parents and their children

RATS WITH	UNDER THE SAME ROOF	COMPATIBILITY RATING
Rat	mutual understanding	✓✓✓
Ox	close	✓✓
Tiger	fretful	✓✓
Rabbit	the relationship improves with age	✓✓✓
Dragon	lots in common	✓✓✓✓
Snake	some clashes of temperament	✓✓
Horse	obvious differences from the start	✓
Sheep	misunderstandings	✓✓
Monkey	lots of laughs together	✓✓✓✓
Rooster	more intellectually than emotionally matched	✓
Dog	strong attachments	✓✓✓✓
Pig	amicable	✓✓✓

RATINGS ✓ uphill struggle ✓✓ some complications
✓✓✓ easy bonding ✓✓✓✓ on the same wavelength

Lovers and spouses

THE RAT LOVER

Rats are attractive people with bags of personal magnetism that draws members of the opposite sex like bees around a honeypot. The Rat himself (or herself) can hardly fail to notice all those admiring glances. If, as the Chinese say, there are very few poor Rats, then there must be even fewer who don't fairly drip with sex appeal – especially in their younger days. Rat people are romantic and fall in love easily; perhaps this is because single Rats are lonely creatures and are always much happier when they have a partner by their sides.

RAT CHARM

One of the Rat's biggest assets is charm. Rats can melt a person's heart with a smile. Add that to their flirtatious nature and you can easily see how they make conquests. And, as Rats are made for the night life, they have plenty of opportunities to meet up with potential mates and have the odd fling. A quirk among some Rat lovers is that they find it difficult to completely sever emotional ties with former lovers. This can prove a source of friction with a new lover and may jeopardize the development of new relationships. But when the Rat eventually meets and settles down with Mr. or Ms. Right, there will be a deep fulfilment in the warm intimacy of the relationship.

THE RAT LOVE PARTNER

Rats like to lead but are so active and lively-minded that they need a love partner who can match up to them. The system of Chinese horoscopes tells us which Animals are compatible and which are antagonistic and suggests whether our relationships have the potential to be successful. This applies to all relationships in life, including those at work. Marriages are made in heaven, so the saying goes. But while the heavens can point the way, the rest is up to us.

The panel on the right shows how the other Animals are suited to the Rat as a partner.

ABOVE *To please a Rat, do something on impulse. Wining and dining never goes amiss, but going to the races or a flight in a hot-air balloon would be fun.*

PARTNERS IN LOVE

RAT ♥ RAT
A successful partnership – especially in business. Great buddies, but bound to compete!

RAT ♥ OX
Sexually thrilling but disastrous in marriage. Better as a love affair.

RAT ♥ TIGER
Expect some dramatic clashes of temperament. Lots of friendship but little true passion.

RAT ♥ RABBIT
The Rat thinks Rabbits lack spunk. Conversely, Rats themselves thrive on adventure. Result? Frustration.

RAT ♥ DRAGON
A brilliant relationship – plenty of understanding and passion. Star-tipped for happiness.

RAT ♥ SNAKE
If these two Animals work on the differences in their characters, they could learn a great deal from each other.

RAT ♥ HORSE
No love lost between these two.

RAT ♥ SHEEP
An uphill struggle at times, though it could be made to work with goodwill on both sides.

RAT ♥ MONKEY
A shared outlook and a common understanding.

RAT ♥ ROOSTER
More scratchy conflict here than there is love.

RAT ♥ DOG
Rats find Dogs dull, but this match can achieve a stable union.

RAT ♥ PIG
A roller-coaster relationship. Terrific companionship and attraction, but watch those bills!

LOVE PARTNERS AT A GLANCE

RATS WITH:	TIPS ON TOGETHERNESS	COMPATIBILITY
Rat	beware rivalry	♥♥♥
Ox	mutual appreciation	♥♥♥
Tiger	learn to compromise	♥♥
Rabbit	on different wavelengths	♥
Dragon	on cloud nine	♥♥♥♥
Snake	an alluring fascination	♥♥♥
Horse	an unstable union	♥
Sheep	at odds	♥
Monkey	irresistible magnetism	♥♥♥♥
Rooster	too many differences	♥
Dog	mutual respect	♥♥
Pig	great happiness and good friends	♥♥♥

COMPATIBILITY RATINGS: ♥ *conflict* ♥♥ *work at it*
♥♥♥ *strong sexual attraction* ♥♥♥♥ *heavenly!*

EAST MEETS WEST

♈ ARIES RAT

These are self-confident, adventurous, go-getting people who cannot pass up a challenge. Charming and affable, Aries Rats can also be irritible and short-tempered, especially with those who cannot keep up the pace.

♉ TAUREAN RAT

Taurean Rats are formidable people. Plodding and methodical on the surface, their razor-sharp minds never miss a trick and they never lose sight of their goals. Traditionalists at heart, making money and accumulating wealth fuels their drive.

♊ GEMINI RAT

Gemini Rats are blessed with the gift of the gab, communicative, articulate, and perceptive. Quick, clever, but easily bored, they thrive on change and variety, and are at their happiest with their fingers in many pies. They tend to be indecisive, however.

♋ CANCERIAN RAT

Cancerian Rats like to maintain their individuality and to stand out from the crowd. Money and material comforts are important to them, but what they value more than anything is a close-knit family with whom they can feel loved, protected, and secure.

♌ LEONINE RAT

The Leonine Rat is a charismatic figure, dynamic, generous, and responsive. Enthusiasm, coupled with high moral standards and the ability to make wise judgements, guarantees that this Rat will go far. People respect Leonine Rats and are drawn to their magnetic personalities.

♍ VIRGO RAT

With gifts for research and analysis, an exquisite eye for detail, and the ability to make minute assessments, the hard-working Virgo Rat will find satisfaction in any occupations where critical faculties and painstaking investigation are required. There is something naive and idealistic about them that attracts lame ducks to their sides.

♎ LIBRAN RAT

Doubly charming, Libran Rats make very smooth operators. These people are sophisticated, elegant, and refined. Highly cultured and urbane, they are drawn to music and the arts. Pleasant in speech and manner, Libran Rats excel in the diplomatic corps, in advertising, and PR.

♏ SCORPIO RAT

Scorpio Rats are the strong, silent types, driven by their emotions. Few would suspect quite how deep this Rat's feelings go. These people have a powerful aura, an intensity that enables them to channel and focus their energies, and a perspicacity that gets right to the heart of the matter.

♐ SAGITTARIAN RAT

Happy-go-lucky, Sagittarian Rats breeze through life and yet are realists who couple wisdom with far-sightedness. They can spot an opportunity at thirty paces, and are quick to size up the implications and to act. On the whole, these Rats are lucky but they all have itchy feet.

♑ CAPRICORN RAT

Industrial, prudent, tenacious, Capricorn Rats are intensely ambitious and make meteoric progress in their chosen occupations. These people are realists, who expect their hard work and practical application to be recognized and rewarded. They may not be romantic or sentimental, but they are faithful and true.

♒ AQUARIAN RAT

Somewhat unconventional, and more tolerant of human foibles, these Rats are outgoing and spontaneous. They are community-minded, far-sighted, and, more selfless than other Rats, are prepared to work for the betterment and well-being of mankind.

♓ PISCEAN RAT

This Rat is sensitive, caring, and perceptive, and especially excels as a personal consultant or in the counseling profession. Piscean Rats are artistic and creative, but tend to lack self-confidence and need to be part of a team.

Famous Rats

Rat people, coming first in the Animal sequence, like to take the lead, or at least to be ahead of everyone else. They are charming, bright, alert, innovative, and quick to seize an opportunity.

◄ Buddy Holly

The American singer, songwriter, and guitarist, who founded the band the Crickets, and who died in a plane crash at the age of only 23, was a great innovator. In the 1950s, he was the first to add drums and a strong beat to country music, and became one of the earliest and strongest influences in the world of rock and pop. He also dramatically changed the composition of the band, introducing the line-up that is now so familiar of two guitars, bass, and drums.

▼ Thomas Hardy

The novels of the famous English writer were extremely innovative and advanced for their time, shocking the urban middle classes with their descriptions of the poor living conditions of rural folk and, worse still, with open references to love outside marriage.

◄ Diego Maradonna

Another nimble-footed Rat, the internationally famous Argentinian soccer player Maradonna led his team to victory at the World Cup in Mexico in 1986. Indisputably a great player, running this way and that in truly Rat-like fashion and needing several men from the other team to guard him, he grasped every opportunity that came his way. It has been claimed he even grasped the ball to help it into the net at one point, putting paid to England's hopes of winning.

▼ Lauren Bacall

Smooth, cool, sophisticated, bright, and with that charm and charisma so typical of Rat-born people, this actress is highly regarded for her performances that are polished and intelligent. This is a performer who throughout the course of her long career has never shown a temperamental side and has always been approachable in public.

▲ Gene Kelly

Nimble-footed like the Rat, Gene Kelly is best known for his dancing (and acting) in cinema musicals. There is something Rat-like about his polished and professional performances, in which every move is calculated. As a dance-director he was also a great innovator in this field and was awarded a special Oscar in 1951 for his major contribution to the development of the musical.

The Ox

The Ox personality

People who are born under the influence of the Ox are blessed with equilibrium and tenacity. The typical Ox has great endurance and strength of character. Few could match their determination and persistence once they have set their mind on a goal. As the mighty Ox inexorably draws the plow through the soil hour after hour, so Ox people quietly labor at their daily tasks unremittingly and without complaint. They know that the way to succeed is by slow, sustained effort, and they certainly don't believe in get-rich-quick schemes.

THE SIGN OF THE OX

The chief characteristics of people born under the sign of the Ox are shown in the panel below, right. Practical, industrious, and down-to-earth, Ox people are driven by a compulsion to work hard and have no truck with free-loaders, nor with the lazy. They are both trustworthy and trusting but not particularly outgoing, often preferring self-reliance to reliance on other people. However, other people can rely unreservedly on Ox people, who are always as good as their word and as dependable as clockwork in their habits. And while they do not particularly feel the need for light-hearted friendships, they form very strong bonds with their partners and families, and make good, lifelong friends.

Though they have a philosophical turn of mind, once people born under the sign of the Ox have made up their mind over an issue, neither heaven nor earth can make them change it. This causes them to be accused at times of pig-headedness and inflexibility, but these are the same qualities that enable the Ox to be staunch, upstanding, and forthright. These qualities contribute toward integrity and the Ox's ability to shoulder responsibility.

AMBITION

Ox types are great traditionalists, drawn by the familiar rather than by the excitement of the unknown. But beneath their unpretentious, placid exterior lies not only a heart of gold, but also a strong will and a clever, determined mentality, powered by a driving ambition to succeed.

YEARS OF THE OX

The Ox would have been first in the cycle but for the clever and corner-cutting Rat. So Ox years are second in the sequence and recur every twelfth year thereafter. As the Chinese New Year starts on a different date each year, it is essential to check the calendar to find the exact day on which each Ox Year begins.

1901 ★ 1913 ★ 1925
1937 ★ 1949 ★ 1961
1973 ★ 1985 ★ 1997

ABOVE LEFT AND BELOW
Like their animal counterpart, Ox people are strong, tenacious, and forebearing.

FACTS ABOUT OXEN

People born in the Year of the Ox share specific characteristics that are common to all other Oxen. To say that someone is an Ox is simply a short-hand way of describing that individual's personality. Here are the salient features associated with this sign.

OX FACTS
Second in order ★ *Chinese name – NIU, sign of industry*
Hour – 1am–2:59am ★ *Month – January*
Western counterpart – Capricorn

CHARACTERISTICS
Honesty ♥ *Loyalty* ♥ *Sincerity* ♥ *Steadfastness*
Integrity ♥ *Popularity* ♥ *Reliability*

Stolidity ✱ *Stubbornness* ✱ *Inflexibility* ✱ *Sulkiness*
Impatience ✱ *Narrow-mindedness*

IN YOUR ELEMENT

The characteristics of people born under the Ox sign, which recurs once every 12 years, are tempered by one of the 5 Chinese elements of Metal, Water, Wood, Fire, and Earth overlaying a 5-year cycle of characteristics on the original 12-year cycle.

THE METAL OX 1901 AND 1961

Ox people who are ruled by Metal work harder, and more conscientiously, than even the other Oxen. They always show a determination, and sheer tenacity, that will brook no interference as they labor to achieve their aims. Like all Oxen, they are completely honest and reliable, but they have a rigidly stiff upper lip that makes it difficult for them to show emotion. These Oxen are as strong as iron, and they have a will to match. Unfortunately, these very qualities can make them insensitive to the feelings of those around them, but the other side of the coin is that they are never afraid to speak up to defend what seems to them to be right.

THE WATER OX 1913 AND 1973

The Water element brings more fluidity and flexibility to the Ox sign. Water Oxen are as hard-working as ever, and particularly methodical, but they are perhaps quicker-thinking and certainly are more open and sensitive to other people than other elemental Oxen. They are much more prepared than the average Ox type to consider other people's points of view and take their ideas onboard, so that they get on well when working with others. They generally understand other people's feelings too, and this makes them tend to be much easier to live with. The patience and integrity that are the salient characteristics of the Ox's nature are still present in full measure, and this ensures their popularity and success with friends, colleagues, and family.

THE WOOD OX 1925 AND 1985

Tolerant and fair-minded, these are the least obdurate of the Oxen tribe and the most willing to accept change. With a more open attitude towards others, they appreciate the value of co-operative teamwork, and other members of the team respect Wood Ox people for their high principles. They have a great deal of self-confidence, which gives them an air of confirmed authority, and

means that they are often elected as leaders or spokes-people. They also have a quicker temper than other Ox people, as well as being outspoken and prepared to stand up and be counted. These Oxen are particularly loyal and devoted to those they love and make staunch and loving friends and relations.

THE FIRE OX 1937 AND 1997

As a rule, Ox folk are not quick off the mark, but being born under the Fire element gives them uncharacteristically dynamic qualities. Their leadership capabilities are made more obvious by the touch of fire in their natures, and this ensures them positions of authority at work and in the community – which is just as well, as they often have a strong urge to dominate. They have the mental ability to be extremely objective, but these Ox people can have hot tempers, and can often also be unusually impulsive in their actions. The danger in this is that they may brush aside things or ideas that are valuable by making hasty decisions and actions. Though tending to be impatient, Fire Oxen are loyal folk and stoutly devoted to their family.

THE EARTH OX 1949 AND 2009

The most reliable and industrious Oxen belong to this group. The Earth element helps them to temper many of their negative characteristics. These Oxen are shrewd and have good judgement, which can make them successful in financial matters. They are aware of their limitations, but nevertheless purposeful and keen to get on in their own slow way. Other people tend to look up to Earth Oxen because of their obvious qualities of reliability, integrity, and sincerity, their modest and realistic ambitions, and their readiness to shoulder the plow and work hard and sensibly to achieve their aims. Honest and loyal to their friends and loved ones, like all the other Oxen, they will toil uncomplainingly to provide their families with a secure and comfortable environment.

Health and habitat

HEALTH AND CONSTITUTION

People born under the sign of the Ox usually have strong constitutions. However, they also have a tendency to be workaholics, and they should try to ease up and rest more. Many Ox folk work in sedentary occupations, and would benefit from making a point of finding some time each day for exercise. They are often prone to problems affecting the bones and joints – especially the knees – and need to take special care of these areas. However, Ox people are basically strong and robust, and, according to ancient wisdom, should be blessed with long life.

THE OX AT HOME

For Ox people, home is their castle and retreat – a place of tranquillity for themselves and their loved ones. The Ox person's house may not be very stylish or fashionable, but it will be very comfortable. As the Ox is basically an outdoor type, and also quite studious, plants and gardening books will be in evidence. Ox people prefer to live in the country, or, if in town, to have a house with a large garden. Although violet is the Ox color, this is not often used in interior design. Instead, a combination of dusky pinks and blues are favored colors, although some Ox people may prefer a color scheme that gently reflects Nature, with gold, moss green, and burnt umber predominating. But since the sign of the Ox is associated with January, winter colors might be more appropriate.

Career and wealth

THE OX AT WORK

Capable, honest, and conscientious, Ox people toil single-mindedly at their chosen task. Colleagues will marvel at their methodical approach and rely on their high standards. They enjoy routine and are efficient and well-organized at work, and particularly well-suited to occupations that allow them to specialize. They actually prefer working for large corporations, as such organizations offer the security the Ox person requires, but they nevertheless work best alone within these companies, since Oxen can be rigid in their views and unhappy working as part of a group.

FINANCE AND THE OX

Oxen believe in security, and are normally unlikely to take any wild risks where money is concerned. They are also careful in their spending habits. But hard work and a fairly simple lifestyle ensure that they accumulate money steadily, which they then invest wisely, if conservatively, to cushion their old age.

ABOVE LEFT *No Ox person is afraid of hard work, and these people usually have few health problems.*

COMPATIBLE BUSINESS PARTNERS

Whether Oxen benefit from, or constantly conflict with, their business partners depends, as in all relationships, on whether their Animal signs are harmonious or antagonistic to each other. Taking into consideration the compatibility of the elements between themselves and their working colleagues can also be very useful.

OXEN RULED BY	BENEFIT FROM	ARE ANTAGONISTIC TO
Metal	Earth Roosters	Fire Tigers
Water	Metal Rats	Earth Horses
Wood	Water Pigs	Metal Sheep
Fire	Wood Oxen	Water Dogs
Earth	Fire Snakes	Wood Monkeys

Compatible Friends

Although each individual person is unique, Chinese astrologers are very precise about which Animals have a general shared understanding and which have characters that are antagonistic to one another. Oxen may wish to note which signs are more likely to provide lasting friendship and which they would find unsettling.

BEST FRIENDS	MORTAL ENEMY
Roosters	*Sheep*
Snakes	

Leisure and pleasures

The Ox is a lover of stability, a great traditionalist and a homemaker. Rarely would you expect an Ox person to be an extrovert pleasure-seeker. They are happiest in the peace of their own home territory.

Likes and Dislikes

OXEN LIKE

Color Preference
Violet

Gems and Stones
Jade, emerald, moss-agate, lapis-lazuli

Suitable Gifts
Tapestry kit, kitchen gadgets, CDs, cookbooks or gardening books, slippers, bonsai tree, crossword books

Hobbies and Pastimes
Marathon-running, body-building, sculpture, gardening, pot-holing, music, sewing, baking

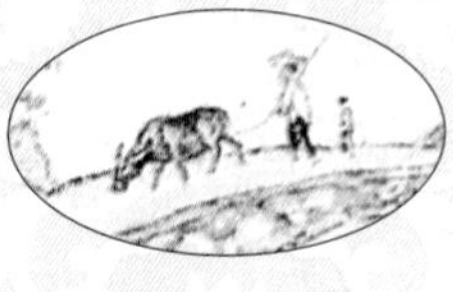

Just as people born under the same Animal sign share a similar character and outlook on life, so they also have similar tastes. As two Oxen get to know each other, they will soon discover that they have many likes and dislikes in common.

OXEN DISLIKE

Making small talk at parties

Feeling insecure

Living without creature comforts

Playing silly games

ABOVE *Ox people tend to be robust, and many of them enjoy outdoor team sports.*

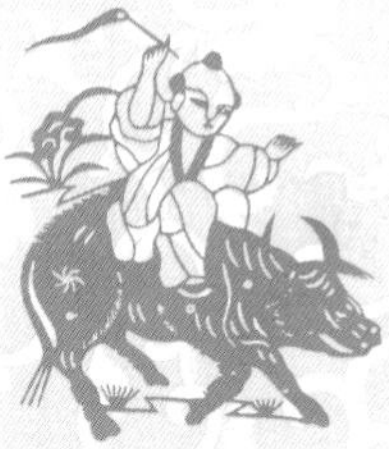

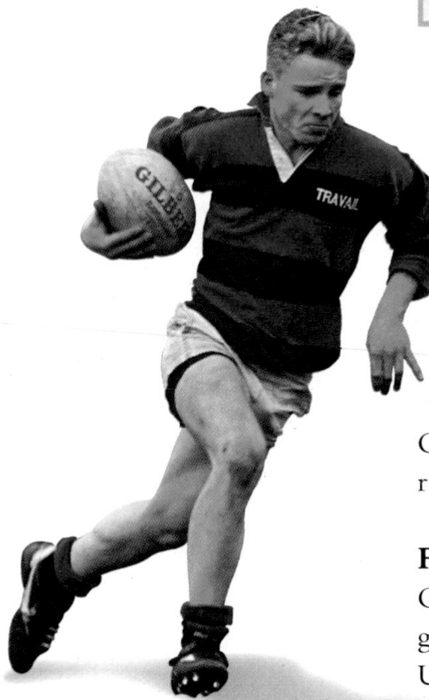

The Ox on vacation

In truth, Oxen are great home-lovers and, once settled, they generally like to stay put, so they probably do not suffer quite so much from wanderlust as people born under other signs do. They are very happy in their own locality, just staying at home, and perhaps spending their summer vacations catching up with the odd spot of interior decorating that the pressure of work has not allowed them to get around to. And of course there is always the garden. Whether they are digging, planting flower beds, or simply sitting out in a deck chair with a cold beer within reach, it is all seventh heaven to them. Should they want to get away, however, Ox people are most likely to be attracted to the hills and mountains, open plains, and rugged cliffs.

Friends and foe

Oxen are not the most gregarious of people. They tend not to mix happily in social gatherings, but prefer their privacy and a certain anonymity away from the public gaze. Unlike the Rat, the Monkey, or the Rooster, the Ox person tends not to have a bulging address book, preferring a few close and loyal friends to a large network of acquaintances. Oxen can sparkle at social occasions, however, when the urge takes them; but more often than not they dislike chit-chat. These are cautious creatures and unlikely to spark up friendships on the spur of the moment. Instead they take their time and like to be sure of their companions before they throw in their lot with them. Their friends, therefore, will be few, but staunch and life-long. A stable marriage and close family provide all the companionship they really need.

Ox parents and babies

Oxen make deeply caring and protective parents. People born under this sign will happily and unselfishly beaver away from dawn to dusk in order to provide a stable and secure environment in which their precious offspring may thrive.

In return, however, the Ox mother and father demand that their youngsters should be courteous, respectful, and obedient. In comparison to other parents, Oxen can appear strict and authoritarian. They are traditionalists and believe in good, old-fashioned values. A good education is especially close to their hearts, and life under the Oxen roof is much more harmonious if offspring are attentive at school and willing to learn. Nothing pleases the Ox father more than a child who brings home an excellent report card. Firm but fair, Ox-born individuals believe that discipline is important in life, and when they set rules and regulations, they expect their children to adhere to them. In the Ox parent's scheme of things, rebelliousness is like a red rag to a bull – and a raging bull is not a pretty sight!

Many Oxen – female Oxen, especially – tend to have children fairly early on in their lives, and then devote themselves totally to their growing families. As a result, Ox mothers can often find it enormously difficult to cut the apron strings when their young fledglings eventually leave the nest.

THE OX BABY AND CHILD

Children who are born under the sign of the Ox are placid and amenable. They develop into solid, independent, resourceful children, happiest when left to their own devices. If disturbed or provoked in any way, or forced to do something against their will, they are prone to sulk or throw a tantrum. In general, Ox-born children are shy, and for many, childhood is a solitary, even lonely, experience, either because they like to keep themselves to themselves or because of a wide discrepancy in the ages of their siblings.

At school, all Oxen display a strong, practical side to their natures from even the earliest age, and all subjects with a manual or constructive edge to them will appeal to these youngsters. Art and music, too, will capture their creative imaginations. These are robust little individuals who will acquit themselves well on the sports field, too. Polite, dutiful, and hard-working, young Oxen are affectionate children and are respectful of their elders.

OX PARENT/CHILD RELATIONSHIPS

For some parents, their children's personalities harmonize perfectly with their own. Others find that no matter how much they may love their offspring, they are simply not on the same wavelength. Below are the compatibility ratings between Ox parents and their children

OXEN WITH	UNDER THE SAME ROOF	COMPATIBILITY RATING
Rat	proud parent, dutiful child	✓✓✓
Ox	chip off the old block	✓✓✓
Tiger	little understanding	✓
Rabbit	domestic contentment	✓✓✓
Dragon	some difficulties to overcome	✓✓
Snake	entwined	✓✓✓
Horse	lack of understanding	✓
Sheep	too sensitive by half	✓
Monkey	lots of fun	✓✓✓✓
Rooster	happy parenting	✓✓✓✓
Dog	little real contact	✓
Pig	harmony reigns	✓✓✓

RATINGS ✓ uphill struggle   ✓✓ some complications
✓✓✓ easy bonding   ✓✓✓✓ on the same wavelength

ABOVE *Ox people are devoted parents, but good discipline is strictly instilled in their children.*

OPPOSITE *When it comes to matters of love, Ox people are not to be hurried.*

Lovers and spouses

THE OX LOVER

Oxen dislike small-talk. They don't enjoy parties much and could probably count all their friends on one hand. They are not really gregarious and would much rather be at home reading a good book. In love, too, an Ox is a person of few words. Big-hearted, yes, and deeply loving, but verbally demonstrative? Emphatically not! An Ox will take a long time to make up his or her mind about choosing a mate because Oxen hate change, and need to find someone who is rock-steady in order to make a stable marriage. Oxen never rush into things and they are simply not the flirtatious kind. So once they are committed they will probably be faithful and true.

MARRIAGE

Unfortunately, however, many Ox marriages do fall apart after a few years, possibly because the dominant Ox is too bossy or too inflexible. Perhaps it's because, when things go wrong, Oxen tend to blame everyone except themselves. But if an Ox is lucky or careful, and has chosen wisely, the couple can build a close-knit family group to which the Ox will devote himself or herself, and which will bring a great deal of happiness.

THE OX LOVE PARTNER

Ox people are strong, silent, and reliable, but they do tend to take it for granted that they will be the leader in a partnership. Some of the other Animals may even find them stubborn and intransigent. The system of Chinese horoscopes can give an indication of which Animals are compatible and which are antagonistic, and this tells us whether our relationships – in business and in love – have the potential to succeed. But, according to Chinese beliefs, while the heavens can point the way, the rest is up to us. The panel (right) shows how the other Animals are suited to having the Ox as a partner.

PARTNERS IN LOVE

OX ♥ RAT
Sexually thrilling but disastrous in marriage. Consequently, better as a love affair.

OX ♥ OX
A good, solid relationship – but where's the pizzazz?

OX ♥ TIGER
The Chinese say that this is one of the worst matches possible, yet despite the disharmony that's likely to result, you are drawn to each other nevertheless.

OX ♥ RABBIT
This union promises a contented domestic life. In business you're too laid-back to make it work.

OX ♥ DRAGON
When it comes to stubbornness, you've met your match here, and essential give-and-take is lacking.

OX ♥ SNAKE
Sympathetic, understanding, loving, on the same wavelength – you've got it all!

OX ♥ HORSE
Better in business together than in bed.

OX ♥ SHEEP
Even though your bodies may meet, your minds won't and it's certain your hearts never will.

OX ♥ MONKEY
When this relationship works, life can be fun, fun, fun!

OX ♥ ROOSTER
Sexy. Passionate. Sizzling. Good match for a happy and successful relationship.

OX ♥ DOG
Not much in common between you two and neither is truly comfortable with the other.

OX ♥ PIG
Plenty of sexual attraction and some shared attitudes can produce harmony.

LOVE PARTNERS AT A GLANCE

OXEN WITH:	TIPS ON TOGETHERNESS	COMPATIBILITY
Rat	*mutual appreciation*	♥♥♥
Ox	*solid but stolid*	♥♥
Tiger	*a clash of temperaments*	♥
Rabbit	*soft and gentle*	♥♥♥
Dragon	*first attraction, then deadlock*	♥
Snake	*simply sublime*	♥♥♥♥
Horse	*confrontational*	♥
Sheep	*in your dreams!*	♥
Monkey	*a complementary match*	♥♥
Rooster	*blessed by the gods*	♥♥♥♥
Dog	*odds against, but a glimmer of hope*	♥♥
Pig	*worth persisting with*	♥♥

COMPATIBILITY RATINGS: ♥ *conflict* ♥♥ *work at it*
♥♥♥ *strong sexual attraction* ♥♥♥♥ *heavenly!*

EAST MEETS WEST

ARIES OX

Aries Oxen are achievement-oriented and attain success by persevering. They charge through life, brooking no opposition. In love too they are dominant; subtlety is not their game, and only a strong, honest, practical, and down-to-earth partner will make a perfect match.

TAUREAN OX

Immovable and implacable, Taurean Oxen are perhaps the most steady and, in their way, the most laid-back of all the Oxen. Stubborn and persistent, diligent and methodical, they get what they want through tenacity.

GEMINI OX

These Oxen have spirit, tenacity, and strength of purpose. They are outgoing and like the company of others. Witty and sociable, they excel in business and commerce, and do well in positions of authority.

CANCERIAN OX

Talent, sensitivity, and determination ensure that Cancerian Oxen develop their creative skills to a high degree. At home these Oxen create a beautiful environment, and their partners and family are fundamental to their happiness and well-being.

LEONINE OX

This duality produces leaders, who feel compelled to take charge and control. They also take themselves seriously and throw their whole being into whatever they undertake. Leo brings a buoyant influence to bear on the Ox. Generous, magnanimous, and giving, these people are happiest with an adoring partner at their side.

VIRGO OX

The Virgo's critical eye and the Ox's pedantry merge to produce individuals who are practical and meticulous, but whose skills in dealing with minutiae can develop into fussing over details. Unmatched in honesty, integrity, and ethical correctness, they are responsible and respected. Perhaps not romantic or flamboyant, but faithful and true.

LIBRAN OX

These Oxen make friends easily and are willing to compromise, making them good employers and employees alike. They are amiable, eminently peace loving, and never prone to rocking the boat – idealists who are constantly looking for perfection in life and love.

SCORPIO OX

Drive, determination, and cool, calculated logic characterize the Scorpio Ox. These Oxen will strive and toil to reach their goal. In love, Scorpio Oxen are passionate and intense, but they hide the seething cauldron of their emotions beneath a calm exterior.

SAGITTARIAN OX

These Oxen have Sagittarian vision and far-sightedness. They are born lucky, prone to taking calculated risks, but shrewd and quick to size up a situation. With these talents they can reach prestigious positions in life and accumulate a large amount of money in the process.

CAPRICORN OX

Capricornian Oxen are made of true grit, resolute, and implacable. Sustained effort enables them to accumulate wealth and achieve a comfortable life. Conservative, rock solid and responsible, Capricorn Oxen work hard to provide security and comfort for their loved ones.

AQUARIAN OX

The eccentric Aquarian Ox is light of spirit. This is not easily reconciled with the solid, constant, and predictable nature of Oxen, and members of this dual sign are a law unto themselves. Free-thinking and intelligent, they like variety, both at work and in their love lives.

PISCEAN OX

Sensitivity and introspection temper the craggy toughness of the Ox to produce an intricate personality, with a bottomless well of creative talent and perspicacity. Piscean Oxen are artistic and content to work behind the scenes, rather than leading the team.

Famous Oxen

Ox people are known for their endurance and strength of character. They will work hard and unfalteringly to attain their goals in life, and are steady, reliable, and steadfast. They are usually great traditionalists and will always stand up and speak up for what they believe is right.

Hans Christian Andersen

Hans Christian Andersen, the Danish writer, is another artistically gifted Ox whose resoluteness of purpose and application to his work enabled him to rise from his humble origins as the son of a cobbler and a washerwoman to being an internationally respected writer. His love of tradition is evidenced by his use of Danish folklore as the source of nearly all his tales.

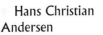

Margaret Thatcher

Margaret Thatcher, now Baroness Thatcher of Kesteven, became leader of the British Conservative Party in 1975 and was British Prime Minister from 1979 to 1990. Even those who disagreed with her policies could not dispute that she demonstrated strong powers of leadership and Ox-like determination. Super-conservative and a staunch supporter of traditional values, she quickly made herself known for her tough, uncompromising determination.

Jackie Collins

The books of the Ox-born popular writer Jackie Collins sell by the million in over 30 countries.

Despite her indisputably glamorous image she is a stalwart and methodical hard worker. When she has set her mind on producing the next bestseller, nothing will deflect her from her purpose in providing a true and honest reflection of the Hollywood lifestyle.

Nikki Lauda

The Austrian former racing driver has the Ox's reliability, and the determination – stubbornness, even – to achieve what he has resolved to do. He also has the Ox's gift of integrity and popularity. After the accident in 1976 in which he was badly burned, he went on to be runner up in the Fomula One motor racing World Championship. Later he set out to build a successful second career and, since his retirement from driving, now runs his own airline.

Meryl Streep

The Ox-born Meryl Streep is a gifted actress whose hard work and application are matched by her talent. Her studious approach to her work has enabled her to master a variety of accents to perfection and to present a wide range of characters in a completely convincing way, while her own unique quality still shines through in each performance.

The Tiger

The Tiger personality

The Tiger is said to be lucky and Tiger characters are colorful, dynamic, and attractive. The Chinese say a Tiger in the house is the best insurance against fire, theft, and evil spirits and this is perhaps because, as well as being lucky, Tigers are courageous and alert, and they fight bravely.

THE SIGN OF THE TIGER

Tigers are not impressed by power or money. They like being straight with everyone, and expect people to be straight with them in return. Yet at the same time, they are sensitive to the opinions of others and need their approval – which is generally guaranteed by their engaging personalities. But when a Tiger person feels let down and senses disapproval or criticism, or fails in some scheme that had been leapt into with great enthusiasm, he or she can become very depressed and low.

Nevertheless, like all felines, Tigers always leap up again for the next challenge and generally land on their feet. Their indomitable energy means that they cannot help burning the candle at both ends and they can dissipate their energy or act rashly or over-enthusiastically.

FIGHTING SPIRIT

Tigers are also incorrigibly competitive – they simply cannot pass up a challenge, especially when honor is at stake, or they are protecting those they love. Tigers are unpredictable, and it would be unwise to underestimate their reactions. They may appear cool, but they have the Big Cat's instincts to pounce at a moment's warning. Natural leaders, they have a strong sense of their own dignity, and if they find themselves in the ranks, they can be stubborn and obstinate. In positions of power they can be difficult though stimulating bosses. Tigers are intelligent, alert, and far-sighted. They have their fingers on the pulse. Good strategists and tacticians, they often have a hidden agenda. As long as they do not risk their luck too often, and keep their restless nature under control, their tactics usually pay off in life.

YEARS OF THE TIGER

Third in the cycle, Tiger Years follow on from the Ox and recur every twelfth year thereafter. As the Chinese New Year does not fall on a fixed date, it is essential to check the calendar to find the exact day on which each Tiger Year begins.

1902 ★ 1914 ★ 1926
1938 ★ 1950 ★ 1962
1974 ★ 1986 ★ 1998

ABOVE *Tigers are full of enthusiasm and optimism, and even their rash ventures usually turn out well.*

FACTS ABOUT TIGERS

People born in the Year of the Tiger share specific characteristics that are common to all other Tigers. To say that someone is a Tiger is simply a shorthand way of describing that individual's personality. Here are the salient features associated with this sign.

TIGER FACTS

Third in order ★ Chinese name – HU, sign of courage
Hour – 3am–4:59am ★ Month – February
Western counterpart – Aquarius

CHARACTERISTICS

Courage ♥ Enthusiasm ♥ Boldness ♥ Sociability
Energy ♥ Optimism

Volatility ✖ Impulsiveness ✖ Impatience ✖ Hot-headedness ✖
Vanity ✖ Disobedience

IN YOUR ELEMENT

The characteristics of people born under the sign of the Tiger, which recurs once every 12 years, are tempered by one of the 5 Chinese elements of Metal, Water, Wood, Fire, and Earth overlaying a 5-year cycle of characteristics on the original 12-year cycle.

THE METAL TIGER 1950 AND 2010

The Metal element brings extra sharpness and a quick-silver speed of thought and action to the Tiger. Tigers born in the Metal year like to be different and to stand out in a crowd. With heightened assertiveness and competitive spirit, they fix their sights firmly on the top and are determined and talented enough to get there. A handsome breed, they can sometimes suffer from Tiger tempers and changes of mood, which they need to keep under control. They should also try not to let themselves get carried away in following the urge of the moment without thinking things through.

THE WATER TIGER 1902 AND 1962

The Water element has a calming effect, so these Tiger types are calmer and more placid than their fellow cats. Their ability to take people's feelings and ideas on board makes them very reasonable and understanding. They are also endowed with great insight and strong powers of intuition, which gives them excellent judgement. The Tiger habit of watching and waiting before leaping can make these Tigers appear unable to make up their minds. They might occasionally find themselves snoozing and watching the ripples, instead of going for the prize they had in mind.

THE WOOD TIGER 1914 AND 1974

Better able to work as part of a team, Wood Tigers don't feel that tremendous Tiger urge to take charge or to dominate the scene. The Wood element gives solidity and stability, and with this comes a warmth of character and thoroughly agreeable nature, which means that Wood Tigers are always popular with their friends. They are also generous with their time and their possessions. They may have less of the Tiger flare, but they bring a

solid, practical approach to any problem. They can allow their natural ability to command make them sit back and let others do the work. They should beware of their somewhat volatile tempers and short attention spans, as they are less able than some of their fellow cats to right themselves for a landing and to get back on track.

THE FIRE TIGER 1926 AND 1986

Colorful, active, and dramatic, Fire Tigers are alight with passion, enthusiasm, vitality, and verve. They are outgoing, communicative, and optimistic and always ablaze with the excitement of the latest scheme. They have the Tiger's inborn powers of leadership in full portion, and a natural ability to inspire other people with their own enthusiasm. They often have a natural wit, too, and powers of oratory to crown their charismatic and persuasive personalities. Fired with their own excitement and an endless supply of energy, they can even seem melodramatic, and they may not be able to understand more cautious or down-to-earth approaches in others.

THE EARTH TIGER 1938 AND 1998

Realistic, practical, and down-to-earth, Earth Tigers tend not to get swept away quite so readily by their own enthusiasm and excitement. They have the sense of responsibility that other Tigers need to cultivate and are not so easily distracted from one brilliant scheme to another. A steadier approach to life in every way, along with the ability to apply themselves to projects for longer periods, brings success through sustained effort. They must be careful not to lose their sense of humor, and not to ignore the needs and feelings of others along the way.

All those who are born
in the Year of the Tiger
share not only similar
talents and inherent skills,
but also the same kind of
aims and ambitions in life.
The occupations
that best suit the Tiger
mentality and abilities
are listed here.

TIGERS MAKE EXCELLENT

*Actors ★ Comedians
Musicians ★ Racing drivers
Chauffeurs ★ Explorers
Pilots ★ Artists ★ Writers
Air hostesses ★ Travel agents
Advertising agents
Lecturers ★ Politicians
Missionaries ★ Office
managers ★ Members
of the armed forces
Sales personnel*

RIGHT *Tigers can put
their health at risk by using
up too much energy without
pacing themselves.*

COMPATIBLE BUSINESS PARTNERS

Whether Tigers benefit from, or constantly conflict with,
their business partners depends, as in all relationships, on
whether their Animal signs are harmonious or antagonistic
to each other. Taking into consideration the compatibility of
the elements between themselves and their working
colleagues can also be very useful.

TIGERS RULED BY	BENEFIT FROM	ARE ANTAGONISTIC TO
Metal	*Earth Dogs*	*Fire Oxen*
Water	*Metal Pigs*	*Earth Snakes*
Wood	*Water Tigers*	*Metal Roosters*
Fire	*Wood Horses*	*Water Rats*
Earth	*Fire Dragons*	*Wood Monkeys*

Health and habitat

HEALTH AND CONSTITUTION

Tigers live as though life were a series of sprinting races, tackling everything in short
bursts of energy and then collapsing with exhaustion. Normally their energy levels are
soon back to full strength, but with this approach their long-term health can suffer.
They need to learn how to pace themselves in order to keep active longer and to
prevent early burn-out. They are blessed with a resilient constitution and recover
quickly from any spells of ill-health, but they owe it to themselves to take things at a
steadier pace. Apart from this long-term danger, the main health problems Tiger people
are likely to encounter are accidents and injuries due to impulsive action.

THE TIGER AT HOME

Tigers like to be different, and this
applies especially to their homes,
where their originality and flair can
be seen at their best. Tigers have a knack
of creating atmosphere with color and light.
Their bold spirit of adventure is reflected in their
experimental décor. Their love of travel will be in
evidence with treasures from far-flung places:
Shaker tablecloths, Tibetan prayer mats, African
carvings, all mixed exuberantly. Unusual designs
are blended in their own inimitable style.

Career and wealth

THE TIGER AT WORK

With their active and alert intelligence, Tigers
are fast learners and have the ability to pick up
skills quickly. All Tigers like a challenge and this,
coupled with their restlessness, explains why they tend
to change careers more often than other Chinese Animals.
Those Tigers who do not dramatically change their occupations from time to time tend to juggle with several
jobs all at the same time instead. Most Tigers display a
natural brand of dominance or leadership and perform
best when they find that their work puts them in
positions of power and influence.

FINANCE AND THE TIGER

Luck plays a large part in a Tiger's finances. Tigers like
to spend, and also to share. They can be rash with
money, but they know they can make more whenever
they need it. Somehow, as a reward, they manage to find
a pot of gold just when it seems they should be heading
for skid row. They may lose a fortune in their time, but
they will often end up with two.

LIKES AND DISLIKES

TIGERS LIKE

Color Preference
Mid-green

❖

Gems and Stones
Ruby, diamond, cat's eye

❖

Suitable Gifts
Crime novel, Mah Jongg set, exotic cookbook, gliding lesson, travel guides, manicure set

❖

Hobbies and Pastimes
Action sports, amateur dramatics, noisy parties, the latest fashions, bridge and chess, adventure films, detective stories, photography

Just as people born under the same Animal sign share a similar character and outlook on life, so do they share similar tastes. As two Tigers get to know each other, they soon discover that they have many likes and dislikes in common.

TIGERS DISLIKE

❖

Having to compromise

❖

Not being in charge

❖

Bad manners

❖

Not getting the support they believe they deserve

Leisure and pleasures

THE TIGER ON VACATION

Tigers need to feel the edge of danger, to see life in the raw. Never one to stay at home, for a Tiger, challenge is the name of the game. A vacation packed with adventure and excitement will thrill Tigers and recharge their batteries, too. Driving long distances satisfies the Tiger's need to burn rubber. At a moment's notice, they could go overland to the Far East or pony trek through the forests of Europe. For a dare they might shoot the white rapids, rappel, or fly into the blue. At other times they would enjoy visiting the Pyramids, going on safari, basking in Bali, or having a ball in Honolulu. On vacation, they party until late, dance until dawn, and then, because they are sun lovers, make sure to leave some time for hanging around on the beach. Soaking up the heat is guaranteed to have the Tiger sizzling in the sand!

FRIENDS AND FOE

Cheery and full of bonhomie, those born under this, the third Animal sign of the Chinese Zodiac, have the gift of lifting the spirits of even the gloomiest individual they happen to meet. With that sort of disposition, Tiger-born folk have no real difficulty in striking up new friendships. Which is just as well, because a Tiger without a friend is quite a miserable soul! Indeed, like the Dragon, the Monkey, and the Rat, Tigers are in their element surrounded by a faithful following of companions.

As friends, Tiger types are exceptionally warm and spontaneously generous – both financially and with their time and attention. Should a friend drop by for a much-needed chat, the Tiger will immediately down tools and offer a welcome cup of coffee, a ready ear, a sympathetic word, a box of tissues, and a broad shoulder to cry on. Few friends could truly be as supportive and encouraging, as funny and full of surprises, or as genuinely concerned as the Tiger.

ABOVE *With their bright spirits, Tigers always attract new friends.*

COMPATIBLE FRIENDS

Although each individual person is unique, Chinese astrologers are very precise about which Animals have a general shared understanding and which have characters that are antagonistic to one another. Tigers may wish to note which signs are more likely to provide lasting friendship and which they would find unsettling.

BEST FRIENDS	MORTAL ENEMY
Horses	*Monkeys*
Dogs	

Tiger parents and babies

Tiger parents, just like their feline counterparts, are fierce protectors of their young and would lay down their own lives in order to defend their little ones. Distinctly caring and devoted, Tiger parents are warm and affectionate. They lavish their brood with treats and often spoil them with their generous hearts. Tiger parents can be playful as kittens, joining in family games with great relish. And, on the whole, they do enjoy being in their children's company, having a good laugh and sharing a joke together. But there are times when, like all Big Cats, adult Tigers will roar with rage if one of their offspring has gone just a little too far, or is disrespectful. Open-minded and experimental these human felines may be, but they will not, under any circumstances, tolerate bad manners, rebellious behavior, and a lack of respect for their elders and betters!

These parents take their role as instructors of the young very seriously, and they are staunch believers in a good education for their children. When their offspring are little, Tigers will tell them stories, and relate tales about their own childhood and experiences, in the hope that this will impart some wisdom or moral values. Children learn through example, Tigers say, and members of this Animal sign are determined to be the best role models going.

BELOW LEFT *As parents, Tigers love family fun, and romp and play happily with their young.*

ABOVE *Family life will always be colorful with Tiger parents – full of caring, warmth, and strong moral examples.*

THE TIGER
BABY AND CHILD

Youngsters born under the sign of the Tiger are happy and endearing little creatures. As children, they have irrepress-ible energy and hurl themselves passionately at life. Boys will like sports and girls become intrepid tomboys. From an early age, these youngsters possess a fine competitive edge to their natures and cannot pass up a dare, just as surely as their older fellow Tigers cannot refuse a challenge. Bright, intelligent, socially skilled, and affectionate, these youngsters have an insatiable curiosity about life and their environment. In class, they are drawn to subjects that allow them to express their colorful characters and vivid imaginations freely.

TIGER PARENT/CHILD RELATIONSHIPS

For some parents, their children's personalities harmonize perfectly with their own. Others find that no matter how much they may love their offspring, they are simply not on the same wavelength. Below are the compatibility ratings between Tiger parents and their children.

TIGERS WITH	UNDER THE SAME ROOF	COMPATIBILITY RATING
Rat	needs time to reach understanding	✓✓
Ox	a struggle	✓
Tiger	similar outlook	✓✓✓
Rabbit	happy days	✓✓✓
Dragon	proud parenting	✓✓✓✓
Snake	each pulling in different directions	✓
Horse	lots in common	✓✓✓✓
Sheep	affectionate although different aspirations	✓✓
Monkey	at odds	✓
Rooster	divergent ideas	✓
Dog	strong loving bonds	✓✓✓✓
Pig	many peaks but also a few troughs	✓✓✓

RATINGS ✓ uphill struggle ✓✓ some complications
✓✓✓ easy bonding ✓✓✓✓ on the same wavelength

Lovers and spouses

THE TIGER LOVER

Tigers are attractive creatures, passionate and strong. As lovers, they are romantic and ardently sexy. Spontaneous, flirtatious – they never quite lose that spark of excitability. And, with the unpredictability of a jungle cat, they carry that *frisson* of excitement around them, that hint of danger that is so irresistible. In too static a relationship, a Tiger will start pacing like a caged animal, and restlessness and curiosity may win the day. This has earned Tigers the reputation for not being the most faithful of the Chinese Animals.

Tigers need a partner who will give them a good run for their money and keep them guessing just enough to maintain their interest. But they draw a great deal of their strength from their family, and from the bonds of a loving union. Perhaps this is why so many Tigers marry young.

LIFE WITH A TIGER

Once committed, Tigers should watch their assertive nature, since they tend to like to dominate. Also, they should try not to upset their partner with outspoken comments. But these are minor faults in comparison to the benefits a Tiger brings to a relationship: warmth and generosity of spirit, that old-fashioned insistence on courteousness, a huge appetite for life, and a spontaneous enjoyment of sex and love-making.

THE TIGER LOVE PARTNER

Tigers thrive on excitement, and need a partner who can stand the pace. The Tiger's love companion must be able to understand his or her ups and downs – to go along with the action and to give comfort and support when the Tiger confidence is temporarily shattered. The system of Chinese horoscopes is very specific about which Animals are compatible and which are antagonistic, and this tells us whether our relationships – in business or in love – have the potential to be successful, but the rest is up to us. The panel (right) shows how the other Animals are suited to the Tiger as partner.

ABOVE *The famous Tiger passion makes for tantalizing love partners who may be tempted to roam.*

PARTNERS IN LOVE

TIGER ♥ RAT
Expect some dramatic clashes of temperament. Lots of friendship but little true passion.

TIGER ♥ OX
The Chinese say this is one of the worst matches possible, but you are drawn to each other nevertheless.

TIGER ♥ TIGER
With two such dominant, individualistic creatures, there are bound to be fireworks.

TIGER ♥ RABBIT
You're good for each other.

TIGER ♥ DRAGON
A gutsy combination with plenty of sparks to fuel the passions.

TIGER ♥ SNAKE
Different outlook, different lifestyles, and different objectives all suggest little meeting of minds.

TIGER ♥ HORSE
Plenty of high jinks in this high-octane relationship ensure an exciting life together.

TIGER ♥ SHEEP
Lots of respect but too much walking on eggshells for comfort.

TIGER ♥ MONKEY
You're likely to drive each other up the wall!

TIGER ♥ ROOSTER
Misunderstandings create problems.

TIGER ♥ DOG
Mutual respect and admiration make this a solid union and a winning team.

TIGER ♥ PIG
Friendship, shared interests, and a good sense of humor bode well for your union.

LOVE PARTNERS AT A GLANCE

TIGERS WITH:	TIPS ON TOGETHERNESS	COMPATIBILITY
Rat	*learn to compromise*	♥♥
Ox	*a clash of temperaments*	♥
Tiger	*too much jostling for the upper hand*	♥♥
Rabbit	*your differences weld you together*	♥♥♥
Dragon	*a dynamic duo!*	♥♥♥
Snake	*odds against*	♥
Horse	*hot and spicy*	♥♥♥♥
Sheep	*work, yes – marriage, no*	♥♥
Monkey	*deeply frustrating*	♥
Rooster	*talk or walk*	♥♥
Dog	*solid!*	♥♥♥♥
Pig	*good humor keeps you smiling*	♥♥♥

COMPATIBILITY RATINGS: ♥ *conflict* ♥♥ *work at it*
♥♥♥ *strong sexual attraction* ♥♥♥♥ *heavenly!*

ARIES TIGER

Aries Tigers are mini-tornadoes who go through life cramming as many activities into the day as they possibly can. Feeling trapped is the Aries Tiger's nightmare. These larger-than-life people are nevertheless caring and heroic, ever ready with courage and passion in equal measure.

TAUREAN TIGER

Steadier and more down-to-earth than the average Tiger, Taurean Tigers can apply themselves practically to all tasks. They can sustain the pace and are able to keep their shoulders to the wheel long enough to bring their dreams to reality. Their relationships are stable yet passionate.

GEMINI TIGER

Gemini Tigers like to be on the move. They hunger for new places and new faces. Intelligent and witty, they are the life and soul of the party, but easily bored. Being tied to one place, one job, or even one person is not on this Tiger's agenda.

CANCERIAN TIGER

This is a romantic individual who is both soft and sensitive, beneath a crusty shell, and spirited and impetuous. So this is an individual like a jungle cat, who, underneath, is just a tender-hearted old puss and who really needs a stable, loving relationship and a secure home.

LEONINE TIGER

A dynamic combination, the Leonine Tiger is all feline – bold, courageous, fervent, and charismatic, powerful of personality and noble of bearing. This Tiger commands respect, and rises to the top as if by divine right. In the true spirit of *noblesse oblige,* these majestic people go about their duties with fervor and magnanimity.

VIRGO TIGER

Virgo caution acts as a brake to feline impetuosity. Tigers are not famed for their love of the minutiae, but the Virgoan Tiger can become a stickler for the finer points and will excel in professions where an eye for detail is a must. Virgoan Tigers can also be mighty selective when it comes to relationships.

LIBRAN TIGER

These Tigers live by justice, and fair play and make good judges, administrators, diplomats, and politicians. But they have a notorious repuation for dithering when it comes to their own lives.

SCORPIO TIGER

No-one lives so intensely as the Scorpio Tiger, whose emotions run unfathomably deep. These are forceful people, strong-minded, and extremely focused, and they do not like to be contradicted.

SAGITTARIAN TIGER

Colorful characters with a huge appetite for life, Sagittarian Tigers are extrovert and adventurous. But they are also impulsive, and can act before having properly considered the consequences. Freedom and independence are vital to their well-being.

CAPRICORN TIGER

From an early age these Tigers realize that success comes through hard work and will put in long hours to achieve the status and position they think is justly theirs. Conservative and law abiding, they do not mind toeing the line. Work comes first, love and relationships second.

AQUARIAN TIGER

Aquarian Tigers flout rules and regulations, and convention, and take a dispassionate view of the world. They have a knack of bypassing emotions in order to get to the heart of the matter. This ability to rationalize their feelings makes these Tigers come across as emotionally distant.

PISCEAN TIGER

Soft, tender and gentle, Piscean Tigers are more amenable than most, despite the fiery passions that lurk beneath the surface. They are patient and sensitive, but if they set their sights on a partner they are determined to stake their claim.

Famous Tigers

Tiger people are bold and sociable, energetic and enthusiastic. They can also be volatile, impulsive, and hot-headed, and certainly unpredictable. High-octane people with courage and talent, who will not be afraid to go their own way.

Christina Onassis

Daughter of Aristotle, Christina certainly showed her fighting spirit throughout her life, attempting to assert her independence and escape the possessiveness of her much-loved father. Born to a life of luxury, ideal for her Tiger temperament, she traveled the world and enjoyed the party spirit. When she inherited her father's empire she gained her opportunity to display her natural leadership style.

▽ Princess Anne, the Princess Royal

Princess Anne is one of the most independent of the British royal family, who just gets on and does her own thing. Her adventurous spirit and the support she inspires are Tiger qualities that have helped her to be particularly effective in the charity work she tirelessly engages in to support the cause of poor children throughout the world.

▲ Demi Moore

This Tiger-born actress is probably as well known for her self-publicity, not least being photographed in the nude, when pregnant, for a glossy magazine cover, as for her work. This is not to deprecate her talent, for she has acted in well over a dozen films of the 1980s and 1990s. But somehow Tigers can't help attracting – and sometimes also seeking – attention.

◁ Groucho Marx

Another quick-witted, epigrammatic, charismatic Tiger, Groucho Marx had the Tiger sparkle in his eyes, and also – it is said – the Tiger temper, from which his name (i.e. grouchy) is derived. An attention-grabbing Tiger individualist to the tip of his cigar.

▲ Oscar Wilde

Oscar Wilde was brilliant, flamboyant, charismatic, and, for his time, amazingly brave about his sexual preferences. This, and his restless spirit, his devotion to individualism, and espousal of the the cause of artistic freedom, are all associated with the sign of the Tiger – as are his quick-witted, epigrammatic conversational gifts.

The Rabbit

The Rabbit personality

Rabbit folk are quiet, private individuals, sensitive and shy. People who are born into this sign tend to shun the limelight, and prefer to take a behind-the-scenes, rather than a high-profile, approach to life. Not that this means, however, that they are in any way reclusive – in fact, they're quite the reverse. Rabbits are very social creatures, always ready to enjoy a good chat and happy in the company of others in formal and informal situations. Simply, they are comfortable being just one of the crowd, and have no wish to stand out or show off.

THE SIGN OF THE RABBIT

The chief characteristics of the sign of the Rabbit are shown in the panel (below, right). Above all, this is the sign of peace, so Rabbits are the least aggressive of all the Chinese Animals and will go out out of their way to avoid unpleasantness of any kind. Even when angry or upset, they never raise their voices or get out of control. But this rarely happens, because Rabbit people are born with a built-in gift for diplomacy that enables them to extricate themselves with great tact from any potentially troublesome situation.

Rabbits may be quiet, and even apparently fail to notice what is going on in many tense situations, but other people need not be misled into thinking that they are not sharp-witted; to be a good diplomat requires intelligence and psychological penetration. It also requires powers of persuasion and cunning. Despite their supreme good manners and genuine love of peace, Rabbit people are masters and mistresses of finesse!

STYLE AND FASHION

The Chinese Rabbit is synonymous with style and culture, and this is expressed in all aspects of its life. Chic and sophisticated, Rabbits look as if they have just stepped out of the pages of the latest fashion magazine, and are to be seen in all the best restaurants. They also generally have a strong artistic vein, which means that Rabbits tend to dominate the world of music and the arts. They look after their creature comforts in an artistic way too, and their homes are expressions of their good taste and love of fine things.

YEARS OF THE RABBIT

Fourth in the cycle, Rabbit years follow on from Tiger years and recur every twelfth year thereafter. As the Chinese New Year does not fall on a fixed date, it is essential to check the calendar to find the exact date on which each Rabbit year actually begins.

1903 ★ 1915 ★ 1927
1939 ★ 1951 ★ 1963
1975 ★ 1987 ★ 1999

ABOVE LEFT AND BELOW
The Rabbit is a quiet and peace-loving Animal who is also sociable and artistic.

FACTS ABOUT RABBITS

People born in the Year of the Rabbit share specific characteristics that are common to all other Rabbits. Rabbits are also known as Hares, and below are listed the salient features associated with this sign.

RABBIT FACTS
Fourth in order ★ Chinese name – TU, sign of peace
Hour – 5am–6:59am ★ Month – March
Western counterpart – Pisces

CHARACTERISTICS
Wisdom ♥ Astuteness ♥ Prescience ♥ Docility
Thoughtfulness ♥ Refinement

Cunning ✖ Possessiveness ✖ Fussiness
Obsession ✖ Snobbery

IN YOUR ELEMENT

he characteristics of people born under the Rabbit sign, which recurs once every 12 years, are tempered by one of the the 5 Chinese elements of Metal, Water, Wood, Fire, and Earth overlaying a 5-year cycle of characteristics on the original 12-year cycle.

THE METAL RABBIT 1951 AND 2011

The Metal element gives Rabbits born in this year a much stronger presence, more resilience and tenacity than the average, often rather timid, Rabbit. Strongly intuitive, and also ambitious, Metal Rabbits can be shrewd, even cunning, in their dealings. In everything they do their feelings run very deep, and their love affairs can become intense without the Rabbit showing much outward expression of this state of affairs. This quality affects working relations, too, and without necessarily showing it, Rabbits can become intensely involved with their colleagues and with the work itself – especially since they are accomplished in the arts and often work with other creative people and on projects that require considerable application and dedication.

THE WATER RABBIT 1903 AND 1963

Sensitive and amenable, Water Rabbits will often go along with the flow to avoid disagreement, since conflict of any kind upsets them deeply. They may at times seem quiet and inward-looking and sometimes prefer to seek their own company, but in the main they are friendly and easy-going. They have great sensitivity, and to those they live and work with they show a supportive and empathetic disposition that attracts people to them. But they do need to learn to avoid letting others take advantage of their kind and trusting nature. Their sensitivity applies to themselves as much as to others, and they can be over-sensitive at times, and all-too easily hurt.

THE WOOD RABBIT 1915 AND 1975

Wood Rabbits have the Rabbit love of peace in extra measure. Even though these Rabbits are popular, kind, and generous, people tend to see the Wood Rabbit as a typical fence-sitter – someone who is uncertain and indecisive. However, much of this may be attributed to a desire for peace and to an inborn kindness which makes these Rabbits particularly reluctant to hurt or upset anyone. Active and sociable, preferring to live life as part of a group, the Wood Rabbit is one of life's givers, always prepared to help, support, and care for those in need. It would help the Wood Rabbit at times to speak up a little more strongly and let his or her views and feelings be known, as these Rabbits can be too accommodating for their own good.

THE FIRE RABBIT 1927 AND 1987

Outgoing, enthusiastic, and bold, the Fire element makes these the most dynamic and magnetic of the Rabbit tribe. They have a tendency to get up and go and a strongly adventurous streak in their natures which, added to their Rabbit skills in diplomacy, often leads to success in life. They can, however, be unexpectedly fiery and temperamental in their emotions, even though they will go to great lengths to avoid emotional or unpleasant confrontations, and are usually good at hiding their feelings under a veneer of real charm. They can, when they choose, be outspoken in expressing their feelings and preferences – for a Rabbit – but they love fun and good-humored relationships, and are not usually going to spoil this by showing their temperaments in public.

THE EARTH RABBIT 1939 AND 1999

Practical, serious, persistent, and hard-working, the Earth influence makes people born in these years logical and level-headed as well as prudent and careful. These sterling qualities, and their ability to give sound advice, ensure for Earth Rabbits the trust and respect of all who know them. They are quite materialistic and like domesticity and security in life. A comfortable home and, above all, a loving partner are absolutely essential to their well-being. These Rabbits can also be quite calculating, and they like to accumulate wealth in their own slow, modest way. They are pretty shrewd too, and can quietly put their own interests first while working to achieve their desire for security and stability in life.

CAREERS FOR RABBITS

All those born in the Year of the Rabbit share not only similar talents and inherent skills, but also the same kinds of aims and ambitions in life. The occupations that best suit the Rabbit mentality and abilities are listed here.

RABBITS MAKE EXCELLENT

Therapists ★ Psychiatrists
Doctors ★ Ophthalmologists
Herbalists ★ Masseurs
Solicitors ★ Judges
Diplomats ★ Campaigners
Teachers ★ Writers
Publishers ★ Designers
Actors ★ Musicians
Administrators ★ Welfare
workers ★ PR agents
Fashion designers
Beauticians

RIGHT *Their love of harmony and balance means that Rabbits usually create graceful homes and make good negotiators.*

COMPATIBLE BUSINESS PARTNERS

Whether Rabbits benefit from or constantly conflict with their business partners depends, as in all relationships, on whether their Animal signs are harmonious or antagonistic to each other. Taking into consideration the compatibility of the elements between themselves and their working colleagues can also be very useful.

RABBITS RULED BY	BENEFIT FROM	ARE ANTAGONISTIC TO
Metal	*Earth Sheep*	*Fire Dragons*
Water	*Metal Dogs*	*Earth Roosters*
Wood	*Water Rabbits*	*Metal Horses*
Fire	*Wood Snakes*	*Water Tigers*
Earth	*Fire Pigs*	*Wood Monkeys*

Health and habitat

HEALTH AND CONSTITUTION

Despite the fact that Rabbit folk are said to be blessed with longevity, they do have a delicate constitution. Physiologically they are prone to allergies and stomach ailments. Psychologically, they are sensitive and tend to suffer badly when living under adverse conditions or emotional pressure of any kind. A notorious love of creature comforts may also mean that some Rabbit folk fail to get enough exercise. They should make a point of getting out into the fresh air as part of a regular routine.

THE RABBIT AT HOME

All Rabbits have an intense love for their homes, where security and comfort are important. Right at the top of the list are style and elegance, because living in uncongenial surroundings makes Rabbits severely depressed. Order, neatness, and lack of clutter are essential, and, for the Rabbit, less is definitely more. Rabbit people's homes are tastefully furnished, reflecting their delicate sense of beauty. Green is the favored Rabbit color and the use of jade or sage green produces an air of cool, chic refinement that characterizes Rabbits' good taste. With their artistic skills, Rabbits create a graceful environment, filling their homes with pretty things, paintings, and antiques.

Career and wealth

THE RABBIT AT WORK

Rabbits are likely to be found in professions that demand their negotiating and management skills. Renowned for their diplomacy and discretion, they also have good communicative skills. The diplomatic corps, the church, teaching, and public relations all suit Rabbit people, with the security of a well-regulated organization to back them up. But with their sense of beauty and artistic inclinations, many Rabbits find their niche in music, literature, or the arts, perhaps in an orchestra, writing historical novels, acting, or working in publishing.

FINANCE AND THE RABBIT

Rabbit people are usually careful and clever when it comes to financial matters. They also tend to be fairly lucky. Much of their money is tied up in their homes and possessions. They are more likely to invest in things than in the stock market, and a terrific nose for genuine antiques and works of art enables Rabbits to make some wise investments in these areas.

Leisure and pleasures

THE RABBIT ON VACATION

Rabbits are culture vultures and they spend their lives looking for peace and beauty. Gentle by nature and with a creative eye, they take great delight in the interior decoration of their homes and would be quite content to spend their vacations scouring craft shops, antique fairs, or salvage yards in the hope of finding just the right painting, the choice ornament, or the appropriate architectural piece to match their decor. To satisfy their cultural needs, a city steeped in history such as Paris, Florence, or Athens would be high on a Rabbit's sight-seeing agenda. Alternatively, because many born under this sign are blessed with literary or artistic skills, taking a course in painting or writing would give the Rabbit a great deal of pleasure. Sitting in an olive grove overlooking the scintillating azure waters of the Mediterranean, with a sketch book in one hand and a glass of fine wine in the other, would be sheer bliss for the Rabbit.

LIKES AND DISLIKES

RABBITS LIKE

Color Preference
Pale Green

❖

Gems and Stones
Pearl, crystal, emerald

❖

Suitable Gifts
Hamper of luxury food, tapestry kit, fine wine, historical novels, original print, CDs

❖

Hobbies and Pastimes
Reading, writing, gardening, cooking, painting, hiking, sailing, gossiping

Just as people born under the same Animal sign share a similar character and outlook on life, so do they also have similar tastes. As two Rabbits get to know each other, they soon discover that they have many likes and dislikes in common.

RABBITS DISLIKE

❖

Macho behavior

❖

Sudden change thrust upon them

❖

Excessive physical contact

❖

A messy environment

LEFT *These people are sociable, but choose their friends with care.*

FRIENDS AND FOE

Rabbits are not given to pushing themselves forward and grabbing the spotlight as a Dragon person might. Nor are they comfortable leading the way like the Rat, or being the most popular person on the block like the Monkey. Yet they are sociable creatures and they like being in the company of others. It is simply that Rabbits are low-profile people and happy to be one of the crowd. Indeed, so strong is the compulsion to identify themselves with a group that people born in a Rabbit year tend, more than most, to belong to a variety of clubs and associations. Perhaps this is because all Rabbits are choosy about their friends, and membership of an institution provides them with an excellent source of like-minded individuals with whom they can link up. As friends, Rabbit people are kind and sympathetic, with terrific shoulders to cry on, and making wise counsellors into the bargain. There is nothing Rabbits enjoy better than a good old gossip session with their friends!

COMPATIBLE FRIENDS

Although each individual person is unique, Chinese astrologers are very precise about which Animals have a general shared understanding and which have characters that are antagonistic to one another. Rabbits may wish to note which signs are more likely to provide lasting friendship and which they would find unsettling.

BEST FRIENDS	MORTAL ENEMY
Sheep	*Roosters*
Pigs	

LEFT *Sailing in a beautiful yacht on a calm sea would be a pleasant occupation for a Rabbit person.*

ABOVE *Rabbit parents often like to dress their babies up, and, although loving, may behave quite formally.*

RABBIT PARENT/CHILD RELATIONSHIPS

For some parents, their children's personalities harmonize perfectly with their own. Others find that no matter how much they may love their offspring, they are simply not on the same wavelength. Below are the compatibility ratings between Rabbit parents and their children.

RABBITS WITH	UNDER THE SAME ROOF	COMPATIBILITY RATING
Rat	some friction	✓✓
Ox	mostly supportive to each other	✓✓
Tiger	differences of opinion	✓✓
Rabbit	harmony reigns supreme	✓✓✓✓
Dragon	creative togetherness	✓✓✓
Snake	a loving relationship	✓✓✓✓
Horse	a gulf between them	✓
Sheep	easy on both sides	✓✓✓✓
Monkey	some sleepless nights	✓✓✓
Rooster	rebellion in the ranks	✓
Dog	a tender understanding	✓✓
Pig	comfortable	✓✓✓✓

RATINGS ✓ uphill struggle ✓✓ some complications
✓✓✓ easy bonding ✓✓✓✓ on the same wavelength

Rabbit parents and babies

The Chinese say the Rabbit is the sign of fertility, and many Rabbit-born individuals do have large families. But however many children Rabbit mothers or fathers choose to have, a happy family life is central to their scheme of things. These individuals make loyal and supportive parents, although it is interesting to note that they can at times appear cool and aloof. Many youngsters of Rabbits can remember times when their parents seemed somewhat distant or even remote. And yet these parents are very protective of their young, sometimes verging on the point of being a little over-possessive of them, too.

When the children are little, the Rabbit mother will dress them in stylish clothes, and both parents will insist on politeness and good manners. Unlike a Tiger or a Rooster parent, Rabbits of both sexes are more likely to give in to the demands of their youngsters just for the sake of a quiet and peaceful life – because people born in the year of the Rabbit always find squabbles and conflict disagreeable – especially so when their children reach those difficult teenage years!

With the deeply caring instinct that comes naturally to all members of this sign, Rabbit parents nurse their little ones tenderly and patiently through all their childhood illnesses. Rabbits always have time for their children as they grow older, too, and provide a ready ear to listen to their children's problems and wise counsel to guide them throughout their lives.

THE RABBIT BABY AND CHILD

Young Rabbits are soft and tender, physically, mentally, and emotionally. Sensitivity is one of the main characteristics associated with this sign, producing delicate emotions that are quick to rise to the surface in the Rabbit infant. Hence, Rabbit babies cry easily, and as boys and girls at school they tend to get upset more than most. As a consequence, the Rabbit child is likely to be teased and branded as a "cry baby" at school. Moreover, young Rabbits, and especially so the males, are strongly bonded to their mothers – an affinity they maintain throughout life.

Perhaps more than those born under any other sign, children born in a Rabbit year particularly need routine and a stable environment in order to thrive. At school, they will quickly develop a flair for artistic subjects, and many of them excel in music.

Lovers and spouses

THE RABBIT LOVER

The Rabbit lover would never dream of wearing his heart on his sleeve. The Rabbit seems aloof, yet underneath is sensual and loving – a tough façade protects a tender interior. Rabbit folk are romantic yet realistic, generous yet mercenary. Rabbits are strongly Yin and, whether male or female, are in tune with the feminine part of their psyche. Their mothering instinct compels them to nurture others, and they have an innate love of home and family.

YIN DOMINANCE

Yin dominance brings out a sentimentality prevalent in the Rabbit nature. Soft, romantic, and nostalgic, Rabbits are easily moved and at times find it difficult to hold back the tears. They are prone to mood swings, too, being easily influenced by the company they keep and the environment they are in. The merest hint of confrontation is misery for a Rabbit.

Rabbits are beautiful, charming, and genteel. Suave and sophisticated or sleek and refined, anyone would consider a Rabbit an asset to have by their side. Despite their cool demeanor, they have a reputation for being highly sexed, but although they may sow a few wild oats when young, most Rabbits, once committed, remain with their partners for life.

ABOVE *Rabbit people make calm and affectionate partners who are nevertheless deeply passionate.*

THE RABBIT LOVE PARTNER

The sensitive and gently mannered Rabbit needs a partner with warmth, and would not be averse to someone with a little cash in the bank either, for Rabbit tastes can be expensive. A partner who shares this good taste and love of quality living would make an ideal match. The system of Chinese horoscopes shows which Animals are compatible and which are antagonistic and whether our relationships have the potential to be successful. But while the heavens can point the way, the rest is up to us. The panel (right) shows how the other Animals are suited to the Rabbit as a partner.

PARTNERS IN LOVE

RABBIT ♥ RAT
Rats rattle Rabbit's nerves, so for a quiet life it's best to give this partner a wide berth.

RABBIT ♥ OX
This union promises a placid and contented domestic life together.

RABBIT ♥ TIGER
You're good for each other.

RABBIT ♥ RABBIT
An easy combination between two affectionate, well-mannered, highly-cultured individuals. Bound for success.

RABBIT ♥ DRAGON
Your differences will either unite or divide you.

RABBIT ♥ SNAKE
Deep passions make this one heck of a sexy combo!

RABBIT ♥ HORSE
Despite conflicts, you could just about put up with each other.

RABBIT ♥ SHEEP
True love, shared interests, respect, understanding. You've got it all!

RABBIT ♥ MONKEY
This can end in tears.

RABBIT ♥ ROOSTER
You're opposites in almost every possible aspect.

RABBIT ♥ DOG
You've got a lot going for you here.

RABBIT ♥ PIG
Warm, close, happy, and comfortable together. Tipped for enduring love.

LOVE PARTNERS AT A GLANCE

RABBITS WITH:	TIPS ON TOGETHERNESS	COMPATIBILITY
Rat	on different wavelengths	♥
Ox	soft and gentle	♥♥♥
Tiger	your differences weld you together	♥♥♥
Rabbit	twin souls	♥♥♥♥
Dragon	learn to give and take	♥♥
Snake	great sex	♥♥♥
Horse	difficult but achievable	♥♥
Sheep	blissful	♥♥♥
Monkey	heartbreak hotel	♥
Rooster	nothing in common at all	♥
Dog	rock steady	♥♥♥
Pig	shared togetherness	♥♥♥♥

COMPATIBILITY RATINGS: ♥ *conflict* ♥♥ *work at it*
♥♥♥ *strong sexual attraction* ♥♥♥♥ *heavenly!*

EAST MEETS WEST

ARIES RABBIT

Active and independent, the Aries Rabbit's tendency to be constantly searching for opportunities means several changes of direction throughout life. More energetic than the average Rabbit, they actively pursue their ambitions while coming across as cool and relaxed. Essentially these people need to be given their own space.

TAUREAN RABBIT

These are acquisitive and industrious people, whose main aim in life is to obtain as many creature comforts as they can and who need to live and work in a gracious and refined environment. Next comes security, which means a healthy bank account.

GEMINI RABBIT

Chatty and sociable, a low boredom threshold means that Gemini Rabbits need constant stimulation. They are rarely short of something to say and are popular members of their set. Witty and highly amusing, they are at their best in the center of a crowd.

CANCERIAN RABBIT

For the Cancerian Rabbit home is where the heart is. These people are strongly attached to their roots and their early conditioning, and form a close bond with their parents – especially their mothers. Cancerian Rabbits are sensitive, sentimental, idealistic, and easily hurt.

LEONINE RABBIT

With the Lion's noble bearing and the Hare's finesse, these are confident individuals, refined and poised, with good manners, and blessed with a charismatic personality that makes them extremely popular with their friends and fellow workers alike.

VIRGO RABBIT

These are practical and capable individuals who can turn a hand to almost anything. Also punctilious types, they can verge on the fussy side. Neat and orderly, efficient and organized, they do everything in a thorough manner.

LIBRAN RABBIT

This mixture produces a polished individual, someone of good taste who is fond of gracious living. Charming and cultured, suave and sophisticated, those born under this influence are social butterflies with delicate manners.

SCORPIO RABBIT

These Rabbits are connoisseurs, many choosing to work in the antiques business or art world. They play their cards close to their chests, but beneath their cool detachment lies depth of feeling and strength of character.

SAGITTARIAN RABBIT

These Rabbits are more spirited and adventurous, and less stay at home. The normally sentimental Rabbit is made light-hearted, less moody, and more optimistic and care-free. They have a broad perspective and a visionary outlook.

CAPRICORN RABBIT

Practical and ambitious, Capricorn Rabbits are extremely industrious. Status is important to them and their patient efforts are rewarded by positions of power and prestige. Not over-demonstrative, they are loyal and steady.

AQUARIAN RABBIT

Aquarian Rabbits are more outward-looking. These are intelligent individuals, who are blessed with imagination and vision. As Aquarians they are interested in the acquisition of knowledge rather than in wealth and material possessions. But as Rabbits they like to surround themselves with beautiful things. Invariably they end up very comfortably off indeed.

PISCEAN RABBIT

With sensitivity, astuteness, idealism, adroitness, loving kindness, and finesse, the Piscean Rabbit is a creature of infinite complexity and creative talent. Not high-powered, these Rabbits are comfortable in low-key professions or in occupations where they can put their creative skills to good use. They thrive in peaceful, harmonious settings.

Famous Rabbits

These people are famous for their love of peace and their apparent docility, but they are nevertheless not to be underestimated. They can be shy and sensitive, but they are also sociable, wise, and capable of springing a surprise, too.

▼ Orson Welles

Rabbits are artists, and they are also sophisticated and capable of being almost obsessively attentive to detail. This filmmaker, although his works are few in number, is acknowledged to be one of the greatest artists of the cinema. His work is meticulously planned, with every detail flawlessly worked out to perfection.

▲ King Henry V

We think of Henry V as the boisterous prince who became a glittering leader and led the English to victory over France at the Battle of Agincourt – not exactly the peace-loving, shy Rabbit type at all. But this prince was also a diplomat, or perhaps gifted with Rabbit shrewdness, for he managed to win a peace treaty that gave him effective control of France. And on his marriage to Catherine of Valois, daughter of the French king, he was officially recognized as heir to the French throne.

▼ Elisabeth Schwarzkopf

Many Rabbits are great connoisseurs of the arts and many take up careers in music, art, or literature. They often have the gift of great sensitivity of interpretation, and some, like Elisabeth Schwarzkopf, the great operatic and lieder soprano, rise to the top of their chosen art form.

▲ Arthur Miller

This is the Rabbit who sprang a surprise. A quiet, sophisticated, intellectual who won the prize of prizes in Marilyn Monroe, Arthur Miller may look slightly bashful, but the reserved smile speaks of a deeply romantic nature, and behind those severe glasses there is a slightly rakish look.

◀ Billie Holiday

Lady Day, the great blues and jazz singer who first became famous when she was only 18 and who sang with all the best big bands during her twenties, had that Rabbit mix of outward aloofness and inner sensuality, cool facade and deep tenderness. She also had the Rabbit's sophistication of appearance and manner.

In her case, her inner tenderness and vulnerability were overstrained by the demands of her artistic gifts, and drugs brought her career to a tragic early end.

The Dragon

The Dragon personality

The Dragon is a creature of myth and legend. Colorful and exotic, symbol of good fortune and emblem of power, the Oriental dragon is always regarded as a sacred beast – the reverse of the archetypal malevolent monster that Westerners of old felt compelled to seek out, defeat, and slay. In Eastern philosophy, the Dragon is held to be a bringer of good fortune and a holder of authority, and those people born in Dragon Years are therefore to be honored and respected.

YEARS OF THE DRAGON

Fifth in the cycle, Dragon Years follow on from the Rabbit and recur every twelfth year thereafter. As the Chinese New Year does not fall on a fixed date, it is essential to check the calendar to find the exact date on which each Dragon Year actually begins.

1904 ✴ 1916 ✴ 1928
1940 ✴ 1952 ✴ 1964
1976 ✴ 1988 ✴ 2000

THE SIGN OF THE DRAGON

The key to the Dragon personality is that these folk are the free spirit of the Zodiac and a law unto themselves. Having to conform is anathema to the Dragon. To him or her, rules and regulations are made only for other people. Restrictions squeeze stone dead the creative spark that at every turn is ready to flame into life. Dragons need to be as free as the wind and clouds that are their domain.

The Dragon is a gorgeous creature, as colorful and flamboyant as a gilded dragon in a Chinese pageant. A dynamo of energy, a supreme extrovert, gifted, original, exciting, and utterly irrepressible, everything Dragon folk do is on the grand scale – big ideas, extravagant gestures, massive ambitions. But they don't behave this way for show, it is simply their nature. And because they have confidence and enthusiasm and are fearless in the face of challenge, they almost invariably meet with success.

Dragons, one way or another, usually make it to the top. However, Dragon people need to beware of their own natures. Too much enthusiasm and too much beating of Dragon wings can leave them exhausted and their ambitions unfulfilled, and their Dragon pride can prevent them from accepting help from other people, even though they will always give aid when it is needed.

Dragons are always able to attract friends through their generous natures, their style, and sheer magnetism, but they can be rather solitary people at heart. A Dragon's self-sufficiency can mean that he or she feels no real need for close bonds with other people.

ABOVE *The Dragon is the great non-conformist and charismatic presence in the Chinese horoscope.*

FACTS ABOUT DRAGONS

People born in the Year of the Dragon share specific characteristics that are common to all other Dragons. To say that someone is a Dragon is simply a shorthand way of describing that individual's personality. Here are the salient features associated with this sign.

DRAGON FACTS

Fifth in order ★ *Chinese name – LONG, sign of luck*
Hour – 7am–8:59am ★ *Month – April*
Western counterpart – Aries

CHARACTERISTICS

Originality ♥ *Self-assurance* ♥ *Resourcefulness*
Adaptability ♥ *Valor* ♥ *Enthusiasm*

Arrogance ✖ *Tactlessness* ✖ *Hot-headedness* ✖ *Criticism*
Unpredictability ✖ *Quick-tempered*

IN YOUR ELEMENT

The characteristics of people born under the Dragon sign, which recurs once every 12 years, are tempered by one of the 5 Chinese elements of Metal, Water, Wood, Fire, and Earth overlaying a 5-year cycle of characteristics on the original 12-year cycle.

THE METAL DRAGON 1940 AND 2000

Honest but intolerant, gutsy but inflexible, straightforward but insensitive, these Dragons have a steely strength as well as the Dragon fire. Metal Dragons succeed in everything by sheer grit and defiance. They are tough, and they respect those who can stand up to them; but weaker mortals get short shrift from these Dragons. They make a powerful ally in times of trouble, but they are ferocious as opponents. Metal Dragons can often ruthlessly subdue others by strength and the sheer force of their personalities. They are always looking for action, and things are never better than when they are defending a principle or conviction in which they have unshakeable faith. They like to lead, and others are often drawn to follow them, but even if their charisma finds them no support they will fight on alone.

THE WATER DRAGON 1952 AND 2012

Water has a calming influence on the Dragon's bold and fiery temperament. It may not quench the Dragon's fire, but it enables the Dragon to direct it more thoughtfully, and makes this kind of Dragon more sensitive to others and more cooperative. Because these Dragons know the art of patience and do not have the same burning desire to be the focus of attention as other Dragons, they are better able to stand back from things and take an objective view of the situation. Thus they make wise judgements and are much more prepared to see eye-to-eye with other people. Even so, their actions can go wrong because of a lack of basic research and from not seeing one project through before starting on another one.

THE WOOD DRAGON 1904 AND 1964

Wood has a moderating influence and also brings practicality and imagination to this sign. Inquisitive and open-minded, Wood Dragons always enjoy discussing new ideas and are receptive to other people's points of view. They are creative and inventive as well as practical, and they appreciate art in all its forms. Generally less egotistical than most Dragons, and with an ability to get on with other people, Wood Dragons have all the gifts required to build a successful and contented life for themselves. They still have the talent for being outspoken, and can at times be a bit too pushy and insistent to please everyone, even in the most friendly dispute or cooperative venture.

THE FIRE DRAGON 1916 AND 1976

The Fire Dragon is a force to be reckoned with. This is a Dragon multiplied by two, and a powerful dynamo this can be! The Fire Dragon can go for the burn and accelerate from cool to explosive in under 60 seconds. In some ways the Fire Dragon is always his or her own worst enemy. These Dragons cannot help having the conviction that they are super-important and right about everything. When they really are right, of course, their combination of enthusiasm and energy is a great asset to the cause; but although they value objectivity, they do not always apply the best judgement, and sometimes jump to the wrong conclusion. They also suffer from impetuosity and quick tempers. But when they can manage to keep their temper, passions, and competitive spirit under control, they can have a powerful influence on others.

THE EARTH DRAGON 1928 AND 1988

Logical and level-headed, Earth Dragons have a flair for organizing, and they make excellent managers. They still have the Dragon urge to dominate and be looked up to, but they are sociable, approachable, and cooperative, and, compared to other Dragons, less inclined to breathe fire or to erupt like a volcano at the least provocation. Earth Dragons will work hard and purposefully to succeed at their aims in life. The Earth element adds a reasonable and realistic note to the Dragon's character, and a larger portion of self-control, and normally the Earth Dragon is worthy of the respect he or she commands. In life and in love, these Dragons take their responsibilities seriously.

Health and habitat

HEALTH AND CONSTITUTION

Dragons are blessed with good health, despite the fact that they run on high-octane energy, burn the candle at both ends, and take breathtaking risks. They are among the most robust of the Animal signs, but they can suffer ill-health as a result of stress. They commonly suffer from tension headaches, and depression or hypertension can be prevalent in Dragons – caused by emotional storms. They can help themselves by keeping their fiery natures under control, getting some routine into their lives, and taking forms of exercise that calm the mind and spirit as well as tone the body.

THE DRAGON AT HOME

Dragons are not the most domestic of creatures, and may be happier out in the world than in a state of domesticity. Nevertheless, with their creativity and aesthetic sense, they can enjoy making an impressive home. It has to be somewhere that can express their flamboyant characters. A Dragon's home needs to be as big and imposing as the Dragon personality, providing space for the fiery Dragon breath.

Career and wealth

THE DRAGON AT WORK

Of the Dragon's many talents, it is originality that stands out the most. The Dragon is distinctly creative and a genius at lateral thinking, always able to see new avenues where others can see only brick walls. Dragons are highly adaptable and are suited to many occupations, especially if they can be in the limelight. In any of the many fields that the enterprising Dragon may decide to work in, he or she will always take a fresh and radical approach. Dragons work hard, but they do not enjoy taking orders; they should avoid jobs that involve too much routine, and should gravitate instead toward work in which their self-sufficiency can be an asset.

FINANCE AND THE DRAGON

Dragons are big spenders, but they are generous with others as well as with themselves. They do not know the meaning of the word "hoard," and accumulating money does not interest them either. Many Dragons will readily take huge risks with their capital, and sometimes bet on their shirt and lose it. However, they were born with the Midas touch, and rare is the Dragon who remains penniless for long. A Dragon person will always be honest and straight in financial dealings and can always be trusted.

LEFT *Meditation and yoga can calm the over-active Dragon and help to prevent stress.*

COMPATIBLE BUSINESS PARTNERS

Whether Dragons benefit from or constantly conflict with their business partners depends, as in all relationships, on whether their Animal signs are harmonious or antagonistic to each other. Taking into consideration the compatibility of the elements between themselves and their working colleagues can also be very useful.

DRAGONS RULED BY	BENEFIT FROM	ARE ANTAGONISTIC TO
Metal	Earth Snakes	Fire Tigers
Water	Metal Monkeys	Earth Sheep
Wood	Water Roosters	Metal Oxen
Fire	Wood Rats	Water Rabbits
Earth	Fire Dragons	Wood Horses

Leisure and pleasures

LIKES AND DISLIKES

DRAGONS LIKE

Color Preference
Greenish-blue

❖

Gems and Stones
Opal, sapphire, amber

❖

Suitable Gifts
Pack of Tarot cards, camera, executive toy, a copy of the I Ching, mirror, a family crest, mobile phone

❖

Hobbies and Pastimes
Show jumping, computer programming, public speaking, fossil hunting, astrology

Just as people born under the same Animal sign share a similar character and outlook on life, so do they also have similar tastes. As two Dragons get to know each other, they soon discover that they have many likes and dislikes in common.

DRAGONS DISLIKE

❖

Being ordered around

❖

Unnecessary bureaucracy

❖

Being told their ideas won't work

❖

People who don't put one hundred percent effort into their undertakings

COMPATIBLE FRIENDS

Although each individual person is unique, Chinese astrologers are very precise about which Animals have a general shared understanding and which have characters that are antagonistic to one another. Dragons may wish to note which signs are more likely to provide lasting friendship and which they would find unsettling.

BEST FRIENDS	MORTAL ENEMY
Rats	*Dogs*
Monkeys	

RIGHT *Whatever the Dragon does on vacation, it is bound to be something adventurous and unusual.*

THE DRAGON ON VACATION

Dragons are attracted by the unusual, the unorthodox, and the bizarre. No self-respecting Dragon would want to walk in the footsteps of the average tourist. Instead, they take great pleasure in seeking out-of-the-way destinations, or, if close to home, then locations that are off the beaten track. But Dragons also like (and need) thrills and spills, which they might find by taking an impromptu Winter break to go skiing. In the Summer, they might go rappelling, parascending, or hang gliding. They could put their courage to the test and ride the longest roller coaster in the land. And because they are attracted to the mysteries of the world, a tour of the wonders of the World would leave the Dragon marveling at humankind's audacity and ingenuity as well as the marvels of nature. But Dragons are also fundamentally sentimental at heart, so retracing their childhood haunts, perhaps, or taking a second honeymoon would bring immense pleasure, too.

FRIENDS AND FOE

Dragons are always popular people, but, because of the richness of their personalities, they seem to manage, throughout their lives, to gather as much criticism as they do admiration. With their tempestuous characters and fiery natures, Dragons are certainly not the most comfortable friends for those of a sensitive or timorous disposition. But those people who know and love the Dragon find him or her kind and benevolent, a true champion, and a terrific ally in times of trouble. Never a fair-weather friend, once these dynamic creatures have pledged their allegiance to someone they will never let that person down. In the Dragon philosophy, a friend is a friend for life. Honest as the live-long day, Dragon people are renowned for their integrity and are, on the whole, extremely trusting souls. Little does it occur to them that others, however, may not be quite so ethical. Discovering that someone in whom they had placed their trust has been using trickery or guile leaves Dragons sadder but a good deal wiser in life.

Dragon parents and babies

Because people born in the Year of the Dragon are so busy climbing the ladder of success, making a name for themselves, or accumulating their wealth, they tend to delay having children until later than many people of the other Chinese horoscope signs. In comparison to others, parenting does not come naturally or easily to the Dragon-born individual. However, when Dragons do become parents, they approach it with as much gusto as they do everything else. They are as proud of their offspring as they are any of their other achievements – and they are never backwards in letting people know about their little ones' talents, the accomplishments, the excellent report cards and, of course, the good looks of their fine offspring.

Dragon folk are renowned for their generosity, and lavish their children with toys, equipment, and spending money. It has been remarked about them that, rather than physically spending time with their children, they shower them with material rewards instead. But when all is said and done, Dragons take their parental responsibilities seriously. They are kind but firm, ambitious for their children's future, and protective of their welfare. Should any problem upset them, or mishap befall them, the Dragon will brandish his or her metaphorical sword and, in typical avenging-angel style, promptly set off to redress all wrongs.

THE DRAGON BABY AND CHILD

Like their adult counterparts, children born in the Year of the Dragon have colorful characters and larger-than-life personalities. Independent from the start, these little infants soon make their needs known. Noisy and active, it pays to begin stimulating their rich imaginations while they are still in their cots. It is this imagination and their curiosity about their environment that can land young Dragons in hot water many times throughout their school days, for these children, hungry to experience all that life holds for them, are easily misunderstood and may be considered mischievous or hyperactive. Sometimes Dragon children are loners who withdraw into their own world of make-believe.

Either way, Dragon children need special attention and careful handling in order to bring out the best in them. Their creative talents must be encouraged, even if this means extra tuition in whatever subject they show promise.

DRAGON PARENT/CHILD RELATIONSHIPS

For some parents, their children's personalities harmonize perfectly with their own. Others find that no matter how much they may love their offspring, they are simply not on the same wavelength. Below are the compatibility ratings between Dragon parents and their children.

DRAGONS WITH	UNDER THE SAME ROOF	COMPATIBILITY RATING
Rat	much pride in each other	✓✓✓
Ox	little understanding	✓
Tiger	lots of thrills	✓✓✓
Rabbit	opposing viewpoints	✓
Dragon	like father, like son	✓✓✓✓
Snake	few problems	✓✓✓✓
Horse	differing attitudes	✓✓
Sheep	too sensitive	✓
Monkey	mutually fulfilling	✓✓✓✓
Rooster	some clashes of temperament	✓✓✓
Dog	difficulties arise	✓
Pig	loving but hard work	✓✓

RATINGS ✓ uphill struggle   ✓✓ some complications
✓✓✓ easy bonding   ✓✓✓✓ on the same wavelength

BELOW *The colorful Dragon character makes a generous and proud parent, with plenty of ambition for his or her offspring.*

OPPOSITE *Dragons can be exasperating people, but their many good qualities ensure that they are always loved.*

Lovers and spouses

On the negative side, for a start, the Dragon is a consummate egotist and a show-off who loves the limelight; modesty is not one of the Dragon's assets. Then there is the Dragon temper, which is the worst of all the Chinese Animals. Dragons can be dogmatic, domineering, and bombastic. They hate taking advice from anyone, are quick to rebuke their nearest and dearest, and can be hopelessly tactless and insensitive to their partners.

IRRESISTIBLE ATTRACTION

Why do people love Dragons so much? Because they are warm and generous, charismatic, and irresistibly attractive, and so strong and courageous that standing beside them drives away fear. Their irrepressible exuberance makes the sun shine on the bleakest day, and they generate excitement wherever they go. They are wild and impulsive and can make others realize their dreams. People love them because they simply feel better when Dragons are around.

Dragons fall in love at the drop of a hat, but are in no hurry to give up their independence – indeed many Dragons remain confirmed singletons. But an intelligent, witty, and amusing companion may well intrigue the Dragon enough to make him or her want to tie the knot. And once Dragon folk become committed, they are unlikely to ever roam again.

THE DRAGON LOVE PARTNER

It takes someone tough, clever, or extremely easygoing to be a Dragon's partner, because, despite their deep-down sentimentality and their superficial irresistibility, they can be rude, moody, and downright insensitive. Many people will feel the need to retire when the Dragon's fiery temper has been provoked.

The system of Chinese horoscopes is very specific about which relationhips have the potential to be successful, in love and in business. But while the heavens can point the way, the rest is up to us. The panel (right) shows how the other Animals are suited to the Dragon as a partner. Like-minded people match up best.

PARTNERS IN LOVE

DRAGON ♥ RAT
A brilliant relationship – plenty of passion, mental rapport, and understanding. Tipped for happiness and success.

DRAGON ♥ OX
When it comes to stubbornness, Dragons meet their match here. Where's the give-and-take essential for a happy marriage?

DRAGON ♥ TIGER
A gutsy combination with plenty of sparks to fuel the passions and the fire.

DRAGON ♥ RABBIT
Your differences will either unite or divide you.

DRAGON ♥ DRAGON
If you learn to share the limelight, the world will be your oyster.

DRAGON ♥ SNAKE
Clever and crafty, flirty and quick-witted – you fit together like two pieces of a jigsaw.

DRAGON ♥ HORSE
A powerful chemistry bonds you two sexually. Reach understanding and you'll have one heck of a partnership!

DRAGON ♥ SHEEP
Despite the sexual attraction, in the long run you're not suited for each other.

DRAGON ♥ MONKEY
You think alike and understand each other – a combination destined to be happy and successful.

DRAGON ♥ ROOSTER
You two exquisite creatures make a gorgeous pair, but your mega-egos tend to get in the way.

DRAGON ♥ DOG
A truly tempestuous affair – not recommended for peace of mind.

DRAGON ♥ PIG
A caring, sharing, and deeply loving partnership.

LOVE PARTNERS AT A GLANCE

DRAGONS WITH:	TIPS ON TOGETHERNESS	COMPATIBILITY
Rat	on cloud nine	♥♥♥♥
Ox	first attraction, then deadlock	♥
Tiger	a dynamic duo!	♥♥♥
Rabbit	learn to give and take	♥♥
Dragon	depends – either heaven or hell	♥♥
Snake	mirror images	♥♥♥
Horse	great sex	♥♥♥
Sheep	different destinies	♥
Monkey	refreshingly alive	♥♥♥♥
Rooster	never a dull moment	♥♥
Dog	keep walking if you want to stay healthy	♥
Pig	sooooo comfy	♥♥♥

COMPATIBILITY RATINGS: ♥ conflict ♥♥ work at it
♥♥♥ strong sexual attraction ♥♥♥♥ heavenly!

EAST MEETS WEST

ARIES DRAGON

These Dragons tend to attract good fortune. With high-octane drive and enthusiasm they cram as much as they can into their day. They are upwardly mobile individuals, and they always get what they want.

TAUREAN DRAGON

Taurus brings the Dragon down to earth, adding strength of purpose and tenacity. Taurean Dragons will work hard and consistently to acquire the material comforts and high standards of living that are essential to their well-being.

GEMINI DRAGON

These are life's performers, relishing the company of others and at their best center-stage. Gemini Dragons can pull off several tasks at once and juggle any number of conversations successfully but undertaking anything in depth is not really their style.

CANCERIAN DRAGON

Cancer Dragons have refined tastes and are accomplished in one art form or another, and their homes act as showcases of their talents. These are less self-interested Dragons, caring and sensitive, and for them a close relationship and settled home life are essential to happiness.

LEONINE DRAGON

As well as being King of the jungle, the Lion is King of the Western zodiac. The Dragon is the sign of the Emperor, the ruler of the dynasty. Leo Dragons have an innate sense of nobility, and are born leaders. They are flamboyant and consummate show-offs, but their warmth and joie de vivre make them irresistibly attractive.

VIRGO DRAGON

Status and position matter a great deal to the Virgo Dragon, and he or she is prepared to work hard to reach them. With these organized and efficient people all aspects of life are carefully planned and nothing is left to chance. The Dragon's erratic tendencies are quelled and the Virgo Dragon has a steady, practical approach to life.

LIBRAN DRAGON

The Libran Dragon is a stylish creature, cultured and refined. Charm is this Dragon's greatest asset and draws people like a magnet. Libra stays the hand of the impulsive Dragon, and the Libran Dragon is a champion of the people and a great believer in fair play.

SCORPIO DRAGON

Colourful and exotic, Scorpio Dragons are mighty people with legendary ardour and zeal, and deep, intense emotions. They put their all into everything they do. When they love they love exclusively and expect the same from their partners.

SAGITTARIAN DRAGON

Open and forthright, the Sagittarian Dragon's honesty, though well-intentioned, can be insensitive. Impulsive, and sometimes indiscreet, these Dragons' exuberant gusto sweeps everyone and everything along. They have an infectiously cheering, optimistic view of life.

CAPRICORN DRAGON

These Dragons are practical, hard-working, and down-to-earth, with a driving desire for success. They will work all hours and slowly but surely climb to the top. For them, love and romance take second place, but once committed, they are highly responsible and dutiful partners.

AQUARIAN DRAGON

Idealistic and unconventional, outlandish and far-sighted, these Dragons delight in the shock of the new. They are intellectuals first and foremost, individualistic and eccentric, and born ahead of their time. Tolerant and broad-minded, they are loved by all.

PISCEAN DRAGON

With Piscean sensitivity added to Dragon brashness, these individuals are still colorful of character and ardent, but less self-centred and more responsive to the needs of others. Nevertheless the Dragon drive is still present beneath that seemingly placid surface.

Famous Dragons

Dragons are a law unto themselves. Confident and fearless when faced with a challenge, they have fiery, airy qualities and are full of ardor and exuberance. Warm, energetic, and charismatic, they are are loved, admired, and followed, but they can be loners at heart.

Sarah Bernhardt

This Dragon-born French actress towered over other actors, both male and female. Her powerful stage presence in the tragic roles she portrayed held people in thrall, and she was in demand in Europe and the United States. Even after she had had to have her leg amputated she traveled the Western world giving her astonishing performances to a full house wherever she went.

Faye Dunnaway

This American actress came to fame with a Dragon-like whoosh with her spirited and fiery performance as Bonnie in her first major film, Bonnie and Clyde in 1967. Even in photographs she shows the charisma for which the Dragon-born are famed. In her somewhat erratic career she has gone her own way, not falling into the lap of Hollywood and taking on very few roles with a Dragon-like unpredictability.

Paul Getty

The famous billionaire president of the Getty Oil Company had the Dragon's talent for success, surrounding himself with wonderful things. He amassed an astonishing art collection, expressing a Dragon-like love of the biggest and the best. As a Water Dragon he also had the ability to make wise judgements – which certainly paid off. The Getty Museum is one of the world's most prestigious art galleries.

Joan of Arc

One of history's most extraordinary women, with the dedication to fight to her death for the cause she believed in with such passion and clung to with such dedication, Joan of Arc had the charisma to keep armies of grown men behind her. This young girl was the Dragon of Dragons.

Pele

Edson Arantes do Nascimento, the internationally famous soccer player known simply as Pele, brought his Dragon brilliance to the game for over 20 years. During his career, he scored over 1,200 goals, and in his home country of Brazil he still has the status of national hero.

The Snake

YEARS OF THE SNAKE

Sixth in the cycle, Snake Years follow on from the Dragon and recur every twelfth year thereafter. As the Chinese New Year does not fall on a fixed date, it is essential to check the calendar to find the exact date on which each Snake Year actually begins.

1905 ★ 1917 ★ 1929
1941 ★ 1953 ★ 1965
1977 ★ 1989 ★ 2001

ABOVE *Slow and deep yet fast to rise and act when the situation requires it, the Snake is endowed with mystery.*

The Snake personality

ncient Chinese wisdom holds that having a Snake in the household is always a good omen, since it means the family will never starve. Whether this is because Snake-born folk are shrewd in business, intuitive in their dealings, or tenacious over their assets, one way or another they manage to attract money. It is unsurprising, therefore, that they are known as the guardians of the treasure. However, this need not refer simply to wealth; metaphorically, it may allude to the Snake person's wisdom and depth of understanding.

THE SIGN OF THE SNAKE

The Snake is the philosopher, the mystic of the astrological signs – perceptive, intuitive, even psychic. Snakes are indisputably attractive. It is not simply the fact that they are so chic, so cultured, so sophisticated and refined, so cool and composed in a crisis, but also that they are enigmatic. And who can resist a mystery?

A PRIVATE PERSON

Calm, reserved, quiet, and contemplative, the Snake is a very private person who likes to play his or her cards very close to the chest. Often appearing to others as secretive and inscrutable, the Snake is in fact a subtle worker, adept at imperceptibly insinuating himself or herself into the desired position, and at handling other people with Machiavellian precision and skill. The minds of Snake people are forever at work – either pondering deeply on abstract and abstruse subjects, or simply plotting how to ensure that things turn out the way they want.

Communication is not the Snake's strong point – certainly not at the superficial, everyday level. But at the same time, Snakes are renowned for their intuitive powers, on which they concentrate their energies. Their line of business is communicating with deeper truths – or with the unknown. Snake people are unpredictable, although they have their own logic. They often appear to hold other people at arm's length, although when they are in love they can be extremely possessive.

FACTS ABOUT SNAKES

People born in the Year of the Snake share specific characteristics that are common to all other Snakes. To say that someone is a Snake is simply a shorthand way of describing that individual's personality. Here are the salient features associated with this sign.

SNAKE FACTS
Sixth in order ★ Chinese name – SHE, sign of sagacity
Hour – 9am–10:59am ★ Month – May
Western counterpart – Taurus

CHARACTERISTICS
Subtlety ♥ Insight ♥ Shrewdness ♥ Discretion
Wisdom ♥ Compassion

Pride ✖ Indolence ✖ Manipulation ✖ Vanity
Malice ✖ Possessiveness

IN YOUR ELEMENT

*I*n addition to the Animal signs that recur once every 12 years, the 5 Chinese elements of Metal, Water, Wood, Fire, and Earth also play their part. This means that a 5-year cycle of characteristics is overlaid on the original 12-year cycle. The Snake birth year is the first guide to the personality as determined by the Chinese horoscope, but the characteristics of each generation of Snake are slightly modified by one of the elements, depending on the overlaying of the 5-year cycle.

THE METAL SNAKE 1941 AND 2001

Snakes influenced by the Metal element have extra-strong willpower and are always to be found on their guard. With an inborn appreciation of the luxurious things in life, they also have a gift for spotting openings and opportunities that will enable them to gratify their heartfelt desires. These Snakes know how to get their feet under the table so swiftly and so silently that others never even notice until the deed is done. Money is important to them, but comes only second to the need for the good things in life. Though they can be open with others – and generous, too, at times – they tend to act alone according to their instinctive qualities.

THE WATER SNAKE 1953 AND 2013

With highly developed intuitive faculties and strong psychological insights, Water Snakes can be powerfully psychic. They are extremely practical, and are also intellectual, and their forte lies in the management and organization of people and institutions. Water Snakes have good business minds, strong powers of concentration, and great determination, and will go hell-for-leather in seeking to attain their most cherished ambitions. Perhaps even more than the other elemental Snakes, the Water Snake has great secrecy in his or her manner. Water Snakes have a tendency to keep things to themselves, and yet with their family and close friends they are always loving and their fidelity is renowned.

THE WOOD SNAKE 1905 AND 1965

Probably the kindest, most amenable, and altruistic of the elemental Snakes, Wood Snakes are not quite as narcissistic as the rest. The Wood element brings stability, and gives these Snakes a love of their family and their home. They have a good circle of friends, despite enjoying the quiet life, and their opinions are respected by friends and family alike. They should learn to take – and seek – the advice of others, too, instead of always coping alone. Wood Snakes have the Snake's deep intellect, coupled with good understanding, and are genuinely concerned for others. Many are prepared to share their knowledge for the good of humankind and exhibit their leadership qualities in this arena. They also have exquisite taste and excellent powers of discrimination.

THE FIRE SNAKE 1917 AND 1977

Magnetic and charismatic, Fire Snakes are also rather outspoken, ambitious, and more extroverted than other Snake people. Fire brings energy and confidence, and Fire Snakes have got what it takes to become influential leaders in many walks of life. They have tenacity as well as leadership qualities, and, with their powers of persuasion, they have people hanging on their every word. Like many Snakes, they have a good, if often wry or sly, sense of humor which balances their tough qualities. The desire for money, power, and fame drives them ever onward and upward, and they can also be rather self-centered and find it difficult to trust or even to value other people.

THE EARTH SNAKE 1929 AND 1989

With their logical, down-to-earth approach, Earth Snakes are not troubled with the characteristic paranoia that afflicts so many other Snakes. Consequently, they have a relaxed and more outgoing manner and are more trusting and friendly, perhaps even more considerate and honest, than many others of their breed. They may be less likely to take risks, but they have the Snake's affinity with money and will succeed in the world of high finance by dint of their own sustained efforts and sensibly calculated investment instead of by taking risks that just happen to come off. These Snakes are sensible, hard-working, and reliable. But shrewdness is their greatest asset.

Health and habitat

HEALTH AND CONSTITUTION

Snakes need plenty of time and space of their own and are prone to stress complaints if they are forced to endure rush and bustle. It is best for Snakes to steer clear of noisy, chaotic situations, since these always upset them and frazzle their nerves. These people need calm at all times. Some people may enjoy the adrenaline surge that goes with physical challenge and conflict, but not Snakes. If they want to stay healthy, Snake people should never burn the candle at both ends. Plenty of rest and sleep is the Snake's formula for a long life.

THE SNAKE AT HOME

In the Snake household, refinement prevails; in decorations and choice of furnishings, quality comes before quantity every time. Though red is the color associated with the Snake sign, if Snakes choose to use it in their decorative schemes it will be applied subtly – muted shades confirm the Snake's sense of stylish elegance. Textures are chosen for their sensual feel, furniture for its deep comfort, and artefacts for detail and effect, which altogether spell luxury. One house never seems to be enough for Snakes; they either move several times or have more than one home.

Career and wealth

THE SNAKE AT WORK

These people often change career at least twice, and are unlikely to be attracted by mundane jobs. Whatever they do, they bring concentration, an eye for detail, and laser-like precision to the job. Snakes take things quietly, and may appear lazy, but in fact they are extremely conscientious and can act super-fast when necessary. They have organizational skills and the ability to put their finger on the problem or find a solution to a difficult situation. They like to sort things out on their own, and can at times seem secretive or ruthless.

FINANCE AND THE SNAKE

Financially, as long as Snake people follow their true instincts, they are likely to be successful. However, they need to avoid impulse-buying or making rash financial judgements because, although they are intuitive, they make poor gamblers and wild speculation, for a Snake, can bring disaster.

COMPATIBLE BUSINESS PARTNERS

Whether Snakes benefit from or constantly conflict with their business partners depends, as in all relationships, on whether their Animal signs are harmonious or antagonistic to each other. Taking into consideration the compatibility of the elements between themselves and their working colleagues can also be very useful.

SNAKES RULED BY	BENEFIT FROM	ARE ANTAGONISTIC TO
Metal	*Earth Rats*	*Fire Dogs*
Water	*Metal Rabbits*	*Earth Horses*
Wood	*Water Oxen*	*Metal Tigers*
Fire	*Wood Roosters*	*Water Sheep*
Earth	*Fire Snakes*	*Wood Monkeys*

ABOVE *The Snake has an affinity with the Orient, with things luxuriant, sensual, and exotic.*

Leisure and pleasures

THE SNAKE ON VACATION

Above all else, Snakes like to wallow in luxury. In fact, wallowing is quite an appropriate term to use where Snake-born individuals are concerned, since the most notorious character fault associated with this sign is indolence. One of the greatest pleasures for people born in the Year of the Snake is simply doing nothing. On vacation, Snakes of all ages seek complete rest and relaxation. Health clubs, particularly if exclusive, would suit the Snake well, and both male or female members of the sign would take full advantage of the treatments on offer. Visiting the flotarium, for example, enjoying the benefits of hydrotherapy, reflexology, or aromatherapy would certainly provide the relaxation a Snake requires.

Alternatively, some Snakes might choose to get away from it all, to rent a villa on a remote Aegean island or a log cabin in the wilderness. Others might turn their attention to spiritual matters and join a retreat or contemplate the meaning of life as they commune with Nature.

FRIENDS AND FOE

Though generally quiet and solitary creatures, Snakes are not averse to social get-togethers – especially if the occasion is a big function or an elegant dinner party. And, while Snakes do not enjoy small talk, they like nothing better than a good old gossip – particularly if it happens to be spiced with a liberal pinch of intrigue or scandal. Since they are highly selective about whom they allow into their affections, Snakes do not make friends easily. The few they do allow into their inner sanctum, however, remain close friends for life. But even these chosen ones can find it difficult to forge a truly intimate understanding with their Snake companions, for Snakes are enigmatic creatures who play their cards very, very close to their chests.

In any relationship, Snakes cannot bear to be crossed. If they are, they will become spiteful and vituperative. Make no mistake – the Snake-born individual will always go to great lengths, no matter how long it takes, to even the score.

COMPATIBLE FRIENDS

Although each individual person is unique, Chinese astrologers are very precise about which Animals have a general shared understanding and which have characters that are antagonistic to one another. Snakes may wish to note which signs are more likely to provide lasting friendship and which they would find unsettling.

BEST FRIENDS	MORTAL ENEMY
Oxen	*Pigs*
Roosters	

ABOVE RIGHT *Snake people need time to relax and time alone, away from everything.*

LIKES AND DISLIKES

SNAKES LIKE

Color Preference
Red
❖

Gems and Stones
Topaz, jasper, bloodstone
❖

Suitable Gifts
Solitaire, pack of Tarot cards, binoculars, religious icon, worry beads, snakeskin wallet, bath oil, diamond brooch, stamp collection, marble bust
❖

Hobbies and Pastimes
Fishing, numismatics, photography, visiting churches, diving, painting, scrying, astrology, orienteering

Just as people born under the same Animal sign share a similar character and outlook on life, so do they also have similar tastes. As two Snakes get to know each other, they soon discover that they have many likes and dislikes in common.

SNAKES DISLIKE

❖
Noisy crowds
❖
Being crossed, whether in business or in love
❖
Making mistakes
❖
Being disturbed

Snake parents and babies

It is said that the sensual nature of the Snake-born individual will encourage him or her to form intimate relationships with several different partners throughout life. So perhaps it is because of this that, more than most other Chinese signs, Snake households tend to be filled with an assortment of children and stepchildren from second, and sometimes even third, marriages. But, regardless of the circumstances, Snakes are in general devoted to their offspring, prepared to sacrifice a good deal to ensure the happiness and welfare of their young.

That droll sense of humor so typical of people born in the Year of the Snake stands them in good stead when dealing with their offspring. Because these people have the knack of seeing the odd or absurd side of things, Snake mothers and fathers can often defuse a potentially explosive situation simply with a wry quip or a funny aside. Though they dearly love and instinctively protect their children, perhaps the most difficult aspect of parenting for the Snake is handling noisy or rumbustious scenes. Adult Snakes are not given to the rough-and-tumble, and any hint of unrestrained boisterousness has them running for peace and quiet. Restoring order, laying down the law, or dishing out the discipline, therefore, tends to fall on their partner's shoulders – who is, hopefully, not another Snake.

THE SNAKE BABY AND CHILD

Snakes, on the whole, keep themselves to themselves and even when young, the children of this sign tend to be solitary creatures, preferring to play quietly on their own to running around in a boisterous gang. These youngsters are notoriously slow starters, and they really need to be allowed to develop in their own time. Consequently, at school many young Snakes will need extra tuition, a gentle helping hand to explain a lesson they might not have understood properly, or a word of encouragement to guide or coax them into developing their latent talents.

When upset, children born of this sign have a tendency to sulk. They are also inclined to harbor a grudge and, if sorely crossed, they can actually turn vicious and strike out as suddenly and as effectively as a viper in the wild.

ABOVE AND LEFT *The Snake household can contain a confusing mix of offspring from previous partners, and from partners' previous partners!*

OPPOSITE *The Snake in love is intensely possessive and devastatingly seductive.*

SNAKE PARENT/CHILD RELATIONSHIPS

For some parents, their children's personalities harmonize perfectly with their own. Others find that no matter how much they may love their offspring, they are simply not on the same wavelength. Below are the compatibility ratings between Snake parents and their children.

SNAKES WITH	UNDER THE SAME ROOF	COMPATIBILITY RATING
Rat	independence will win the day	✓✓
Ox	fairly sound	✓✓✓
Tiger	clashes	✓
Rabbit	much contentment	✓✓✓
Dragon	happy families	✓✓✓✓
Snake	of like minds	✓✓✓
Horse	too diverse	✓
Sheep	indulgent	✓✓✓
Monkey	what the eye doesn't see	✓✓✓✓
Rooster	on the whole, constructive	✓✓
Dog	cuddly	✓✓✓
Pig	uninspired	✓

RATINGS ✓ uphill struggle ✓✓ some complications
✓✓✓ easy bonding ✓✓✓✓ on the same wavelength

Lovers and spouses

THE SNAKE LOVER

Sleek, sultry, and passionate, the Snake is the original *femme fatale* or the dark, brooding hero about whom romantic novels are written. All Snakes are physically beautiful and devastatingly sexy. Always stylish and well-groomed, they have that certain something that people find so alluring, but can't quite put their finger on. Snakes are truly seductive, and bewitch and intoxicate those around them. They exude a feeling of intense emotional energy and pent-up sexual power.

Snakes are extremely discriminating and selective when it comes to the people they date and their choice of partner. In any relationship they are a decided asset, not only because of their good looks, their charm, and their refined tastes, but also because of their clever, incisive minds, physical responsiveness, and oddball sense of humor.

PASSION AND INTRIGUE

In love, Snakes can become intense, jealous, and possessive, yet they are not averse to the occasional extramarital affair. They adore intrigue and the thought of a secret love tryst fills them with a *frisson* of excitement. However, if a Snake is crossed or betrayed, a ruthless and vituperative side to the Snake nature will emerge and he or she will go to any lengths to get even.

THE SNAKE LOVE PARTNER

Not everyone can take a Snake. Their mix of closeness, passion, and jealousy, with a slight remoteness and the way they play their cards close to their chests, can put off people with more easygoing natures. But Snakes have

much to offer the right partner, with their depth of wit and wisdom, their appreciation of life's luxuries, and their strong, deep feelings.

The Chinese system of horoscopes can show us which relationships have the potential for success and the panel (right) shows how the other Animals are suited to the Snake as a partner.

PARTNERS IN LOVE

SNAKE ♥ RAT
If you both work on the differences in your characters, you could learn a great deal from each other.

SNAKE ♥ OX
Sympathetic, understanding, loving, on the same wavelength – you two have got it all!

SNAKE ♥ TIGER
Different outlook, different lifestyle, and different objectives all suggests little meeting of minds.

SNAKE ♥ RABBIT
Deep passions make this one heck of a sexy combo!

SNAKE ♥ DRAGON
Clever and crafty, flirty and shirty – you fit together like two pieces of a jig-saw puzzle.

SNAKE ♥ SNAKE
Intellectually, you make a great match. Emotionally, jealousy gets in the way.

SNAKE ♥ HORSE
Different viewpoints and agendas spell poor prospects.

SNAKE ♥ SHEEP
Terrific friends and sexy lovers.

SNAKE ♥ MONKEY
You'll each be constantly looking over your shoulder at the other.

SNAKE ♥ ROOSTER
What a great team!

SNAKE ♥ DOG
Mutual attraction on sight.

SNAKE ♥ PIG
Alas, little common ground.

LOVE PARTNERS AT A GLANCE

SNAKES WITH:	TIPS ON TOGETHERNESS	COMPATIBILITY
Rat	an alluring fascination	♥♥♥
Ox	simply sublime	♥♥♥♥
Tiger	odds against	♥
Rabbit	great sex	♥♥♥
Dragon	mirror images	♥♥♥
Snake	maintain separate identities	♥♥
Horse	talking helps to sort it out	♥♥
Sheep	deeply satisfying	♥♥♥♥
Monkey	only with cooperation	♥♥
Rooster	solid!	♥♥♥♥
Dog	first comes the physical, then the mental	♥♥♥
Pig	deep divisions	♥

COMPATIBILITY RATINGS: ♥ *conflict* ♥♥ *work at it*
♥♥♥ *strong sexual attraction* ♥♥♥♥ *heavenly!*

EAST MEETS WEST

ARIES SNAKE

The sun in Aries brings the Snake courage and enterprise. Aries Snakes are achievers, and their astuteness enables them to make money. They are generous and liberal with cash and make ardent lovers and happy home-makers.

TAUREAN SNAKE

Tenacious, with long memories, these are not the most active or energetic people, but they have the most incisive of minds. It never pays to underestimate a Taurean Snake. Love, comfort and wealth are essential to their well-being and they will contrive to make sure they get the lot.

GEMINI SNAKE

These mercurial Snakes can slip and slither their way out of the most difficult situation and have such penetration that they can see right to the heart of any matter. They are well read and have a charm, wit and sociability that make them captivating and a sparkling asset at a party.

CANCERIAN SNAKE

These are glamorous, twinkling stars, who strive for kudos and prestige. They will work hard in their chosen way to acquire for themselves and their families the best that money can buy. Deeply domestic, for them family and home are the centre of the universe.

LEONINE SNAKE

Proud individuals with a strong self image and great self-confidence, these Snakes hate deferring to others or coming out second. They need encouragement, approval and admiration to make sure that they function well, but not so much that it goes to their heads.

VIRGO SNAKE

Highly ambitious, industrious, and bossy to boot, Virgo Snakes like to be in charge. With cool efficiency and superb organizational power they will tirelessly give of their energies to improve their status and position. Intellectual and unemotional, in love they are not demonstrative, but they make dedicated home-makers.

LIBRAN SNAKE

These are some of the most attractive people of the Snake clan. With their social graces and persuasive charm Libran Snakes make gracious, considerate, affable, and witty hosts or guests. These people are never short of a suitor, and are idealistic and romantic in love.

SCORPIO SNAKE

This combination produces powerful, enigmatic individuals whose thoughts and feelings are labyrinthine deep. Ultra-guarded, secretive and impossible to fathom, they play their cards extremely close to their chests. Cool and controlled, they are also passionate and possessive and can have a Scorpion sting to their tail if crossed in love.

SAGITTARIAN SNAKE

These highly intuitive snakes are perspicacious and almost clairvoyant. Elegant and classy or suave and debonair, and endowed with great good taste, they succeed by following their instincts. Sagittarian Snakes seek a partner with whom they can share a deep and spiritual relationship.

CAPRICORN SNAKE

Capricorn Snakes patiently and efficiently build their reputation, position and wealth in life with meticulous planning and organization. They steadily bide their time, and go for the best in everything. They may be accused of snobbery, but their hearts are in the right place.

AQUARIAN SNAKE

Intellectual but idealistic, broad-minded but possessive, the Aquarian Snake is full of contradictions. These Snakes need to be loved and to have a supportive partner, but they hate to feel shackled and tied down.

PISCEAN SNAKE

These Snakes are sensitive, soft and sensual, dreamy and kind, receptive and compassionate to others. Delicate emotionally, they take everything to heart. Being ruled by their feelings, they fall in love and commit themselves hook, line and sinker.

Famous Snakes

The typical Snake-born person is smooth and sinuous, sensual and sophisticated, refined and wise, and above all enigmatic. Snake people are laid back and never seem hurried. They usually go for what they want and get it, but they can sometimes seethe with passion.

Mae West

Mae West, of "Come up and see me sometime" fame oozed Snaky sinuosity, both in her films and in real life. Her film persona is almost an archetype of the Snake personality, though with none of the darker undercurrents that can go with this sign and with the droll humor that can be characteristic of the Snake.

Howard Hughes

The famously reclusive film producer, businessman and multimillionaire got what he wanted and built up riches for himself in a most aloof and Snake-like way. He sealed himself off from the world while still controlling his business interests and finances, and succeeded in shrouding himself in mystery even beyond his death. This Snake still remains an enigmatic character to this day.

Martin Luther King, Jr.

The American preacher, civil rights campaigner, and 1964 Nobel Peace Prize winner was an Earth Snake, which is consistent with the openness of his character. The Snake's calm wisdom can be seen in his quiet but determined espousal of non-violence in the pursuance of racial equality.

Two other great leaders alive at the same time and also born under the sign of the Snake were John F. Kennedy and China's Mao Tse-tung.

Greta Garbo

This actress showed many aspects of her Snake inheritance. Her sophisticated, glamorous and aloof sensual appeal gave her a distance that held others off while making her desirable. "I want to be alone" is the wish of the Snake. She could also be said to have some of the Snake's vanity and love of building up treasure.

Grace Kelly

One of those really sophisticated and high-class Snakes, in all her screen performances Grace Kelly was able to give out that subtle hint of inner passion that was all the more tempting for being so much in contrast with the cool exterior. After only six years as a Hollywood actress she shed one of her Snake's skins and became a princess.

The Horse

The Horse personality

Bursting with life, vivacity, and irrepressible enthusiasm, Horse people explode onto the scene, becoming without effort the life and soul of the party, and amusing everyone with their sparkling wit and lively conversation. Then, without warning, they will kick up their heels and head off to the next pasture that takes their eager fancy.

THE SIGN OF THE HORSE

Horse people are indisputably impulsive and highly volatile. Yet they are also intelligent and practical with it. They have razor-sharp minds, enabling them to pick up new skills in the twinkling of an eye, and they are adept at carrying on several conversations at once or at holding down two or three jobs at a time, while attending to whatever is on hand.

LIFE AT A GALLOP

Most people find Horse folk as attractive as they are elegant, always at home in social situations, and full of verve and vigor. They can get to grips rapidly with new facts, ideas, and situations, and are open, honest, and completely without guile. But they like a challenge, and sometimes fail to stick with things when they see a new fence in the distance to jump. While Horse people are dependably loyal to friends and colleagues, and particularly to partners, they like to keep their freedom and independence – even though they may only want to graze under a tree or gallop over the hills alone.

On the whole, the Horse is likeable and trustworthy – neither shy and over-sensitive, nor egotistical – a good companion and a good leader, without being bossy. But Horse people can have fits of stubborness, in which they show their self-centered side. They also have a temper and a fierce kick. They can find themselves exploding in a sudden rage, which, however justifiable the provocation, will usually seem out of all proportion to it. Afterwards, the Horse person feels full of regret, but not everyone else will be able to understand and forgive the episode.

YEARS OF THE HORSE

Seventh in the cycle, Horse Years follow on from the Snake and recur every twelfth year thereafter. As the Chinese New Year does not fall on a fixed date, it is essential to check the calendar to find the exact date on which each Horse Year actually begins.

1906 ★ 1918 ★ 1930
1942 ★ 1954 ★ 1966
1978 ★ 1990 ★ 2002

ABOVE *The energetic Horse is a great juggler of projects, but also at times erratic and whimsical.*

FACTS ABOUT HORSES

People born in the Year of the Horse share specific characteristics that are common to all other Horses. To say that someone is a Horse is simply a short-hand way of describing that individual's personality. Here are the salient features associated with this sign.

HORSE FACTS
Seventh in order ★ Chinese name – MA, Sign of elegance and fervour
Hour – 11am–12.59pm ★ Month – June
Western counterpart – Gemini

CHARACTERISTICS
Vivacity ♥ Stamina ♥ Wit ♥ Independence
Cheerfulness ♥ Refinement ♥ Friendliness

Selfishness ✖ Volatility ✖ Impatience
Inconstancy ✖ Vanity ✖ Recklessness

IN YOUR ELEMENT

he characteristics of the Horse, as determined by the Animal sign that recurs once every 12 years, are also subtly modulated by one of the 5 Chinese elements of Metal, Water, Wood, Fire, and Earth, which overlay a 5-year cycle of characteristics on the original 12-year cycle. The Horse birth year is the first guide to the personality, but each generation of Horse is slightly different.

THE METAL HORSE 1930 AND 1990

Twice as adventurous, independent, and freedom-loving as the average Horse, and with a great enthusiasm for any challenge, the Metal Horse has a fear of being trapped that makes him or her shun all form of commitment. This Horse is a born rover, and is always reluctant to put down roots or to settle in a stable relationship. Consequently, he or she tends to change jobs and partners frequently. This type of Horse is particularly attractive to others, with a hint of a wild and untamed spirit, and in fact makes a good, warm friend as long as the Horse knows he or she is able to head off alone when the fancy takes hold.

THE WATER HORSE 1942 AND 2002

The fluidity of the Water element brings great adaptability, and the Water Horse can make the most of circumstances, whatever they may be. But this is also the most indecisive of the equine tribe. The Water Horse tends to make frequent changes of mind and follow a new direction at a toss of the mane. This behavior can be confusing to colleagues and partners, who thought they knew where they were. At its best, it gives a sense of spontaneity and keeps people exitedly on their toes, but it can also make the Water Horse seem irritatingly or bafflingly inconsistent. Still, the Water Horse is always cheerful and has a sparkling wit and a marvellous sense of humor, which makes this Horse always in demand.

THE WOOD HORSE 1954 AND 2014

This stabilizing influence helps to temper the Horse's inconsistency and adventurousness, making the Wood Horse less skittish than most. As a consequence, Wood Horses are generally more predictable than other Horse folk, and better able to control excessive equine restlessness and take a more disciplined approach to life. Ultimately, this brings professional success and stability in personal relationships. All Horses will work hard, but Wood Horses perhaps tend to stick to the task in hand more readily than other Horse types, and work cooperatively with others. They are intelligent and good-humored – but even so, the Horse nature balks at any hint of being dominated by anyone else.

THE FIRE HORSE 1906 AND 1966

The Fire Horse is a breed apart – volatile, flamboyant, and passionate. There is a strong, wild streak in this Animal that makes him or her want to live life on the edge. The Chinese say that the Fire Horse leaves a trail of devastation behind wherever it goes. Given this nature, Fire Horses fall into one of two groups: they are either hugely fortunate and successful or deeply miserable and unlucky. Fire Horses typically love change and action. They have great flair, but not much sticking power. Fire infuses their temperaments, and they are never lukewarm about anything, but are always ready to drop one burning torch in favor of the next. A force to be reckoned with if you happen to irritate them, Fire Horses are engaging, but a little awesome.

THE EARTH HORSE 1918 AND 1978

A more stable brand of Horse, and perhaps with a bit of the cart horse rather than the purebred racer in their nature, Earth Horses will work methodically towards a chosen goal. Although in love matters they can be fickle at times, they are never recklessly impulsive, and usually weigh up the consequences of any action before they decide to take it. This can bring about indecisive traits, as the Earth Horse will consider everything so carefully and see all the pros and cons. At work, and on a broad canvas, the Horse ability to grasp things quickly is still in evidence, but in smaller matters these Horses can beat around the bush, as if they can't make up their minds. Kindness, adaptability, and good humor guarantee them easy and happy relationships.

Health and habitat

HEALTH AND CONSTITUTION

When it comes to health, those born under the sign of the Horse are literally as "strong as a horse." Their optimistic outlook and positive attitude keep them hale and hearty, while their active lifestyles ensure that they get plenty of exercise and fresh air to keep them fit. If denied the outdoor life they love, they feel under par, and should always make a point of finding time for outdoor exercise, even if it is only in the park. Horse people need to learn to relax a little, and to beware the Horse tendency to turn to alcohol and nicotine when under pressure.

THE HORSE AT HOME

There is always a warm welcome to be found at the house of the Horse, since Horses like nothing better than spending a convivial evening chatting and dining in good company in their own homes. Evidence of their skill in handicraft will be found there in plenty, as will be the many projects left undone when something more exciting came along. Golds and oranges, their favorite colors, are used imaginatively to create a vibrant, stimulating environment that is practical as well as comfortable. Housework, however, is not one of the Horse's favorite hobbies.

Career and wealth

THE HORSE AT WORK

With their agility of mind and boundless energy, and a great ability to pick up new skills at a glance and to try anything once, Horse people are suited to almost any career they wish to choose, as long as routine and taking orders are not involved. They like to work in areas that bring them into contact with plenty of people, but their independence and self-reliance make them prefer to be in control. It is to the world of communications that they are perhaps best suited, since they have an inherent talent for communicating, a genius for getting through to other people, and often a considerable gift for languages as well.

FINANCE AND THE HORSE

Horses are as irrepressible in financial matters as in other areas of their life. When it comes to money, they make it and they spend it. Money brings them huge enjoyment, but they are not avaricious, or overly concerned about it. When they have it, they have a good time spending it. When it's gone, they simply go out and make some more. Often they will take risks and gamble, but more for the fun than for the possible prize.

COMPATIBLE BUSINESS PARTNERS

Whether Horses benefit from or constantly conflict with their business partners depends, as in all relationships, on whether their Animal signs are harmonious or antagonistic to each other. Taking into consideration the compatibility of the elements between themselves and their working colleagues can also be very useful.

HORSES RULED BY	BENEFIT FROM	ARE ANTAGONISTIC TO
Metal	Earth Sheep	Fire Snakes
Water	Metal Dogs	Earth Pigs
Wood	Water Roosters	Metal Rats
Fire	Wood Horses	Water Rabbits
Earth	Fire Tigers	Wood Monkeys

Leisure and pleasures

THE HORSE ON VACATION

People born in the Year of the Horse have itchy feet, so traveling is one of their favorite hobbies. The further they can get away and the faster, the better they like it. Horse-born individuals are impulsive vacationers. They throw together a few essentials and take off on a whim. Whether they take after the thoroughbred or the practical cart-horse, sporting or activity holidays suit them well because, like their animal counterpart, human Horses like to feel the wind in their hair as they gallop across the open range. Camping, caravaning, hiking, and touring by land or sea are also appropriate Horse-type activities. Entertainers par excellence, Horse-born folk love to be entertained themselves. But with their highly original turn of mind, it is the out-of-the-ordinary type of amusement they seek. An avant-garde theatrical performance would fit the bill, dropping in on a jazz festival, or taking a plane to Rio to catch the carnival.

LIKES AND DISLIKES

HORSES LIKE

Color Preference
Flame orange

❖

Gems and Stones
Amethyst, turquoise, topaz

❖

Suitable Gifts
Compass, kite, silk shirt, camera, exotic cookbook, embroidery kit, mobile phone, pedicure, overnight case, Mah Jongg set

❖

Hobbies and Pastimes
Athletics, horse riding, modern dance, theater, playing wind instruments, flying model airplanes

Just as people born under the same Animal sign share a similar character and outlook on life, so do they also have similar tastes. As two Horses get to know each other, they soon discover that they have many likes and dislikes in common.

HORSES DISLIKE

❖

Being ignored

❖

Feeling stuck in a rut

❖

Jealousy

❖

Losing their independence

COMPATIBLE FRIENDS

Although each individual person is unique, Chinese astrologers are very precise about which Animals have a general shared understanding and which have characters that are antagonistic to one another. Horses may wish to note which signs are more likely to provide lasting friendship and which they would find unsettling.

BEST FRIENDS	MORTAL ENEMY
Tigers	*Rats*
Dogs	

ABOVE AND RIGHT *The Horse makes friends easily.*

FRIENDS AND FOE

Though spirited and independent, Horses are also highly gregarious. Despite their flighty and volatile dispositions, they feel miserable if they are alone for any great length of time. In fact, Horse-born folk need to be part of a strong coterie of people, and to have a supportive network of friends around them. Fortunately, with their buoyant personalities, people gravitate toward them, and Horses find it easy to make friends. In those born in the Year of the Horse, an element of the horse's natural herding instinct emerges in a compulsion to join clubs and associations in an attempt to surround themselves with like-minded individuals. Sociability being their strong suit, they derive immense pleasure from meeting up with friends for a good chat, and, despite enjoying competitive activities, just being part of the team is sometimes enough for them.

Horse parents and babies

Those who are born under the sign of the Horse are renowned for their ability to hold down two or three jobs at the same time, to carry on several conversations at once without ever losing track, and to keep disparate projects in the air while attending to whatever matter is currently at hand. If, as all mothers and fathers know only too well, parenting is a multi-task operation, then these inherent talents of the Horse will equip him or her very well when it comes to bringing up baby.

As far as Horse parents are concerned, stimulating their children's imaginations and encouraging them to think for themselves are the two principle tenets to parenting that these people hold close to their hearts. Horse-born mothers and fathers teach their offspring while they are virtually still in their cots to become independent and to value their rights and their freedom.

Some might argue that since Horses buck against shackles and restraints, it is their own personal drive for freedom that forces their children to stand on their own two feet when still comparatively young. Indeed, many Horse-born folk make cool, unsentimental parents, who often put their work, if not before, at least on a par with, their child-rearing responsibilities. But in reality, they are enthusiastic parents whose children grow up with an enquiring mind and an indomitable spirit of adventure.

THE HORSE BABY AND CHILD

A salient feature of Horse-born babies is that they will burble away contentedly to themselves for hours. Talking develops early – and becomes a life-long passion! At school, these youngsters go on to excel in languages and all forms of communication studies.

Children belonging to the sign of the Horse believe in forging their own identities from a very young age, and particularly so if they were born in a Fire year, as this element dramatically magnifies the adventurousness and high spirits of this Animal. Independence is their biggest drive, and they will fight for their rights to liberty and freedom with all their might. If they are restrained or forced to conform by too many strict rules, they will rebel. And they will do it in style. Indeed, Horse-born youngsters, including those who are idyllically happy at home, have a reputation of flying the parental nest just as soon as they are able to do so.

ABOVE *Horse people encourage their children to think for themselves.*

HORSE PARENT/CHILD RELATIONSHIPS

For some parents, their children's personalities harmonize perfectly with their own. Others find that no matter how much they may love their offspring, they are simply not on the same wavelength. Below are the compatibility ratings between Horse parents and their children.

HORSES WITH	UNDER THE SAME ROOF	COMPATIBILITY RATING
Rat	diverse ambitions	✓
Ox	satisfactory	✓✓
Tiger	no generation gap here	✓✓✓✓
Rabbit	conflicting views	✓✓
Dragon	plenty of verve	✓✓✓
Snake	improves with time	✓✓✓
Horse	independence prevails	✓✓
Sheep	mutual understanding	✓✓✓✓
Monkey	lots of respect for each other	✓✓✓
Rooster	at odds	✓
Dog	amicable	✓✓
Pig	comfortable	✓✓✓

RATINGS ✓ uphill struggle ✓✓ some complications
✓✓✓ easy bonding ✓✓✓✓ on the same wavelength

Lovers and spouses

THE HORSE LOVER

The agile, mercurial Horse is the Peter Pan of the Chinese Animal signs, perpetually youthful and breezing through life by following his or her instincts. This is the sign of fervor, and of elegance in speech and appearance. Eloquent and persuasive, the Horse can charm the birds from the trees, and very few can match the Horse's style. Like champagne, the Horse is effervescent and highly intoxicating, and his or her happiness and enthusiasm fill all the people the Horse meets with good cheer. The Horse's capacity to live life to the full inspires others to drink deep of the joys of life.

BLIND IN LOVE

The Horse-born individual is a smart cookie in almost every department of life, but not when it comes to love. Horses fall in love all the time – and always lose their judgement and throw all reason to the wind. The two aphorisms "love is blind" and "marry in haste, repent at leisure" could have been penned especially for the Horse.

Horse people fall in love far too quickly and usually far too often. And every time it's the grand passion. They throw everything over to follow the objects of their desire, and every time they say it's for keeps. However, Chinese astrologers tell us that when it comes to Horses, maturity brings emotional stability, so that's when their relationships are more likely to succeed.

THE HORSE LOVE PARTNER

Horse people love to live life at a headlong gallop. Wherever they go they carry a vortex of high-octane activity around with them. Inexhaustible and indefatigable are terms often used to describe the Horse character, as with seemingly boundless energy these people can cram more into one day than others do into a week of Sundays.

The system of Chinese horoscopes is very specific about which Animal signs offer the potential for successful relationhips with Horse people, in love and in business. The panel (right) shows how the other Animals are suited to the Horse as a partner.

ABOVE Not exactly fickle, the Horse just can't help falling in love again.

PARTNERS IN LOVE

HORSE ♥ RAT
No love lost between you two.

HORSE ♥ OX
Better in business together than in bed.

HORSE ♥ TIGER
Plenty of high jinks in this high-octane relationship ensure an exciting life together.

HORSE ♥ RABBIT
Despite conflicts, you could just about manage to put up with each other.

HORSE ♥ DRAGON
A powerful chemistry bonds you two sexually.

HORSE ♥ SNAKE
Different viewpoints and agendas spell poor prospects for this union's success.

HORSE ♥ HORSE
Two strong-minded, independent individuals suggests little chance of this relationship staying the course.

HORSE ♥ SHEEP
Attraction at first sight is followed by galvanic passion and shared desire. This union is for keeps.

HORSE ♥ MONKEY
A prickly combination, better for friendship than for marriage.

HORSE ♥ ROOSTER
Despite the odd power conflict, you make a great team.

HORSE ♥ DOG
Tipped for lasting happiness, stability, and success.

HORSE ♥ PIG
A laid-back sort of affair with lots of indulgent fun, but who would attend to paying the bills or buying the groceries?

LOVE PARTNERS AT A GLANCE

HORSES WITH:	TIPS ON TOGETHERNESS	COMPATIBILITY
Rat	*an unstable union*	♥
Ox	*confrontational*	♥
Tiger	*hot and spicy*	♥♥♥♥
Rabbit	*difficult but achievable*	♥♥
Dragon	*great sex*	♥♥♥
Snake	*talking helps to sort it out*	♥♥
Horse	*terrific passion but, alas, only short-term*	♥♥
Sheep	*made for each other*	♥♥♥♥
Monkey	*socially, yes, sexually, no*	♥♥
Rooster	*quarrels undermine your love*	♥♥♥
Dog	*you have what it takes*	♥♥♥♥
Pig	*nice, but unrealistic*	♥♥

COMPATIBILITY RATINGS: ♥ *conflict* ♥♥ *work at it*
♥♥♥ *strong sexual attraction* ♥♥♥♥ *heavenly!*

EAST MEETS WEST

🐎 ARIES HORSE

These Horses like to take life at a gallop. They can be courageous leaders or just that bit pushy. New ideas and fresh adventures always grab their attention but there is a danger of a trail of half-finished projects being left behind them. Aries Horses excel where bold strokes and innovative approaches are called for.

🐎 TAUREAN HORSE

The common sense and practical streak of the Taurean makes these Horse-born people more circumspect, security-conscious, and driven by the need for creature comforts, and also more likely to put down roots. They are imaginative, with strong creative talents.

🐎 GEMINI HORSE

Gemini Horses are mercurial, clever, and astute, persuasive and witty. They prefer to know a little about a lot of things. Charming, flirtatious, and with youthful good looks, they are often at the center of attention. Emotionally, they tend to be immature and inconstant in love.

🐎 CANCERIAN HORSE

These big-hearted Horses are less likely than most to kick up their heels and gallop off into the sunset. Cancerian Horses have high standards of excellence and either find the love of their lives when young or go on searching for the perfect but elusive mate in life. This is a big-hearted person with much love to give.

🐎 LEONINE HORSE

This resplendent individual dispenses sunshine all round. Leo Horses are dynamic, high-profile people of regal poise and bearing. They have innate self-confidence and nothing will deflect them from their chosen goal. When a Leo Horse falls in love, he or she is totally blind to reason.

🐎 VIRGO HORSE

These Horses are more sensible, more practical, and more hard-working than most. The Virgo influence steadies the erratic tendencies of the Horse and calms the emotional makeup. Virgo Horses take a mature and responsible attitude to their commitments and love affairs.

🐎 LIBRAN HORSE

Friends play a very important part in the lives of Libran Horses. Their charm, light-hearted banter and effervescent personalities make them highly in demand at all social occasions. Libran Horses have flair, panache, and style.

🐎 SCORPIO HORSE

Scorpio lends powers of concentration that enable these Horses to focus on their ideas and see projects through to the end, while the Horse's zany outlook lightens any Scorpionic intensity.

🐎 SAGITTARIAN HORSE

This is the union of two Horses, both impulsive and free-wheeling. The Sagittarian Horse is an impulsive, larger-than-life extrovert – irrepressibly enthusiastic, ever adventurous, and indefatigably optimistic – who can severely overstretch his or her capabilities.

🐎 CAPRICORN HORSE

The Capricorn Horse is driven by ambition and the need to succeed. Money and status are important to these Horse people, and the industrious influence of the Goat steadies the erratic nature of the Horse. Capricorn Horses are faithful and loyal, and great achievers.

🐎 AQUARIAN HORSE

These are perhaps the most colorful of all Horse-born folk: zany, unconventional, unorthodox, funny, and uniquely eccentric. They always have an eye on the distant horizon and are far-sighted thinkers and talented inventors with a great creative flair.

🐎 PISCEAN HORSE

Pisces adds gentleness, empathy, and a deeply caring instinct to the Horse's brio. Piscean Horses are impressionable people, who can be swept along by ideals or who may spend their lives collecting lame ducks.

Famous Horses

Horse people are vivacious and full of stamina. Cheerful and independent, they are also volatile and sometimes reckless or impulsive. The Horse makes a great master juggler.

Leonard Bernstein

The American musician Leonard Bernstein is best known to many as a larger-than-life conductor, but he spread his musical talents far and wide, and showed his Horse-like characteristics in many ways. He had the Horse's qualities through and through in his cheerfulness, high energy level, and versatility. He was composer of musicals, including *West Side Story*, as well as symphonies and ballets and a memorial mass for J F Kennedy. He was also an accomplished pianist, and active promoter and encourager of young musicians.

Mike Tyson

The US heavyweight boxer Mike Tyson is an example of the athletic Horse. In 1986 he became the youngest world heavyweight champion, and he was world champion holder from 1987 to 1990, boxing with easy strength and agility and pulling a fast punch. No one could dispute his lively character and the way he attracts attention, and he seems to be unpredictable too.

Rita Hayworth

The vivacious Rita Hayworth was a film actress with the healthy good looks of many a Horse-born type. Her vivacity and the variety of her roles are linked to the Horse's qualities. She was married to a Rabbit, Orson Welles. This is said to be a difficult match, and in their case the marriage lasted five years.

Billie Graham

Full of Horse-style energy, the evangelist Billy Graham brought showmanship to prayer and made preaching into an audience-grabbing performance art. Cantering from one venue to the next, he converted people to God in droves with his Horse-like fervor. Could it be that he also showed some of the vanity sometimes associated with this birth sign?

Boris Yeltsin

The Russian president since 1990, Boris Nikolayevich Yeltsin has the animation and leadership qualities attributed to the sign of the Horse. He also has the straightforward manner and straight-talking powers of persuasion linked to this birth animal.

The Sheep

The Sheep personality

For the placid and easygoing Sheep (or Goat, as this sign is sometimes called), life is too short to buck the system. Sheep prefer not to swim against the current, preferring to keep their heads down and let the seasons gently carry them along, while they get on with what they want to do in their quietly creative way. They are often idealistic and impractical, and what Sheep desire most is a peaceful life and a cozy, comfortable home, to be cushioned from strife and protected from hardship and ills, while they keep their minds on nature and art.

YEARS OF THE SHEEP

The Sheep is eighth in the cycle, with Sheep Years following on from Horse Years and recurring every twelfth year thereafter. As the Chinese New Year starts on a different date each year, it is essential to check the calendar to find the exact day on which each Sheep Year begins.

1907 ★ 1919 ★ 1931
1943 ★ 1955 ★ 1967
1979 ★ 1991 ★ 2003

THE SIGN OF THE SHEEP

Essentially, the underlying principles of this sign are all to do with the anima, the "feminine" or Yin side of our natures, the part of us that instinctively urges us to care and nurture, to garner and provide, to love and to cherish. For both male and female members of this troop, their basic nature is peaceable, passive, and receptive. Kind and considerate, gentle and peace-loving, Sheep abhor all forms of confrontation, aggression, or violence. They are happiest among others, and harbor no dreams of being dazzling or of standing out from the crowd. They have no wish to roam. No lust for power lurks in the Sheep's tranquil breast. But in their own quiet way, Sheep can be extremely successful in life, and they sometimes travel farther than they realize as they graze their way over the hills and valleys.

FACTS ABOUT SHEEP

People born in the Year of the Sheep share specific characteristics that are common to all other Sheep. To say that someone is a Sheep is simply a shorthand way of describing that individual's personality. Here are the salient features associated with this sign.

SHEEP FACTS
Eighth in order ★ Chinese name – YANG, sign of the arts
Hour – 1pm–2:59pm ★ Month – July
Western counterpart – Cancer

CHARACTERISTICS
Artistry ♥ Culture ♥ Kindness ♥ Gentleness
Intelligence ♥ Sensitivity

Fussiness ✖ Self-indulgence ✖ Dependence
Sulkiness ✖ Insecurity ✖ Ingratiation

ART-LOVING HUMANISTS

Sheep people have strong humanitarian inclinations, but apart from this they also have a creative eye, which makes them tower head-and-shoulders above the rest in all aspects of the arts. With their strong artistic sensitivity Sheep are frequently drawn to the world of music and the arts. Polished, cultured, and well-mannered, they are a civilizing influence to all around.

To other people, Sheep are kind and generous – almost to a fault, as they can be taken advantage of. Even so, Sheep can get their own way, and through such subtle tactics that the other person often has no idea it has happened.

ABOVE *The idealistic Sheep is a lover of beauty and nature.*

IN YOUR ELEMENT

*I*n addition to the Animal signs which recur once every twelve years, the five Chinese elements of Metal, Water, Wood, Fire and Earth also play their part. This means that a five-year cycle of characteristics is overlaid on the original twelve-year cycle. The Sheep birth year is the first guide to the personality as determined by the Chinese horoscope, but the characteristics of each generation of Sheep are slightly modified by one of the elements, depending on the overlaying of the five-year cycle.

THE METAL SHEEP 1931 AND 1991

On the face of it, Metal gives a hard edge to the Sheep character. These Sheep like to pretend they are hard nuts to crack, but this is actually because they are emotionally as soft as putty and need to build a protective layer around themselves. Those who are in tune with the Metal Sheep will not be taken in by this defensive strategy and will see right through to the Metal Sheep's heart of gold. Metal Sheep would not need their outer armor were they not so deeply vulnerable. They tend to treat others the way they privately feel about themselves, and can be over-protective mollycoddlers to those they care for. The love of art so noticeable in all the Sheep is particularly strong in Metal Sheep.

THE WATER SHEEP 1943 AND 2003

Gentle and compliant, Water Sheep are always content to go along with the flow, and this makes them very easy to live with. Water Sheep are popular and well-liked. They seem to have an aura of "loveability" that makes people fall over themselves to protect and look after them. Like other Sheep, they need to feel safe and protected at home, and usually like to remain in one place. Despite their rather timid natures they are actually articulate and friendly and have a good sense of humor, and they simply need a little more self-confidence. Water Sheep also like to be humored, and when they are not, they can be known to sulk.

THE WOOD SHEEP 1955 AND 2015

These Sheep like to get involved in a diverse range of activities with groups of friends or colleagues, and they are not usually short of friends and acquaintances. Dedicated, compassionate, and empathetic to a fault, they also seem to attract an assortment of strays and people down on their luck who need comfort and support. And this is always readily available, sometimes even to the truly undeserving, and such is this Sheep's compassion that he or she readily responds to others. With such overflowing kindness these Sheep may sometimes be taken for a ride, but more often their goodness is rewarded appropriately. Nevertheless, it might be a good thing if these folk occasionally put themselves first.

THE FIRE SHEEP 1907 AND 1967

Fire lends an interesting spark to the Sheep characteristics. More outgoing and individualistic than other Sheep, Fire Sheep are less likely to need the support and approval of others, and less likely to be hurt and let down if they fail to get it. They stand up for themselves and like to make their own way in life, away from the rest of the flock. Their artistic sense leans toward the theatrical, and having a strong innate sense of drama, many of the Fire Sheep gravitate toward the performing arts. They are lively and imaginative, and enjoy a busy social life with a good circle of friends; but with the Sheep's love of peace and non-violence they can tend to deceive themselves rather than see the unpleasant truth of a situation.

THE EARTH SHEEP 1919 AND 1979

Apart from a slight lack of self-confidence, the Sheep is already a stable character, and the Earth element provides an even stronger grounding effect. The Earth element makes Sheep folk industrious, independent, and resourceful, and also a little on the conservative side. But this Sheep has tenacity – he or she is self-reliant, but also self-indulgent in a domesticated way. Spouse and family are the most important aspect of the Earth Sheep's life and they will work hard for the good of those they love. While prudent and conventional, they are, nevertheless, blessed with a sunny disposition, which enables them to make a good impression wherever they go.

Health and habitat

HEALTH AND CONSTITUTION

Despite having a delicate appearance, the Sheep is pretty robust. Sheep may protest if they are physically uncomfortable, and they take great care over their creature comforts, but their calm disposition protects them from most health problems. What does lay them low, however, is any hint of marital discord, because being loved and supported by an understanding partner is critical to the Sheep's well-being. Should that much-needed love be withdrawn for any reason, the Sheep immediately gets ill; unhappiness just ties the Sheep's stomach up in knots.

THE SHEEP AT HOME

Traditional is the adjective that best describes the Sheep's domestic scene. Sheep revel in the conventional role of homemaker, making jam, arranging dried flowers, making curtains, putting up shelves, and taking turns to rock the cradle. The Sheep person is a strong believer in family togetherness, and his or her house reflects this homely instinct with log fires, comfortable furniture, and the smell of freshly baked apple-pie. Male and female Sheep alike are contentedly domesticated. Their love of comfort and artistic sensitivity are combined in their decor, which is sumptuously elegant, with a classical, timeless look created by their artistic skills. Their love of ease will ensure that their home lacks no modern convenience and time-saving gadget.

Career and wealth

THE SHEEP AT WORK

Sheep people like being part of a group, and have no interest in seeking power and position. If they have to don the mantle of authority they will, and moreover, they will carry out their responsibilities with intelligence and tact. But they are not really comfortable in the position of leader and would not normally seek a high-status job out of choice. Sheep folk are much happier taking a supporting role.

FINANCE AND THE SHEEP

Although Sheep love domestic comfort and security, they are not materialists in the financial sense at all. Yet Sheep people seem to attract money, anyway – and it's just as well, since most of them are outrageous spend-thrifts. Perhaps they have a knack with money, a partner with a healthy bank account, or maybe they are just plain lucky, but they are always well-housed, well-dressed, and, it would appear, well-off.

LEFT *Both male and female Sheep characters are happiest at home, and like to feel settled and secure.*

COMPATIBLE BUSINESS PARTNERS

Whether Sheep benefit from or constantly conflict with their business partners depends, as in all relationships, on whether their Animal signs are harmonious or antagonistic to each other. Taking into consideration the compatibility of the elements between themselves and their working colleagues can also be very useful.

SHEEP RULED BY	BENEFIT FROM	ARE ANTAGONISTIC TO
Metal	Earth Sheep	Fire Monkeys
Water	Metal Rabbits	Earth Roosters
Wood	Water Horses	Metal Tigers
Fire	Wood Pigs	Water Oxen
Earth	Fire Snakes	Wood Dogs

Leisure and pleasures

THE SHEEP ON VACATION

Security is the key to the Sheep-born psyche, so when these people travel they consider safety in numbers to be the prudent approach. Not for them the inaccessible places beloved by the intrepid Rat, nor the spine-tingling adventures sought by the fiery Dragon, nor even the impromptu here-today gone-tomorrow forays of the Horse. Rather, the Sheep prefers to stay with the flock, so Sheep people feel more comfortable going on vacation with a group.

Guided-tours are especially favored by these people, as are vacations with a practical edge, such as a tour of famous gardens, perhaps, or visiting important buildings. But Sheep-born folk are also naturally drawn to water, so vacations by the sea or boating on a lake would be ideal for them. Taking a cruise around the Caribbean, visiting the fjords in Norway, geysers in New Zealand, hot springs in Iceland, spectacular Niagara Falls, or the bejewelled lakes of northern Italy would bring much pleasure to these gentle creatures.

FRIENDS AND FOE

People born in the Year of the Sheep are diplomatic and streetwise. Accomplished in the social graces and able to adapt to whatever company they find themselves in, Sheep folk make excellent hosts and hostesses. Indeed, a party thrown by a Sheep is often the talk of the town! When it comes to the art of socializing, the Sheep comes out on the top of the list of Chinese Animals. But these gentle souls are not the kind of people who show off or wear their hearts on their sleeves, for Sheep-born folk need to be very sure of their territory and of those in their company before they can talk freely about their innermost thoughts and emotions. Consequently, anyone who wants to get to know someone born in a Sheep Year will need to stick around for a while. The few who do, however, will become lifelong friends. The many who do not, simply get added to the Sheep's considerable list of acquaintances.

ABOVE *The love of water is strong in Sheep people. A quiet boating vacation with chosen friends would be perfect.*

LIKES AND DISLIKES

SHEEP LIKE

Color Preference
Pink, purple

Gems and Stones
Moonstone, sapphire, jade

Suitable Gifts
Silk bathrobe, theater tickets, body massage, crystal decanter, cameo brooch, champagne, seashells, peppermint oil

Hobbies and Pastimes
Swimming, tennis, reading, bridge, food, buying clothes, sleeping, movies

Just as people born under the same Animal sign share a similar character and outlook on life, so do they also have similar tastes. As two Sheep get to know each other, they soon discover that they have many likes and dislikes in common.

SHEEP DISLIKE

Being separated from their loved ones

Inefficiency

Conflict and aggression

Not having a partner at their side

Sheep parents and babies

People born under the Sheep influence possess an innate nurturing instinct that enables them to take naturally to their parental duties and responsibilities. Sheep-born mothers and fathers are deeply family-oriented and, if they can, they usually choose to have more than the average number of children. Showering their offspring with affection comes all too easily, and can too often develop into smothering love.

But, just as Sheep are close to their children, so do they also form lasting bonds to their own parents, too, many settling within striking distance from where they themselves were brought up, or possibly even instaling their relatives in an annex to their homes. Sheep love to have an extended family around them and encourage their children to have as much contact with their grand-parents as they do themselves.

Gracious and refined, Sheep parents abhor bad manners, so they give top priority to instilling polite-ness and social grace into their little lambs from the very moment they are born.

THE SHEEP BABY AND CHILD

Children born under the sign of the Sheep have much in common with Rabbits, for these two Animals are highly compatible. Like the Rabbits, Sheep are emotion-ally tender and prone to tears. In fact, little Sheep learn from a very young age that turning on the waterworks often gets them what they want in life – a ploy that many remember throughout adulthood!

These are sensitive youngsters, clingy and dependent but very affectionate. Placid and well-behaved, they enjoy nothing better than snuggling up to a parent and having a story read to them to make them feel protected and secure. Low self-confidence is one of their drawbacks, so all little Lambs need a lot of encourage-ment to enable them to develop their talents. Compliant and respectful, these youngsters shun conflict and aggres-sion. Moreover, since they are family-oriented, they never stray too far from home.

SHEEP PARENT/CHILD RELATIONSHIPS

For some parents, their children's personalities harmonize perfectly with their own. Others find that no matter how much they may love their offspring, they are simply not on the same wavelength. Below are the compatibility ratings between Sheep parents and their children.

SHEEP WITH	UNDER THE SAME ROOF	COMPATIBILITY RATING
Rat	opposing views	✓
Ox	beware temper tantrums	✓
Tiger	better with time	✓✓
Rabbit	warm and sensitive	✓✓✓
Dragon	proud parenting	✓✓✓✓
Snake	supportive ties	✓✓✓
Horse	warm rapport	✓✓✓✓
Sheep	total empathy	✓✓✓✓
Monkey	differing modus operandi	✓✓
Rooster	a robust relationship	✓✓
Dog	long-lasting love	✓✓✓
Pig	love and understanding	✓✓✓✓

RATINGS ✓ uphill struggle ✓✓ some complications
✓✓✓ easy bonding ✓✓✓✓ on the same wavelength

ABOVE *Sheep like to keep the family together, and create strong bonds with both parents and children.*

OPPOSITE *Under the Sheep's family-loving exterior lurks a deeply sensuous and caring lover.*

Lovers and spouses

THE SHEEP LOVER

Sheep fear loneliness, and tend to be shy, self-conscious, and insecure. Sheep-folk are extremely family-oriented, and for them, a loving, intimate relationship is absolutely essential to their happiness and well-being.

Some Oriental astrologers, however, refer to this sign as a Goat and say that Goats are capricious, dissipating their energies by jumping this way and that unless they are tethered. The outcome is the same, as nothing provides a better tether than a loving, stable union.

GAINING CONFIDENCE

True, on a bad day, Sheep can be clingy and dependent, even wheedling and cajoling until they get their own way. But they are romantic creatures through and through, and their soft-hearted, compassionate natures are hard to resist. A supportive partner's encouragement enables the Sheep to develop his or her innate sparkling personality, to have self-confidence, and to become a rounded person, who is witty and amusing.

THE SHEEP LOVE PARTNER

Anyone born under the sign of the Sheep needs to be appreciated by a caring partner, as these people are sensitive and sweet of disposition, and can hide their many talents even from themselves. They flourish with the encouragement of the one they love. With a trusted partner at his or her side, the Sheep or Goat feels protected and secure and has the confidence to shine.

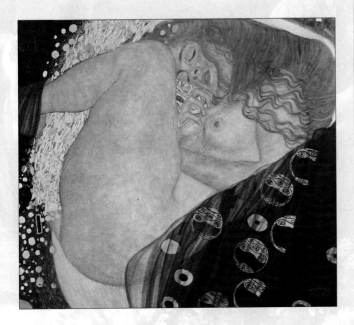

PARTNERS IN LOVE

SHEEP ♥ RAT
An uphill struggle at times, though you could make it work with a bit of goodwill.

SHEEP ♥ OX
Your bodies may meet but your minds and hearts will not.

SHEEP ♥ TIGER
Lots of respect, but too much walking on eggshells for real comfort here.

SHEEP ♥ RABBIT
True love, shared interests, lots of understanding, great respect. You've got it all!

SHEEP ♥ DRAGON
Despite the sexual attraction, you are temperamentally unsuited to each other.

SHEEP ♥ SNAKE
Terrific friends and sexy lovers.

SHEEP ♥ HORSE
Attraction at first sight is followed by galvanic passion and desire. This union is for keeps.

SHEEP ♥ SHEEP
You're a couple of hedonists who understand each other perfectly.

SHEEP ♥ MONKEY
Very different people, but you could make it work by pooling resources.

SHEEP ♥ ROOSTER
Difficulties at every turn give only an average rating for this union.

SHEEP ♥ DOG
A tiresome togetherness.

SHEEP ♥ PIG
Plenty of understanding and mutual love make this a winning team.

LOVE PARTNERS AT A GLANCE

SHEEP WITH:	TIPS ON TOGETHERNESS	COMPATIBILITY
Rat	at odds	♥
Ox	in your dreams!	♥
Tiger	work, yes – marriage, no	♥♥
Rabbit	blissful	♥♥♥♥
Dragon	depends – either heaven or hell	♥♥
Snake	deeply satisfying	♥♥♥
Horse	made for each other	♥♥♥♥
Sheep	recipe for success	♥♥♥
Monkey	learn from each other	♥♥
Rooster	touch and go	♥
Dog	a clash of personalities	♥
Pig	champagne and caviar	♥♥♥♥

COMPATIBILITY RATINGS: ♥ *conflict* ♥♥ *work at it*
♥♥♥ *strong sexual attraction* ♥♥♥♥ *heavenly!*

EAST MEETS WEST

ARIES SHEEP

Aries Sheep are more spirited than the average Sheep, but are still better working in the wings, and are brilliant as the power behind the throne. In love, they are possessive and emotionally demanding, but at their best in a stable relationship with a strong, adoring partner.

TAUREAN SHEEP

Taurean Sheep have expensive tastes, a double helping of materialism and an insatiable desire for creature comforts. Not money-grabbing *per se*, they do put their own comfort and security at the top of the list. For true happiness, they need to be wedded and feather-bedded.

GEMINI SHEEP

Chatty, witty, and sociable, and irresistibly charming, these are brilliant dilettantes. The mercurial element of the Twins lends speed of thought and a retentive memory. The Gemini Sheep spends a good deal of time chatting on the phone and enjoys nothing better than cosy soirées or dinner parties surrounded by friends and family.

CANCERIAN SHEEP

Sensitive, gentle, devoted, and kind, with so much love to give and so much need to be loved, Cancerian Sheep are archetypal family men or women, but prone to anxiety and in need of the support of their families. These Sheep make warm, affectionate children who never stray too far.

LEONINE SHEEP

Leonine Sheep are sunny and fun to be with. The Leo influence brings greater independence and a certain excitement to the normally placid sign. Leo is fair, just, and honorable, always generous and magnanimous, and endows the Sheep with a noble presence and lofty ideals, but also a strong eye for luxury.

VIRGO SHEEP

These Sheep have exceptionally high standards and a naturally critical eye and they can be overly fussy and pedantic. Although there are many situations in which such finesse is needed, this can also work to the Virgo Sheep's disadvantage in matters of the heart.

LIBRAN SHEEP

Intelligent and refined, suave and elegant, Libran Sheep are the epitome of cultured sophistication. They are attractive, desirable, and highly accomplished and everything they undertake is done with style.

SCORPIO SHEEP

Scorpio toughens the sinews of the placid Sheep and gives a more independent and assertive nature. This mixture serves to make Scorpio Sheep magnetically alluring and delicately appealing. Yet underneath that gentle façade, the Scorpio Sheep is as tough as old boots!

SAGITTARIAN SHEEP

As long as they are free to pursue their own interests, Sagittarian Sheep are as happy as Larry, and they tend to have many projects constantly on the boil. These Sheep stand on their own two feet with greater confidence.

CAPRICORN SHEEP

Ambition, drive, industriousness, and practicality give the strength of character necessary to attain this Sheep's worldly aspirations. But Capricorn Sheep are full of surprises: normally as steady as a rock, they now and again let their hair down and behave quite out of character.

AQUARIAN SHEEP

These are people with brilliantly inventive minds who cannot be pinned down. For here is a colorful character and one of Nature's free spirits – ethereal, elusive, and electric. Aquarian Sheep live for the moment and expect others to do the same.

PISCEAN SHEEP

Piscean sensitivity, coupled with the Sheep's creativity, makes for highly accomplished artists. Piscean Sheep are soft and not particularly pushy, and are better able to bring their potential to fruit when with a supportive partner.

Famous Sheep

Easygoing, idealistic and civilized, kind and gentle, sensitive and highly artistic, people born under the sign of the Sheep love their homes and are devoted to their families. At the same time they are often prominent in the world of the arts – which normally draws people with more tempestuous characters.

▲ Leslie Caron
This very feminine dancer and actress with the poised air of quiet tranquillity has the Sheep's artistic talent. She delighted in her home and her children, and in her heyday found the pressure of being an international film star, perpetually on show, at odds with her gentle nature.

▼ Jane Austen
This great English writer was a domestic animal in both her own life and her subject matter. Although her writing was done in a detailed way on a tiny canvas it shows a breadth of understanding of human nature and displays the subtle and sparkling wit that comes readily to the best Sheep when they feel secure and loved. Jane Austen never married, but was devoted to her family and generous and loving with her parents, siblings, nephews, and nieces alike.

▶ Buster Keaton
In his films, this brilliant comedian of the silent screen is always sweet and earnest, dead-pan and hilarious. Like many Sheep, he had great artistic talent and the ability to sparkle when in the limelight. His is the reserved Sheep manner, and the Sheep's perfectionism. He directed all his major films, devised every gag himself, and was his own stuntman in his impeccably timed visual jokes.

▶ Margot Fonteyn
A Sheep-born person of great artistry and interpretive skills, Margot Fonteyn's career as a ballet dancer blossomed during her partnership with Rudolf Nureyev. Her gentle, peace-loving nature must have calmed his Tiger tempestuousness, for theirs was a long and outstanding stage partnership. In her retirement, Margot Fonteyn showed the Sheep love of humanity in her international work for poor and underprivileged children.

◀ Laurence Olivier
One of Britain's outstanding actors, Laurence Olivier (later Lord Olivier) was a truly civilized and artistic Sheep. Despite his talent and powerful presence on stage and screen, he was a person who worked well in a team and did not seek personal attention. For over a decade he was director of the National Theatre company in London, and he upheld a traditional approach to the theater despite directing and acting in contemporary work as well as in traditional repertoire.

The Monkey

The Monkey personality

Quick wits and mental dexterity are the Monkey's trademarks, and Monkeys pride themselves on being able to dance rings around everyone else. With their clever, alert minds, Monkeys catch on quickly and process information in a trice. The typical Monkey person is as bright as a button, nimble of foot, and able to accomplish almost any task – the more intricate and involved the better. With their razor-sharp wits and huge sense of fun, Monkeys are constantly seeking new experiences and fresh challenges to stimulate their senses.

The sign of the Monkey

The chief characteristics of the Monkey are shown in the panel below. Perhaps the key to their personality is that Monkeys possess an irrepressible sense of fun, seemingly from birth, and delight in jokes, tricks, and amusing stories. But they can also be a bit mischievous – especially if they ever get bored. Then they get that naughty glint in their eye and simply have to go and stir something or someone up, just for the sheer fun of it! This done, the Monkey takes a front-row seat and settles down to enjoy the fireworks. What's more, it has to be said that the Monkey may indulge in deceit – just for the pure fun of it – but he or she will call it a trick and not expect you to mind. Curiously enough, you probably won't mind, either.

Monkey curiosity

Some people call it inquisitiveness. Others swear it's downright nosiness. The Monkey will say that it is simply a healthy interest. But however we label it, a Monkey always has an insatiable curiosity.

Monkey people are gifted with great mental powers, but imagination, intuition, and sympathy are not first among them. Somehow, despite their astonishing brightness, they seem always to take things literally and cannot imagine what it is like to be in someone else's shoes. Nevertheless, they are full of goodwill towards their slower fellows, and usually have plenty of friends and admirers. They are good with words and good at problem-solving, but are easily bored or distracted.

Facts about Monkeys

People born in the Year of the Monkey share specific characteristics that are common to all other Monkeys. To say that someone is a Monkey is simply a shorthand way of describing that individual's personality. Here are the salient features associated with this sign.

MONKEY FACTS

Ninth in order ★ *Chinese name – HOU, sign of imagination*
Hour – 3pm–4:59pm ★ *Month – August*
Western counterpart – Leo

CHARACTERISTICS

Imagination ♥ *Ingenuity* ♥ *Resourcefulness* ♥ *Versatility*
Persuasiveness ♥ *Sense of humor*

Mischievousness ✖ *Slyness* ✖ *Restlessness* ✖ *Impudence*
Superficiality ✖ *Mendacity*

Years of the Monkey

Ninth in the cycle, Monkey Years follow on from the Sheep and recur every twelfth year thereafter. As the Chinese New Year does not fall on a fixed date, it is essential to check the calendar to find the exact date on which each Monkey Year actually begins.

1908 ★ 1920 ★ 1932
1944 ★ 1956 ★ 1968
1980 ★ 1992 ★ 2004

ABOVE *The brightest and nimblest Animal of them all is a great communicator and quick-witted.*

IN YOUR ELEMENT

In addition to the Animal signs which recur once every 12 years, the 5 Chinese elements of Metal, Water, Wood, Fire, and Earth also play their part. This means that a 5-year cycle of characteristics is overlaid on the original 12-year cycle. The Monkey birth year is the first guide to the personality as determined by the Chinese horoscope, but the characteristics of each generation of Monkey are slightly modified by one of the elements.

THE METAL MONKEY 1920 AND 1980

Clever, persuasive, and highly ambitious, the Metal Monkey is lively, outwardly warm, and strongly passionate. In business this breed is a complete success story, because Metal Monkeys are determined and prepared to put in a good deal of hard work in order to make it to the top. These Monkeys have ambition and strong will, and also tend to like to go it alone. They have wisdom as well as quick Monkey wits, and are always fully prepared to apply themselves in order to achieve their ambitions. In love their passionate nature reveals itself to the full, and they are also loyal, faithful, and caring.

THE WATER MONKEY 1932 AND 1992

Water adds a strong measure of sensitivity to the Monkey nature, which means that these Monkeys can get easily hurt. To protect themselves, they keep their feelings hidden from others. In general, Water Monkeys keep a great deal under their cloaks, hiding things from others and rarely letting on about their plans. With their talents and qualities they can go one of two ways: if they concentrate on what they are up to and channel their intellectual energies, they can pursue their objectives with patience, method, and success and become original trendsetters and an inspiration to all. If not, however, they will seem fickle and indecisive, and may prefer to meddle in other people's business than to get on with their own.

THE WOOD MONKEY 1944 AND 2004

Wood Monkeys have the typical Monkey acumen and sharpness in full measure and are blessed with powers of logic, instinctive understanding of how things work, and a practical turn of mind. This gives them a talent for science, but they also have a gift for communicating, and it is in the world of communications, linguistics, computers, and information technology that they excel. It could be said that they have more integrity than most other Monkeys and a natural gift for dealing with people. This is useful to them, as they can also be rather ambitious, and they can swing their way into the branches of ever higher trees through their diplomatic dealings with others, combined with their hard work and application.

THE FIRE MONKEY 1956 AND 2016

Fire brings extra energy and determination to the Monkey. What stamina, what daring, and what a uniquely inventive mind the Fire Monkey possesses! These people always strive to gain the upper hand, and like nothing better than a position at the top of the tree. They also love making conquests among the opposite sex, and can be very fickle – just Monkey fun, of course, but this does not always get appreciated by those who take life and love more seriously. At the same time, the Fire Monkey feels strongly about his or her own aims and ambitions in all aspects of life. Fire Monkeys should remember that there is a saying in the East: "The further up the tree a monkey goes, the more you see his bottom." If they use their talents and vitality well, they can be highly successful, popular with all, and loyal to and loved by their chosen partners.

THE EARTH MONKEY 1908 AND 1968

Honest, serious, intelligent, and academically minded, Earth Monkeys like to go by the rule book. They are calmer than others of their tribe, and show concern for and kindness to others. Emotionally reserved and controlled, they are less highly strung than most Monkeys and altogether more dependable. They are honest in all their dealings, and completely devoted to the causes and people they care for. Generally unselfish and reliable, they nevertheless have an ego. They very much appreciate respect, and may even be a bit huffy if this is not handed out. They can be irritatingly law-abiding in a most un-Monkey-like way. As partners they are kind and loyal, very loving, and deeply understanding.

Health and habitat

HEALTH AND CONSTITUTION

As far as the Monkey is concerned, life is too short to be ill. With their indomitable spirit they tend to keep diseases at bay and keep themselves fighting fit. Monkeys generally seem to enjoy extraordinarily good health, and if they are ever ill, usually show amazing powers of recovery. If they succumb to any illness it is likely to be to a nervous disorder or, later in life, to heart or circulatory conditions, due to the fast pace at which they lead their lives. It would be a good idea for most Monkeys to channel a little more of their energy into taking physical, rather than mental, exercise.

THE MONKEY AT HOME

Most Monkey people are more suited to the hustle and bustle of the city than to the peace and quiet of the country. They always like to be at the center of things, feeling the pulse of life around them. Seeing people going past the door or gathering in a city center will keep a Monkey amused for hours. So, a room with a view, in a town house, preferably situated up a hill, would be ideal. Sensible Monkeys use their Monkey intelligence and energy on hobbies, and their homes may even have a special room that is devoted to model railways, computer games, dressmaking, or whatever interesting pastime exercises those busy Monkey wits.

Career and wealth

THE MONKEY AT WORK

Adaptability and a good memory are the Monkey's stock-in-trade. Intelligent and astute, Monkeys pick up skills in the twinkling of an eye and then work out a way of improving the task. If a job can be done in half the time for twice the money, the Monkey is sure to find the way to do it. Many Monkeys work in the world of finance, where they love doing quick deals and the buzz of the stock exchange floor, and many make excellent salespeople, using their communication skills.

FINANCE AND THE MONKEY

Though Monkey people have the knack of making money, they are equally good at spending it. Monkeys are not the best savers in the world, since they live for the moment and tend to let tomorrow look after itself, so occasionally making a wise investment for the future would be a sensible plan.

LEFT *Monkeys like a room with a view, from where they can watch people coming and going.*

COMPATIBLE BUSINESS PARTNERS

Whether Monkeys benefit from or constantly conflict with their business partners depends, as in all relationships, on whether their Animal signs are harmonious or antagonistic to each other. Taking into consideration the compatibility of the elements between themselves and their working colleagues can also be very useful.

MONKEYS RULED BY	BENEFIT FROM	ARE ANTAGONISTIC TO
Metal	Earth Horses	Fire Roosters
Water	Metal Pigs	Earth Sheep
Wood	Water Dragons	Metal Tigers
Fire	Wood Monkeys	Water Snakes
Earth	Fire Rats	Wood Rabbits

Leisure and pleasures

THE MONKEY ON VACATION

People born in the Year of the Monkey enjoy talking more than almost any other pursuit, and consequently need to be constantly surrounded by people. So, when considering vacations, it is not the wild mountains nor the barren plains that attract those who are born under this sign. For these essentially gregarious people it is the urban landscape that draws them. The city, with its bright lights, constant rumble of traffic, and hubbub of people, grabs Monkey people's imagination, sharpens their senses, and revitalizes their spirits. If they had the choice, it would have to be the Big Apple that calls the Monkey-born native. Alternatively, major cities teeming with life, such as London, Paris, Hong Kong, Sydney, or Rome, would satisfy the Monkey's curiosity. And because they are lucky, dicing with fate in Monte Carlo or Las Vegas would add the excitement and the spice that are so necessary to the Monkey's need for stimulation in life.

FRIENDS AND FOE

Sociable and gregarious, the Monkey's bulging address book testifies to his or her huge circle of friends and vast network of acquaintances. Monkeys have a low boredom threshold, so it is essential for them to have as wide a range of contacts with whom they can interact whenever, and on whatever level, they require. No other Animal among the Chinese signs finds it so easy to communicate across all classes, races, or types of people as a Monkey-born individual can. Just as the monkey in the trees of the jungle has a reputation for chattering, so there is nothing that a human Monkey relishes more than being in company, chatting, laughing and sharing the odd joke or two with a group of friends. With their clever minds, their bubbly spirits, and brilliant sense of humor, these folk cannot help but be popular. And, as friends, they are witty, amusing, and thoroughly entertaining companions to have around.

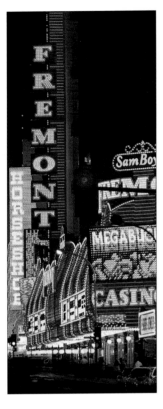

ABOVE *Thrills and nightlife, cities and people are what the Monkey wants from a vacation.*

COMPATIBLE FRIENDS

Although each individual person is unique, Chinese astrologers are very precise about which Animals have a general shared understanding and which have characters that are antagonistic to one another. Monkeys may wish to note which signs are more likely to provide lasting friendship and which they would find unsettling.

BEST FRIENDS	MORTAL ENEMY
Dragons	*Tigers*
Rats	

LIKES AND DISLIKES

MONKEYS LIKE

Color Preference
Yellow, gold
❖
Gems and Stones
Quartz crystal, aquamarine, topaz, agate
❖
Suitable Gifts
Books, gold pen, mobile phone, personal computer, playing cards, a makeover, joke book, puzzle
❖
Hobbies and Pastimes
Playing piano or guitar, table-tennis, poker, word games, dancing, craft-work, karaoke

Just as people born under the same Animal sign share a similar character and outlook on life, so do they also have similar tastes. As two Monkeys get to know each other, they soon discover that they have many likes and dislikes in common.

MONKEYS DISLIKE
❖
Solitude
❖
People who can't take a joke
❖
Being told to shut up
❖
Not being the most popular person on the block

Monkey parents and babies

Having someone who is born in the Year of the Monkey as a parent is more like having another big brother or big sister around. It is said of Monkeys that they have Peter Pan qualities, that they retain their youthfulness throughout their lives and never really grow up. Being so young-at-heart comes in handy as a parent because it enables the parents to relate to their offspring on their own level. There is no generation gap in a family where either the mother or father belong to this sign. Moreover, Monkeys genuinely enjoy being around children, playing their games, sharing their high spirits, and taking part in their discussions. Open-minded, playful, and amusing, if Monkey parents are not chatting or telling jokes to their youngsters, they are probably curled up together on the sofa enthralling their little ones before bed with yet another of their magical stories.

But Monkeys are also party animals with a bulging address book that is a testament to their full social lives. They are not the kind of people who like to stay in every night sipping cocoa by the fire. When it comes along, parenthood slightly cramps the Monkey's style – but not for long, since these ingenious creatures soon work out the most efficient babysitting roster in town. Or else, if the conditions are suitable, they bundle up their babies and, with very little fuss, they simply take them along too.

MONKEY PARENT/CHILD RELATIONSHIPS

For some parents, their children's personalities harmonize perfectly with their own. Others find that no matter how much they may love their offspring, they are simply not on the same wavelength. Below are the compatibility ratings between Monkey parents and their children.

MONKEYS WITH	UNDER THE SAME ROOF	COMPATIBILITY RATING
Rat	strong bonds of affection	✓✓✓✓
Ox	supportive	✓✓✓
Tiger	opposing views	✓
Rabbit	a sensitive bonding	✓✓✓
Dragon	shared rapport	✓✓✓✓
Snake	cool but understanding	✓✓
Horse	some clashes	✓✓
Sheep	positive feelings	✓✓✓
Monkey	like two peas in a pod	✓✓✓✓
Rooster	occasional friction	✓✓
Dog	conflicting ideals	✓
Pig	lots of love between them	✓✓✓✓

RATINGS ✓ uphill struggle   ✓✓ some complications
✓✓✓ easy bonding   ✓✓✓✓ on the same wavelength

THE MONKEY
BABY AND CHILD

Young Monkeys are full of life. Bright, intelligent, and insatiably curious about their universe, they want to know everything that is going on, and find it hard to keep still for long. With their incisive brains and razor-sharp understanding, they are quick to learn, and find school work easy. Indeed, many sail through

exams with apparent ease. Most Monkeys are highly articulate and develop complex social skills from a very young age. But mischievousness and a naughty sense of humor are the Monkey's trademarks, qualities that can land them in hot water at school, for people of this sign cannot help but stir people up just for the fun of it. And when their backs are against the wall, Monkeys can bend the truth in their favor with consummate skill.

ABOVE *A baby with Monkey parents will get bundled up and taken out to dinner.*

OPPOSITE *A carefree love life may typify the Monkey lifestyle, with so many available partners.*

Lovers and spouses

THE MONKEY LOVER

Fleet of foot and nimble of mind, Monkeys can also be fast and loose when it comes to sexual relationships. In fact, of all the astrological Animal signs, this is the·one that has the greatest reputation for promiscuity. Certainly, Monkeys can be flirtatious, especially in their younger days; perhaps this is something to do with boredom, or the need for new experiences. Or perhaps the Monkey sees it as a skill, like a balancing act, to have several lovers and admirers going at the same time.

Monkeys have a sense of mischief, a delight in breaking the rules, impishness, and the ability to bend the truth to their own advantage. There are even times when Monkey folk can be unscrupulous, manipulative, and clever at covering up their traces – skills that they wouldn't balk at using in the pursuit of a lover!

PASSIONATE TEASE

As lovers Monkeys can be passionate and intense. They also know how to be a vamp and a tease. Monkeys know how to charm and allure, how to be funny and provocative, how to amuse and entertain with their sparkling wit and ready repartee. Deeply sensual and fantastically sexy, when the Monkey settles down, he or she is likely to remain remarkably faithful and true.

THE MONKEY LOVE PARTNER

The ideal partner for a Monkey is light at heart and quick of wit. Too much sensitivity will bring the partner to grief, and too much solemnity will not suit the Monkey at all. The panel (right) shows how the other Animals are suited to the Monkey as a partner.

PARTNERS IN LOVE

MONKEY ♥ RAT
A shared outlook and a common understanding equals love for you and your Rat.

MONKEY ♥ OX
When this relationship works, life can be fun, fun, fun.

MONKEY ♥ TIGER
You're likely to drive each other up the wall!

MONKEY ♥ RABBIT
It'll end in tears.

MONKEY ♥ DRAGON
You think alike and understand each other perfectly – a combination destined to be happy and successful.

MONKEY ♥ SNAKE
Intellectually, you make a great match. Emotionally, jealousy gets in the way.

MONKEY ♥ HORSE
A prickly combination, better for friendship than for marriage.

MONKEY ♥ SHEEP
Very different people, but you could make a go of it by pooling your talents and resources.

MONKEY ♥ MONKEY
Brilliant rapport, even if at times you behave like adolescents!

MONKEY ♥ ROOSTER
Romantically, this could be a bit of a damp squib.

MONKEY ♥ DOG
Not a bad shot. With so much desire to pull together, you have plenty going for you.

MONKEY ♥ PIG
Occasional strife heightens the sexual tension between you.

LOVE PARTNERS AT A GLANCE

MONKEYS WITH:	TIPS ON TOGETHERNESS	COMPATIBILITY
Rat	irresistible magnetism	♥♥♥♥
Ox	a complementary match	♥♥
Tiger	too much jostling for the upper hand	♥♥
Rabbit	heartbreak hotel	♥
Dragon	refreshingly alive	♥♥♥♥
Snake	only with cooperation	♥♥
Horse	socially, yes, sexually, no	♥♥
Sheep	recipe for success	♥♥♥
Monkey	together it's just one long summer holiday	♥♥♥♥
Rooster	soooo picky	♥
Dog	cheerfully complementary	♥♥♥
Pig	a colorful affair	♥♥♥

COMPATIBILITY RATINGS: ♥ *conflict* ♥♥ *work at it*
♥♥♥ *strong sexual attraction* ♥♥♥♥ *heavenly!*

ARIES MONKEY

These are among the most garrulous folk around. They are high-profile people for whom being in the company of others is all-important. Amusing and fun-loving, but also active and go-getting, boredom is their biggest enemy.

TAUREAN MONKEY

The Taurean Monkey is a well-adjusted individual, as Taurus steadies the Monkey's jitters. Taurean Monkeys have a *penchant* for luxury and an eye for beauty. In love, life can be difficult, as part of this character wants a steady life and a stable relationship but another part wants freedom and autonomy.

GEMINI MONKEY

These people are doubly clever, versatile, and mercurial – able to process information at the speed of light. A hyperactive handful, they have such energy and verve that they go through life like whirling dervishes. Emotionally, they are miserable without an adoring partner.

CANCERIAN MONKEY

Monkeys like to be here, there, and everywhere, and are not especially noted for their domesticity. The Cancerian influence makes the Monkey more home-loving, with a strong sense of family. Money is important to them, but luckily they are wizards when it comes to finances.

LEONINE MONKEY

Leo and the Monkey are both terrific attention-seekers, with an overwhelming need to be loved and reassured. They are great show-offs, beautiful, and talented, and turning heads wherever they go. In love, they make adoring partners, hard-working, passionate, and true.

VIRGO MONKEY

Detail pleases the Virgo Monkey, who is a perfectionist, endlessly dotting i's and crossing t's. Monkeys are quick as lightning, able to pick up a skill at a glance. With the Virgo influence, these are intelligent individuals with razor-sharp perception, who never miss a trick.

LIBRAN MONKEY

Charm is perhaps the Libran Monkey's most outstanding asset. Libran Monkeys know instinctively how to flatter, sweet-talk, and turn a situation to their own advantage. These folk are subtle and make smooth, slick operators and expert mediators.

SCORPIO MONKEY

Monkeys are fun-loving and, by and large, amusing companions to have around. But Scorpio activates some aspects of the Monkey's negative side. Under this influence, the Monkey's ingenuity can turn to guile; inventiveness to mendacity; dexterity into plain craftiness.

SAGITTARIAN MONKEY

This mix produces lucky, cheerful personalities, clever and deep-thinking. Sagittarian Monkeys like to think big. And why not, when the world is their oyster? With the Archer's far-sightedness and the Monkey's ingenuity, they will succeed at whatever they set out to do.

CAPRICORN MONKEY

Intelligent and hard-working, the Capricorn Monkey is more stable and resolute than most others. This Monkey applies his or her talents consistently, to become formidable in business and invariably successful in life.

AQUARIAN MONKEY

Colorful and eccentric, bright and breezy, and with a razor-sharp intellect, Aquarian Monkeys seek a sharing of minds in their everyday interactions with other people. These Monkeys are born with an immense curiosity and an impressive ability to solve problems.

PISCEAN MONKEY

There is a whimsical delicacy about the Piscean Monkey that belies a clever and calculating mind. Piscean Monkeys are sophisticates, cultured, and refined, and with complex and highly developed talents. But they can also have a certain artificiality or an economy with the truth, and are adept at fabricating stories with words.

Famous Monkeys

So quick that they are gone before you see them coming, Monkeys can be pranksters. They are alert of mind, have a gift for languages and technology, and are very inquisitive. They also need to be on the go. Monkey-born people are also gregarious, adaptable, and astute, and they usually have a great sense of fun.

◀ Joan Crawford

Born Lucille le Sueur, Joan Crawford changed her name to Billie Cassin before settling on Crawford, and was one of America's greatest cinema actresses and stars. Always on the go, and seemingly with the Monkey's gift of good health, she starred in dozens of films from the 1920s until 1970. She revealed her Monkey outlook on life with her remark, "Inactivity is one of the great indignities of life."

◀ Bob Marley

The great Jamaican reggae musician shows the Monkey talent for words and communication. His gifted and easy-sounding lyrics and catchy rhythms convey his meaning with lightness and grace, helping him to communicate his Rastafarian message and the culture of the West Indies to the whole world.

▼ Martina Navratilova

Monkeys are agile and nimble, quick of wit and quick on their feet. Tennis is just the right sport for the Monkey-born, as it demands all these qualities in full and is also highly competitive, which suits the Monkey type. Monkeys are not likely to be team players by nature. Like many Monkey people, Navratilova is colorful on and off the court, and generally manages to win as well as get her own way.

◀ James Stewart

Another active Monkey, who was a workaholic actor, James Stewart began performing on the screen in 1935, and acted in scores of films, working for over 50 years, even appearing (as a voice) in a film in 1991, when he was over eighty. The Monkey speaks in his quote, "If I had my career over again? Maybe I'd say to myself, speed it up a little."

▲ Omar Sharif

The Egyptian actor first became internationally known with his role in the film *Lawrence of Arabia*, and was a great success in the cinema in the 1960s. He seems to have the Monkey's restlessness, as he has never settled down. With his large, dark eyes, he has never found it difficult to attract members of the opposite sex, either, and he is a happy gambler. Sharif is now a professional at bridge and backgammon.

The Rooster

The Rooster personality

Being born under the tenth Chinese Animal sign makes for colorful and flamboyant characters. The Rooster is a feisty individual: tough, resilient, confident, and strong-willed. Rooster people are proud, extroverted, and theatrical. In fact, many Rooster-born folk are downright show-offs, with a tendency to strut a good deal. But to give them their due, they are also honest and plain-speaking; as far as the Rooster is concerned, a spade is a spade, and the Rooster is happy to call it that.

YEARS OF THE ROOSTER

Tenth in the cycle, Rooster Years follow on from the Monkey and recur every twelfth year thereafter. As the Chinese New Year does not fall on a fixed date, it is essential to check the calendar to find the exact date on which each Rooster Year actually begins.

1909 ★ 1921 ★ 1933
1945 ★ 1957 ★ 1969
1981 ★ 1993 ★ 2005

THE ROOSTER SIGN

Roosters are not given to trickery or underhandedness of any sort, and they despise deceit and disloyalty. Rooster people always like to put their cards on the table and they respect those who are candid enough to do the same. Despite this blunt, straightforward streak, the Rooster is not just a plain, honest type of person. Roosters love mixing in society. They are a great success at social gatherings and can be the life and soul of any social occasion. Roosters can be witty, amusing, and entertaining. They are at their happiest in these situations, where they can attract plenty of admiring attention, but they do like being listened to whether others want to or not, and can get angry if they find anyone else trying to enjoy the same role. Roosters like to crow, and are not known for their diplomacy or sensitivity to others. All Roosters like showing off their fine feathers.

FACTS ABOUT ROOSTERS

People born in the Year of the Rooster share specific characteristics that are common to all other Roosters. To say that someone is a Rooster is simply a shorthand way of describing that individual's personality. Here are the salient features associated with this sign.

ROOSTER FACTS

Tenth in order ★ Chinese name – JI, sign of honesty
Hour – 5pm–6:59pm ★ Month – September
Western counterpart – Virgo

CHARACTERISTICS

Resilience ♥ Courage ♥ Passion ♥ Protectiveness
Patriotism ♥ Industriousness

Bluntness ✖ Conceit ✖ Rudeness ✖ Impatience
Aggression ✖ Bossiness

ABOVE *Roosters are dashing and theatrical, and always attract admiring glances.*

PERFECTIONISM

Roosters have a tendency to be melodramatic, and enjoy playing to the gallery. But despite this, they are immensely practical and logical. Perhaps one of the most hardworking of the signs, they possess excellent powers of discrimination and pay attention to detail. With such high standards of excellence they can be perfectionists. The adverse side of this characteristic is over-punctiliousness and a tendency to be fussy, pecking away at problems instead of sorting them out. Other people can find these nit-picking tendencies very irritating.

IN YOUR ELEMENT

*I*n addition to the Animal signs which recur once every 12 years, the 5 Chinese elements of Metal, Water, Wood, Fire, and Earth also play their part. This means that a five-year cycle of characteristics is overlaid on the original 12-year cycle to modulate the character of the Rooster, as shown below.

THE METAL ROOSTER 1921 AND 1981

Metal Roosters can at times seem arrogant and highly opinionated, and people would describe them as cocky. They need to feel important and have a large ego. They have great powers of deduction and rationality and like to analyze every situation they meet. These Roosters need to make sure they do not analyze instead of acting or taking heed of their true feelings. Despite their air of tough self-righteousness, they are idealistic to the hilt and will passionately work to improve the lot of humankind. Learning to compromise, and to tone down their seemingly aggressive behavior would help them in their relationships with other people.

THE WATER ROOSTER 1933 AND 1993

Water gives the Rooster a character that is altogether more reasonable and compliant than others born under this sign. Quieter, calmer, and generally more intellectual than most of the Roosters, Water Roosters still have the typical Rooster powers of rational thinking and analysis, and they excel in the world of science and communications. They have a seemingly constant supply of energy, but they can allow themselves to have an obsessive interest in detail, which can mean that they dissipate this energy and lose track of the point. Water Roosters need to make an effort to maintain their wide vista throughout life; otherwise, their punctilious attention to detail could narrow their field of vision.

THE WOOD ROOSTER 1945 AND 2005

Kind and considerate to friends and family, and able to get along well with others working as part of a team rather than needing to rule the roost, Wood Roosters possess a strong social conscience that drives them to work for good causes and the betterment of society. They will work with boundless energy and enthusiasm for any cause to which they have committed themselves, expecting everyone else involved to do the same. However, they can expect too much of others, not realizing that not everyone has so much energy, and they sometimes offend other people by being critical or speaking too bluntly. Wood Roosters often end up making too many promises and taking on more than they can realistically handle.

THE FIRE ROOSTER 1957 AND 2017

The element of Fire brings great flamboyance to this sign. Image is extremely important to the Fire Rooster, who spends a lot of time preening his or her fine feathers. With their dynamic élan they are also prone to displays of high theatricals. Nevertheless, these Roosters are brilliant organizers, have great willpower, and make natural leaders whom others are happy to follow and respect. They should watch a tendency to bully others in order to fulfill their wishes, though, and need to learn to be a little more diplomatic and tactful. However, a Fire Rooster can generally make a superb leader or manager in any field in which he or she may choose to exercise this Animal's considerable talents.

THE EARTH ROOSTER 1909 AND 1969

Careful, methodical, neat, and tidy, the Earth Rooster is super-efficient. Earth Roosters have penetrating powers of thought and good financial and business sense. They are never afraid to commit themselves or to take on responsibility, and these elemental Roosters will always be prepared to work hard, and expect others to do the same. They have the Rooster's interest in detail, and are particularly good at gathering and analyzing information. They use these talents very efficiently, and have the power to be very successful in life. Earth Roosters have very exacting standards, and also expect others to share them. This can make them less than popular with colleagues or employees at work, and they need to remind themselves that there are other ways of inspiring people and encouraging them to work hard and well if they want to be leaders of a happy and cooperative team.

Health and habitat

HEALTH AND CONSTITUTION

Involvement in sports and a fondness for the outdoors keep Rooster types fit; besides, Roosters are fighters and refuse to let ill-health get the better of them. If they do succumb, their excellent recuperative powers soon have them brimming with vitality again. It is more in the psychological realm that Roosters are likely to suffer, as they can be prone to dramatic mood swings and are always driven by exacting standards. So it is stress and a tendency to over-indulge that Roosters need to watch.

THE ROOSTER AT HOME

Rooster folk tend to be houseproud. With their remarkable organizational skill, love of method, and attention to detail, their homes are always neat and clean, with a place for everything and everything in its place. Hygiene is also of great importance to the Rooster, and an abundance of cleaning agents is a tell-tale sign of their Chinese Animal birthright. They have a habit of forever sorting and rearranging, cleaning out drawers, and moving furniture around, and this either confuses their long-suffering families or drives them completely around the bend. Shades of apricot and peach are the colors associated with the Rooster sign, and these blend well with their preference for classical furniture and traditional decor.

Career and wealth

THE ROOSTER AT WORK

More career-oriented than most other Animals, Roosters are very hard-working, status-conscious, and driven by ambition. Their qualities suit them to a wide variety of occupations, and with determination and indomitable resilience they will stick at whatever tasks they undertake until they have reached their desired goal. This means they often have great success at work and quickly climb the ladder to the top of their chosen professions.

FINANCE AND THE ROOSTER

Roosters seem to have great talent in the financial field, with their keen eye for detail and ability to make bold gestures. Roosters give very sound financial advice to others, especially when it comes to advice on controlling the budget. Yet when it comes to managing their own money, they tend to fall into one of two categories: either they belong to the band of big-hearted Roosters who love spending money and showering their friends with gifts, or they put it all in the bank and gleefully watch it grow.

LEFT *Many Rooster people take up careers in the worlds of ballet and opera.*

COMPATIBLE BUSINESS PARTNERS

aWhether Roosters benefit from or constantly conflict with their business partners depends, as in all relationships, on whether their Animal signs are harmonious or antagonistic to each other. Taking into consideration the compatibility of the elements between themselves and their working colleagues can also be very useful.

ROOSTERS RULED BY	BENEFIT FROM	ARE ANTAGONISTIC TO
Metal	Earth Snakes	Fire Roosters
Water	Metal Oxen	Earth Pigs
Wood	Water Pigs	Metal Tigers
Fire	Wood Sheep	Water Dogs
Earth	Fire Dragons	Wood Tigers

Leisure and pleasures

THE ROOSTER ON VACATION

The fashion-conscious Rooster likes to be seen in all the best places. Exponents of chic, these people pride themselves in keeping abreast of trends and dressing in the very latest fashions. For them, shopping is a great delight, especially if they can visit exclusive stores and spend a few hours browsing through the designer labels. Younger Roosters are drawn to the "in" boutiques like moths to a candle-flame. Roosters are no strangers to Fifth Avenue, to Rodeo Drive, or even the Champs Elysees. Almost paradoxically, though, nature is also a passion for all natives of this sign. Being able to tuck themselves away in a hotel (five-star preferably), in the middle of nowhere would constitute a dream vacation for people of this sign. They could climb the mountains or walk through valleys, sit by a babbling brook, or lie on their backs and conjure images from the clouds scudding across the skies.

FRIENDS AND FOE

It is no secret that Roosters are bossy and outspoken. Add to that the fact that tact is not one of their strongest attributes, and it is easy to understand why their friends need to be pretty thick-skinned! In fact, folk born in the Year of the Rooster are the sort of people who tend to have more acquaintances than really close friends. Perhaps because, as social climbers, they tend to accumulate a wide network of contacts through their work, or perhaps because they are fairly secretive about their personal lives, they allow only a few individuals to get truly close to them. And yet, no one could have a more trusty friend than the Rooster who, at the drop of a hat, will bend over backward to help a friend in need. Those who know them well have long recognized that, beneath the abrasive exterior of the Rooster, beats a heart of pure gold.

LIKES AND DISLIKES

ROOSTERS LIKE

Color Preference
Peach, apricot

❖

Gems and Stones
Diamond, ruby, topaz

❖

Suitable Gifts
Brocade jacket, egg-decorating kit, bonsai tree, garden trug, terrarium, silver hip flask, ebony walking cane

❖

Hobbies and Pastimes
Golf, fishing, dressmaking, singing, gardening, making silk flowers, hiking

Just as people born under the same Animal sign share a similar character and outlook on life, so do they also have similar tastes. As two Roosters get to know each other, they soon discover that they have many likes and dislikes in common.

ROOSTERS DISLIKE

❖

Poor hygiene

❖

Underachievers

❖

Bad manners

❖

Being teased

❖

Taking orders from anyone

COMPATIBLE FRIENDS

Although each individual person is unique, Chinese astrologers are very precise about which Animals have a general shared understanding and which have characters that are antagonistic to one another. Roosters may wish to note which signs are more likely to provide lasting friendship and which they would find unsettling.

BEST FRIENDS	MORTAL ENEMY
Oxen	Rabbits
Snakes	

LEFT *Roosters like to be seen, yet an active vacation in the wilds of nature fits the bill.*

Rooster parents and babies

Think of a brooding hen clucking over her chicks, picking and pecking and tucking them under her wings. In just the same way, parents born under the sign of the Rooster nurture and nourish, protect and care for their youngsters, and do all they can to keep their offspring safe and free from harm. Such zealous protectiveness, however, can at times go too far, and the Rooster parents' natural instincts incline them to want to wrap their children from head to toe in cotton.

In general, Rooster mothers and fathers tend to err on the side of being strict, most believing fervently in discipline. It has been said that, as parents, these people can be insensitive to their children, lacking in understanding and intolerant of ideas or standards of behavior that do not comply with their own. Certainly, Roosters are conformists, and impatient with those who refuse to maintain the status quo. Moreover, these people are sticklers for old-fashioned values, morality, and honesty, so they will insist that their children grow up to be polite and respectful – not only toward their elders and betters, but also to nature and the environment in which they live. But Rooster parents are deeply committed to their children, and unwavering in their care and affection for them. They offer a truly cast-iron guarantee of parental love upon which the Rooster's child can always rely.

ROOSTER PARENT/CHILD RELATIONSHIPS

For some parents, their children's personalities harmonize perfectly with their own. Others find that no matter how much they may love their offspring, they are simply not on the same wavelength. Below are the compatibility ratings between Rooster parents and their children.

ROOSTERS WITH	UNDER THE SAME ROOF	COMPATIBILITY RATING
Rat	detached	✓✓
Ox	solid bonds	✓✓✓✓
Tiger	not the easiest rapport	✓
Rabbit	some irritations	✓✓
Dragon	an interesting relationship	✓✓✓
Snake	differing expectations	✓
Horse	willful tantrums	✓✓
Sheep	loving despite many differences	✓
Monkey	conflicts	✓
Rooster	battles of will	✓✓
Dog	true affection	✓✓✓✓
Pig	strongly supportive	✓✓✓✓

RATINGS ✓ uphill struggle ✓✓ some complications ✓✓✓ easy bonding ✓✓✓✓ on the same wavelength

THE ROOSTER BABY AND CHILD

Like the natives of the sign of the Monkey, children born in the Year of the Rooster are bright, vivacious, alert, and socially adept. For them, interacting with others, and particularly with their elders, is as easy as falling off a log. Indeed, their charm is often one of the qualities that first endears these children to adults. At school, young Roosters are eager to learn, although as a rule this sign is not especially noted for its academic brilliance. But the Rooster is a competitive Animal, with a strong adventurous streak that best manifests itself in sports. Practical subjects, drama, and all situations where social skills are required are the areas in which the young Rooster will particularly excel.

ABOVE *The Rooster parent keeps a close watch over his or her children – to the point of fussing.*

OPPOSITE *Not far below the surface, the Rooster is longing for love.*

LEFT *These parents expect good manners and are ready to set the right example.*

Lovers and spouses

THE ROOSTER LOVER

Rooster emotions tend to be black or white, so they either love or hate – with very little room for gray areas. Theirs is a strong, forceful personality, and although usually candid and open in interactions with others, Roosters tend to keep their emotions firmly under wraps and are reluctant to talk about their innermost feelings. Discretion is definitely the better part of valor for Roosters, and partners can be sure that they would never disclose the details of their intimate sexual exploits.

HEART OF GOLD

Roosters are not the easiest people to live with. And yet, anyone who is prepared to look beyond their bossy, abrasive exteriors will find someone who desperately wants to love and be loved, who is anxious to please and is genuinely kind and generous. For, though tough and uncompromising, a Rooster's heart is made of solid gold.

It is their candor, a virtue prized by Roosters, that can actually damage their relationships, especially if their partner tends towards a sensitive disposition. Never one for mincing his or her words, the Rooster, male or female, can be highly critical, tactlessly carping about other people's shortcomings. Roosters also have a habit of taking the high moral ground with a sanctimonious smugness that would drive all but the meekest saint straight to the nearest divorce court.

THE ROOSTER LOVE PARTNER

A solid and not oversensitive person would make an ideal partner for the Rooster – someone who can shout the Rooster down from time to time, or who will be unconcerned by the crowing, and who will not mind the Rooster's strutting, but feel admiration for his or her firm attitudes. The panel (right) shows which Animals are most compatible with Rooster folk and which relationships will be hard work.

PARTNERS IN LOVE

ROOSTER ♥ RAT
Alas, there's more scratchy conflict than there is tender love between Rats and Roosters.

ROOSTER ♥ OX
Sexy, passionate, sizzling. Good match for a happy and successful relationship.

ROOSTER ♥ TIGER
Misunderstandings between you two strong-minded animals will create problems. Talking about things will help.

ROOSTER ♥ RABBIT
You're opposites in almost every aspect you could think of.

ROOSTER ♥ DRAGON
You're exquisite creatures and make a gorgeous pair, but each of you has a mega-ego, and that tends to get in the way.

ROOSTER ♥ SNAKE
What a winning team!

ROOSTER ♥ HORSE
Despite the occasional power conflict, you really do make a great couple.

ROOSTER ♥ SHEEP
Difficulties at every turn give only average ratings for this union.

ROOSTER ♥ MONKEY
Romantically, this could be a bit of a damp squib.

ROOSTER ♥ ROOSTER
So much self-righteousness in one house can only lead to misery.

ROOSTER ♥ DOG
Not a lot of common ground here.

ROOSTER ♥ PIG
Despite your differences, you two could really make this relationship work.

LOVE PARTNERS AT A GLANCE

ROOSTERS WITH:	TIPS ON TOGETHERNESS	COMPATIBILITY
Rat	too many differences	♥
Ox	blessed by the gods	♥♥♥♥
Tiger	talk or walk	♥♥
Rabbit	nothing in common at all	♥
Dragon	never a dull moment	♥♥
Snake	solid!	♥♥♥♥
Horse	quarrels undermine your love	♥♥♥
Sheep	a recipe for success	♥♥♥
Monkey	soooo picky	♥
Rooster	a disastrous combination	♥
Dog	difficult	♥♥
Pig	worth preserving	♥♥♥

COMPATIBILITY RATINGS: ♥ *conflict* ♥♥ *work at it*
♥♥♥ *strong sexual attraction* ♥♥♥♥ *heavenly!*

EAST MEETS WEST

🦏 ARIES ROOSTER

Clever, witty, blunt, and forthright, Aries Roosters are plain speakers, uncompromisingly honest, and expect others to deliver the plain, unvarnished truth too. They are tough enough to face adversity and they respect those who can give as good as they get.

🦂 TAUREAN ROOSTER

These robust and sober-minded individuals are industrious to the point of becoming workaholics. They are persistent and achievement-oriented and have no time for shirkers. Learning to relax and letting their hair down now and again would help to lighten their serious outlook.

👬 GEMINI ROOSTER

Gemini Roosters can run rings around almost anyone. They know a lot, or so it seems, and they like nothing more than a good debate. Restless and impulsive, they are full of brilliant schemes and ideas, with a talent for organization. A high profile with friends is important to them.

🦐 CANCERIAN ROOSTER

Cancer endows the Rooster with tenderness and softens the spiky edges. The Rooster sign brings efficiency and so the household shines like a new-pin. The more children, pets, and relatives that gather around their feet, the happier and more secure these people feel.

🦁 LEONINE ROOSTER

These two signs can match each other in color, drama, and flamboyance. This is a character who enjoys overtly displaying his or her fine feathers and someone with an undisguised belief in his or her own superiority. But this Rooster is also sincere, loving, and passionate.

🐾 VIRGO ROOSTER

Virgo Roosters excel in tasks requiring a logical mentality. They home in on detail and drive partners to distraction with their exacting standards. Moreover, they can be abrasive in their criticism, even though they mean well. Partners and colleagues need to develop a thick skin.

⚖️ LIBRAN ROOSTER

Mess or unpleasantness of any sort disturbs these Roosters' sensitivities. This applies to emotional embroilment as well as physical clutter. Cool and refined, Libran Roosters take an intellectual approach to life and yet are charming and affable, with many friends and good companions.

🦂 SCORPIO ROOSTER

With strong will and determination, if these Roosters set their sights on something or someone, they refuse to give up until they have it. Their sinister side, although it rarely emerges, lies quite close to the surface, and the Scorpio Rooster's emotions run deep.

🏹 SAGITTARIAN ROOSTER

Cheerful and happy-go-lucky, this Rooster has a jaunty gait and lightness of heart that lift the spirits. Sagittarian Roosters are more tolerant and philosophical than other Roosters, but have a tendency to put their feet in their mouths. They are famed for their idealism and altruism.

🐐 CAPRICORN ROOSTER

Ambition and worldly aspirations drive the Capricorn Rooster to work hard and climb that ladder of success, and these people are practical, super-efficient, and unflappable in a crisis. Status and reputation are top of the agenda to the Capricorn Rooster.

🏺 AQUARIAN ROOSTER

These people like to stand out, to be different, individualistic, or even downright eccentric. Emotionally, they cannot bear to be tied down. Intellectually, Capricorn Roosters need to seek fresh challenges on a daily basis in order to stimulate their active imaginations.

🐟 PISCEAN ROOSTER

Both hard-headed pragmatist and sensitive romantic, the Piscean Rooster is more amenable and less abrasive than many others. Bad feelings or emotional friction of any sort upsets these tamer Cockerels, who are inclined to see things through rose-colored spectacles.

Famous Roosters

Proud, dignified, and flamboyant, but solid, sound, and with a good old heart of gold, Rooster people are straight talking and straightforward, with absolutely no deviousness. And despite their showy side, these people are practical and down to earth and always ready to work hard for their living and to achieve their ambitions.

▷ Dolly Parton

A great Rooster character who displays her fine feathers and is full of happy self-confidence, this is a double Rooster – a singer who can act. Dolly Parton is a great entertainer. She has the persona of someone who can give it to people straight, and she also has a sense of humor and can even make fun of herself, a gift not always found in Rooster people.

◁ Mary Quant

The sign of the Rooster is often linked with fashion, and Mary Quant put British fashion on the map in the 1960s. The flamboyant Rooster is also a traditionalist, and Quant's simple look and new colors were underpinned by well-cut clothes and understanding of the classical couture tradition. She also showed the Rooster gift for finance in running an international fashion empire that grew fast and turned over millions.

▽ Katharine Hepburn

With her self-assured character both on and off screen, Katharine Hepburn is flamboyant almost without realizing it and certainly without meaning to be. One of the key adjectives used to describe the Rooster is often applied to Miss Hepburn: feisty. She has a great Rooster talent for entertaining and can always hold the floor.

▽ Eric Clapton

Many Roosters make good musicians, and Eric Clapton is a musician even other musicians look up to. He applies industry to his art and has remained at the top for decades. He can be the center of attention on stage, but most of all he has shown the Rooster resilience and courage in beating drug addiction and personal tragedy, surviving and staying on top in a tough and demanding industry.

△ Nick Faldo

The British golfer Nick Faldo has helped to make golf into a fashionable, cutting-edge sport. Roosters tend to be competitive, and this leisure activity even enables participants to compete against themselves. The Rooster's love of display is also apparent in Faldo's predilection for stylish clothes.

The Dog

The Dog personality

Caring, unselfish, and altruistic, the Dog is one of life's givers. The Dog person always has a kind word to say, an encouraging remark to offer, and a reassuring smile. Dogs make time for other people, listening to their problems, providing a shoulder for them to cry on, lending them support, and finding some wise counsel from that seemingly bottomless well of common sense philosophy that they possess. Their detractors, on the other hand, might say that they are just nosey, following people around and giving advice when it wasn't asked for. People rarely notice that their Dog friend knows more about them than they know about the Dog. The Dog doesn't like to reveal his or her own problems, and tends to be a bit of a worrier in private.

THE SIGN OF THE DOG

There are times when, because they think they know best, Dogs can be somewhat high-handed, marching in and taking over a situation without waiting to be asked, and twice as forcefully as anyone expected. But such occasions are rare, and it's more often that the Dog's generosity of spirit and genuine concern shine through in every action. For as far as the Dog type is concerned, it is always people that count. Money, power, prestige – none of these things matter to the Dog. For these people, their family and loved ones constitute all the treasure they need, and they have a widespread – and genuine – concern for others.

Dog people specialize. They won't be seen wasting their energy by following each new scent that greets them, and wasting their time on one new thing after another. Once they have chosen a hobby or interest, they stick to it. And they tend to be the same with work – sticking purposefully to their chosen career. It is just as well for them to choose carefully. They need the incitement of knowing that what they are doing is worthwhile, and they may show a slightly lazy streak if they are not motivated enough.

Dogs are disarmingly honest, highly principled, and morally upright, and those who come to know Dogs soon learn to respect their great integrity and to value their warm and faithful friendship.

YEARS OF THE DOG

Eleventh in the cycle, Dog Years follow on from Rooster Years and recur every twelfth year thereafter. As the Chinese New Year starts on a different date each year, it is essential to check the calendar to find the exact day on which each Dog Year begins.

1910 ★ 1922 ★ 1934
1946 ★ 1958 ★ 1970
1982 ★ 1994 ★ 2006

ABOVE *Dogs have strong moral qualities and can be pillars of society.*

FACTS ABOUT DOGS

People born in the Year of the Dog share specific characteristics that are common to all other Dogs. To say that someone is a Dog is simply a shorthand way of describing that individual's personality. Here are the salient features associated with this sign.

DOG FACTS
Eleventh in order ★ Chinese name – GOU, sign of fidelity
Hour – 7pm–8:59pm ★ Month – October
Western counterpart – Libra

CHARACTERISTICS
Reliability ♥ Perseverance ♥ Devotion
Resourcefulness ♥ Unselfishness ♥ Honesty

Introversion ✖ Nosiness ✖ Cantankerousness
Anxiety ✖ Pessimism ✖ Cynicism

IN YOUR ELEMENT

In addition to the Animal signs that recur once every 12 years, the 5 Chinese elements of Metal, Water, Wood, Fire, and Earth also play their part. This means that a 5-year cycle of characteristics is overlaid on the original 12-year cycle. The Dog birth year is the first guide to the personality as determined by the Chinese horoscope, but the characteristics of each generation of Dog are slightly modified by one of the elements, depending on the overlaying of the 5-year cycle.

THE METAL DOG 1910 AND 1970

Uncompromisingly scrupulous and with extremely high standards, Metal Dogs have a serious outlook on life. Fiercely loyal and faithful, once they have shown their allegiance to a person, party, or cause, there is very little that will persuade them to retract. These Dogs have firm confidence in themselves and in the importance of their chosen causes. They are forthright and not afraid to speak their minds, and will back their causes loyally and consistently in word and deed. With the unbending influence of the Metal element, this type of Dog tends to want to have a plan, and to feel a little anxious if the plan seems to be going wrong. Sometimes it would help them to lighten up a little, and not to takes things quite so seriously.

THE WATER DOG 1922 AND 1982

The Water Dog's keen insight, quiet contemplative nature, and powerful psychological penetration make it easy for Water Dogs to appreciate other people's points of view. They are more flexible and easygoing than some of the other Dog people because of the Water influence, but they can also be in need of more control. Their easygoing nature may encourage them to be incautious with money and perhaps be a little less loyal and reliable than the majority of Dogs. However, the Water Dog's friendliness and warmth, tolerance and understanding guarantee that these Dogs will never be short of friends, and they are sure to be among the most popular of people with friends and colleagues alike.

THE WOOD DOG 1934 AND 1994

Wood Dogs are generous by nature and well-balanced by disposition. More adaptable but less independent than other Dogs, they like to live and work as part of a group. The support of others is important to the Wood Dog, as this gives them the sense of protection and support that is so necessary to their well-being. They are loyal to the group and very friendly within it, but they don't go around wagging their tails at all and sundry, and can be shy with new people until they get to know them. They tend to lack self-confidence when outside their chosen group, although they are amiable and well-liked and have very stable characters.

THE FIRE DOG 1946 AND 2006

Fire Dogs make born leaders. This element imparts dynamism, energy, enthusiasm, independence, a strong streak of adventurousness, and tons of charm, with a charismatic personality. An outgoing disposition and creative mentality ensure the Fire Dog popularity and success. Fire Dogs are usually very attractive to people of both sexes and have great self-assurance. Nevertheless, they have the Dog person's sterling qualities of honesty, loyalty, and reliability, and they do not get carried away with their own success. With their adventurous spirits, Fire Dogs are less settled than others and may have a more volatile nature.

THE EARTH DOG 1958 AND 2018

Slow but sure, the solid Earth Dog is a wise and kindly character. The Earth element lends these people innate practicality and invaluable talent when it comes to giving advice and dealing with money. Honesty, objectivity, and impeccable integrity are the trademarks of Earth Dogs. They are good at influencing other people's opinions through their quietly persuasive manners, and they are generally well-regarded by others. The Earth Dog inspires, and deserves, confidence. A great democrat, and always prepared to listen to other people's points of view and weigh the evidence, the Earth Dog will always dispense justice wisely and be thoroughly dependable when placed in positions of power.

Health and habitat

HEALTH AND CONSTITUTION

Their general philosophical acceptance of human nature and the vagaries of life tend to give Dog people resilience and keep their health on an even keel. Because of this they seem to have a remarkable ability to absorb and withstand the buffeting of events that life throws at them. Being happy is the Dog's best protection against disease; otherwise, a tendency to feel deep-seated anxiety can bring out problems associated with the nervous system.

THE DOG AT HOME

Dog-born individuals love their homes to be clean and well-organized, and will spend hours dusting and polishing. But although it is neat and orderly, there is always a comfortable feel about the Dog person's environment. Deep sofas in attractive upholstery simply beg the welcome guest (and the Dog owner) to sit down and take it easy. Dog people go for good taste, so there is nothing showy about their house's interiors. Tradition is important to them and they are more likely to favor conservative styles and will choose solid wood in preference to plastic, wool carpets rather than synthetics, and antiques or traditional furniture instead of modern pieces.

CAREERS FOR DOGS

All those who are born in the Year of the Dog share not only similar talents and inherent skills, but also the same kind of aims and ambitions in life. The occupations that best suit the Dog mentality and abilities are listed here.

DOGS MAKE EXCELLENT

Lawyers ★ Judges
Police officers ★ Teachers
Scientists ★ Nurses
Doctors ★ Surgeons
Carers ★ Welfare workers
Psychiatrists ★ Psychologists
Councillors ★ Politicians
Priests ★ Nuns ★ Clerics
Gardeners ★ Builders
Interior decorators

Career and wealth

THE DOG AT WORK

Cheerful and willing, Dog people are thoughtful and helpful and, whether at the top or bottom of the ladder, often take on extra responsibilities in order to lighten the loads of their colleagues. As a consequence, they are always popular and respected members of the workforce. In positions of responsibility the Dog is a good judge of people, possessing insight and intuition and so thoroughly honest and open that he or she inspires loyalty from the rest of the team.

FINANCE AND THE DOG

Dog people are careful when it comes to money; they work hard and know the value of spending moderately and wisely. The idea of accumulating wealth for its own sake is of little interest to them, although they like to have enough to make themselves comfortable, and can be very generous with friends and family. Dogs are good at conserving their resources and many put a little money by on a regular basis to build up savings for the future.

COMPATIBLE BUSINESS PARTNERS

Whether Dogs benefit from or constantly conflict with their business partners depends, as in all relationships, on whether their Animal signs are harmonious or antagonistic to each other. Taking into consideration the compatibility of the elements between themselves and their working colleagues can also be very useful.

DOGS RULED BY	BENEFIT FROM	ARE ANTAGONISTIC TO
Metal	*Earth Horses*	*Fire Dragons*
Water	*Metal Snakes*	*Earth Roosters*
Wood	*Water Tigers*	*Metal Oxen*
Fire	*Wood Rats*	*Water Sheep*
Earth	*Fire Rabbits*	*Wood Monkeys*

ABOVE LEFT *Dog-born people make good teachers, as they are caring and patient and take their responsibilities seriously.*

Leisure and pleasures

LIKES AND DISLIKES

DOGS LIKE

Color Preference
Pale yellow

Gems and Stones
Moonstone, carnelian, jasper

Suitable Gifts
Window box, rocking chair, puzzle, the latest novel, a massage session, silk flowers, lace tablecloth, red roses

Hobbies and Pastimes
Gardening, craftwork, sailing, dancing, cooking, flower arranging

Just as people born under the same Animal sign share a similar character and outlook on life, so do they also have similar tastes. As two Dogs get to know each other, they soon discover that they have many likes and dislikes in common.

DOGS DISLIKE

Injustice

Letting the team down

Hurting people's feelings

Losing their temper

BELOW AND RIGHT *A family vacation will appeal to the Dog person. Adult Dogs are happy to put others first, and will gladly hang around the beach with the youngsters all day.*

THE DOG ON VACATION

Compulsive observers of human nature, people born in the Year of the Dog could happily while away their time sitting in a café just watching people go by. Whether they choose Prague, Istanbul, Athens, or Amsterdam does not matter. What is important, however, is that the Dog should have the opportunity to take in the local social mores. People born under this sign are very family-oriented, so for them a vacation surrounded by all their favorite relatives would be perfect. And Dogs are really happy to accommodate everyone's tastes and needs, too, whether that involves eating sandy sandwiches on the beach with the little ones, driving the teenagers to a pop concert, escorting the elderly parents to the opera, or enjoying the fresh air with a great-aunt on the boardwalk. Seeing that their loved ones are happy is all the pleasure in life a Dog requires.

FRIENDS AND FOE

No one could wish for a better companion than a person born in the Year of the Dog. Indeed, subjects of this sign are the easiest people to get along with that one is ever likely to meet. Honest, sensible, solid and reliable, Dogs take humanity as it comes – warts and all. Loving and faithful, these people will stand by their friends through thick and thin, rushing to their sides in a crisis, sharing in their joy and sadness, providing commonsense advice and a strong arm upon which they can lean. Dogs are the carers among the Chinese Animals, always ready to give comfort and support to those in need. What makes Dogs so companionable is that they are not ambitious or desirous to take the lead, but just happy to go along with the flow. Moreover, Dogs value their friends and rank their friendships higher than status or wealth.

Dog parents and babies

One of the most caring, responsible, and deeply devoted parents of all the Chinese Animals, Dogs always put their families first. As far as those born under this sign are concerned, to consider others before their own offspring is tantamount to heresy. Staunchly loyal and unwaveringly faithful, Dog-born parents stick by and protect their children through thick and thin.

Dog mothers and fathers will do everything they can to make their homes happy and safe places in which their youngsters can grow and develop. Selflessly and without a word of complaint, they will stay up night after night by a sick child's bedside, patiently holding her hand or mopping his brow and generally giving comfort and reassurance until the fever has passed. Parents belonging to the Dog sign also encourage their children to question and explore, to learn at their own pace, and to find things out for themselves. When they choose their life direction, Dogs wouldn't dream of standing in their children's way. But they let their offspring know that they are there on the sidelines, rooting for them all the way. And their children know, too, with confidence, that their Dog parents will still be there for them if they are ever in need – no matter how small or how big the problem might be.

THE DOG
BABY AND CHILD

Children born under the sign of the Dog are as cute and cuddly as any puppy dog around. Easily pleased, these youngsters are able to amuse themselves contentedly for hours around the house. They are happy to play a quiet game in a corner all by themselves, or to take out a construction toy and build a fantastic wonderland, draw a picture in a sketch book, pick up a stone in the backyard and watch with rapt fascination as the insects go about their lives. Indeed, having a Dog child about the house is no problem whatsoever. Common sense is their greatest virtue, and these children blossom if they are given responsibility. Whether the task involves running an errand or looking after a younger brother or sister, they will carry out their duties efficiently and with maturity, for children of the Dog sign are born to help, and pleasing others gives them the greatest pleasure of all.

ABOVE *The person born in the Year of the Dog is a protective parent who also knows how to give the children freedom.*

OPPOSITE *Though perhaps a little shy at first, the Dog is a loving and devoted partner who can be relied on.*

DOG PARENT/CHILD RELATIONSHIPS

For some parents, their children's personalities harmonize perfectly with their own. Others find that no matter how much they may love their offspring, they are simply not on the same wavelength. Below are the compatibility ratings between Dog parents and their children.

DOGS WITH	UNDER THE SAME ROOF	COMPATIBILITY RATING
Rat	lots of shared contentment	✓✓✓
Ox	each requires own space	✓
Tiger	proud parenting	✓✓✓✓
Rabbit	mutual benefits	✓✓✓
Dragon	opposing ambitions	✓
Snake	misunderstandings likely	✓
Horse	warm ties	✓✓✓
Sheep	needs tenderness	✓
Monkey	obvious generation gap	✓✓
Rooster	much to praise	✓✓✓
Dog	genuine rapport	✓✓✓✓
Pig	positive vibes	✓✓✓✓

RATINGS ✓ uphill struggle ✓✓ some complications ✓✓✓ easy bonding ✓✓✓✓ on the same wavelength

Lovers and spouses

THE DOG LOVER

There is an innate shyness about Dog people that can get in the way of making friends. Perhaps this is because Dogs need to know people well before they entrust them with their affections. Perhaps they are suspicious, with a fear of being hurt and let down. For Dogs are sensitive and emotionally tender – they do not easily throw slights over their shoulders, and consequently their wounds take a long time to heal.

Having found his or her soulmate, the Dog person makes a loyal and true companion. As a lover, Dogs are kind and gentle. Helpful and supportive, they care tenderly for those they love and are always anxious to please. They stick by their partner, sharing all the highs and lows of life, defending and protecting him or her if need be with every fiber of their being.

HONEST DOG

A Dog who is contented and loved is happy to plow his or her own furrow. Dogs are undemanding and have simple needs. Because they find change disturbing, even if they are unhappy in love, they are likely to stay put rather than cast off into the cold unknown. Honesty is the Dog's abiding principle, but harsh truths can do untold damage in a relationship, and Dogs need to learn to deliver their criticisms with tact if they are to avoid being accused of possessing a caustic tongue.

THE DOG LOVE PARTNER

The system of Chinese horoscopes is very specific about which Animals are compatible and which are antagonistic, and this tells us whether our relationships have the potential to be successful. Most people get on well with Dog folk, and they make good partners with many of the other types. A bit on the serious side, and rather down-to-earth, the Dog may find the flashy Rooster or the fiery Dragon tiresome, and there will seldom be love lost between the two, while the Sheep will find the Dog unbending and bring out his or her bossiness.

The panel (right) shows how other Animals are suited to the Dog as a partner.

PARTNERS IN LOVE

DOG ♥ RAT
Despite some dull moments, you can actually achieve a stable union together.

DOG ♥ OX
You don't have much in common and are not truly comfortable with each other.

DOG ♥ TIGER
Mutual respect and admiration make this a winning team.

DOG ♥ RABBIT
Lots going for you here.

DOG ♥ DRAGON
A truly tempestuous affair that's not recommended for peace of mind.

DOG ♥ SNAKE
Mutual attraction on sight.

DOG ♥ HORSE
Tipped for lasting happiness, stability, and success.

DOG ♥ SHEEP
A tiresome togetherness.

DOG ♥ MONKEY
Not a bad shot this. With so much desire to pull together, you've got plenty going for you.

DOG ♥ ROOSTER
Not a lot in common here – difficulties arise all the way.

DOG ♥ DOG
Compassionate, understanding, and harmonious, together you're likely to stay the distance.

DOG ♥ PIG
A solid, amicable, and honest partnership, even if a little unadventurous at times.

LOVE PARTNERS AT A GLANCE

DOGS WITH:	TIPS ON TOGETHERNESS	COMPATIBILITY
Rat	*mutual respect*	♥♥
Ox	*odds against, but a glimmer of hope*	♥♥
Tiger	*solid!*	♥♥♥♥
Rabbit	*rock steady*	♥♥♥
Dragon	*keep walking if you want to stay healthy*	♥
Snake	*first comes the physical, then the mental*	♥♥♥
Horse	*you have what it takes*	♥♥♥♥
Sheep	*a clash of personalities*	♥
Monkey	*cheerful complementarity*	♥♥♥
Rooster	*difficult*	♥♥
Dog	*deep affection*	♥♥♥♥
Pig	*honest and sincere*	♥♥♥

COMPATIBILITY RATINGS: ♥ *conflict* ♥♥ *work at it*
♥♥♥ *strong sexual attraction* ♥♥♥♥ *heavenly!*

ARIES DOG

Aries Dogs are confident of their abilities, enjoy their independence, and are less likely to stay with the pack. Their search for true spiritual rapport prevents them from settling down too early. When they find their life partners they have to learn that a little tact facilitates relationships.

TAUREAN DOG

Taurean Dogs have conservative beliefs and traditional values. They are dedicated and hard-working, towers of strength, pillars of the community, sensible and down-to-earth, and make people feel comfortable and reassured. But they are also stubborn and like things done their way.

GEMINI DOG

Bright, breezy, and intelligent, Gemini Dogs could out-talk anyone. Full of ideas, flexible, and multi-talented, these people are far less intimidated by change than many of the other Dogs. Gemini Dogs positively enjoy the adventure of new experiences.

CANCERIAN DOG

Cancerian Dogs are people of quiet, discriminating tastes. Instinctive home-makers, they are at their happiest at home surrounded by their loved ones. They tend to be sensitive and to suffer from personal insecurities, and need solid, loving partners to provide support and reassurance.

LEONINE DOG

Proud, confident, and dignified, Leonine Dogs come across as worldly-wise and self-assured. None but those truly close to them would suspect that they suffer from inner doubts and a fragile ego. The Leo Dog is genuine, warm, and caring, courteous, noble-minded, faithful, and loyal, but needs the support of a loving partner.

VIRGO DOG

Virgo Dogs are dutiful and responsible. They work hard and dedicate themselves totally to those they love. Steady, quiet, and utterly trustworthy, they carry out whatever task they are given efficiently and without fuss.

LIBRAN DOG

Libran Dogs are extremely charming, very sincere, and genuinely concerned about people. Fair-minded and equitable, at work and in life, they are true egalitarians and believe in fair play for all. But in love, partners fail to come up to the Libran Dog's expectations.

SCORPIO DOG

Scorpio determination brings passion and strength, and these Dogs are some of the most deeply committed people. Their word is their bond. Scorpio Dogs have powerful personalities and prefer to lead than to be led. In personal relationships they give and expect one-hundred percent loyalty, and brook no betrayal.

SAGITTARIAN DOG

Sincerity, warmth of character, and generosity guarantee the Sagittarian Dog a loyal following. More adventurous and fun-loving than most other Dogs, these people like a certain autonomy of action. Being hemmed in, whether mentally or physically, makes the Sagittarian Dog ill.

CAPRICORN DOG

These Dogs are caring, dutiful, and utterly responsible. They run their businesses efficiently, keep their accounts meticulously and their homes impeccably neat, and guard their families assiduously. They are not the most emotionally expressive of people, but they have a heart of gold.

AQUARIAN DOG

Original and somewhat eccentric, the Aquarian Dog is one of the least materialistic people in the world. A staunch upholder of democratic rights and of the rights of the underdog, the Aquarian Dog seeks spiritual fulfilment. These people dedicate themselves to others.

PISCEAN DOG

Happiness for the Piscean Dog centers around a quiet, restful environment, a loving home, and a devoted partner. These are quintessentially peace-loving, sensitive souls, but rather prone to over-anxiety.

Famous Dogs

Dog people are reliable, unselfish, honest, and persevering. They can also gnaw away at bones, and seem at times to enjoy licking their wounds. They can be strongly intuitive, able to sense other people's feelings or impending danger, and they can be pessimistic, always sensing trouble. They value friends and companions more than worldly wealth, but they can also care about friends so much that they may boss them around. They are simple folk, never devious or scheming.

▶ Liza Minnelli

A performing Dog who was thrust into the limelight while still a small child as a stage accessory to her mother Judy Garland, Liza Minnelli is a great trooper of a Dog, with a lot of talent and a very uncertain ego. She is a hard-working and utterly reliable performer who would never let the audience down and who has a warm greeting for the most incidental acquaintance, but she seems to have the Dog tendency to worry and feel insecure.

▶ Sophia Loren

Despite her international fame, this terrifically sexy but very diligent actress has kept a low profile in her private life. Her talents shone under the directorship of her husband, Carlo Ponti, with whom she enjoyed a happy domesticity. And although she worked well with many people, she was a constant partner to Marcello Mastroianni.

▽ Ava Gardner

Ava Gardner was a great film heroine of the 1940s and '50s and an exceedingly glamorous Dog person with her handsome features, and soft, dark eyes often associated with this sign. In hard-working Dog fashion she carried on acting long after her pin-up days were over, and then settled into comfortable retirement. She was good in the Cinderella role of the gifted underdog whose talents were eventually allowed to flourish.

◀ Sylvester Stallone

The character played by Sylvester Stallone in his Rocky films has Dog-like characteristics – good but not very bright; loyal but anxious, wondering whether everything would turn out all right. Stallone is a humanitarian who gets depressed but who will plod on and fight with honesty all the way through the ranks to champion the underdog. He has been described as portraying Rocky as a true naive, or latter-day noble savage, and this certainly picks on some of the Dog's qualities as an old-fashioned sort of person. In the Rambo films Stallone becomes a reliable, devoted companion. And then there are those soft brown eyes!

△ Norman Schwarzkopf

This is the Dog in command. Dog people are worried about security and like keeping order. The U.S. Supreme Commander of the Allied Forces in the 1991 Gulf War shows the orderly and organizing side of the Dog character. Reliable and loyal to the hilt, with a bit of a gruff bark, he planned the Desert Storm campaign with such method that there was victory with very little loss of life on the side of the Allies. As a result of his handling of the Gulf War, he has become a modest hero.

The Pig

The Pig personality

Born with a naturally patient and cheerful disposition, the Pig, or Boar, is an outgoing, jovial character who is able to brighten up and encourage anyone he or she meets. Pig people are by nature kind and caring, with an easygoing manner that belies their resilience and tenacity. Honest as the day is long, they expect others to be just as sincere as they are – which contributes to the Pig's special charm, but which also gives people born under this sign a trusting, almost wide-eyed naivety when it comes to dealing with others.

THE SIGN OF THE PIG

The chief characteristics of people born under the sign of the Pig are shown in the panel (below, right). Always considerate, the Pig is ready to drop whatever he or she may be doing and run to the assistance of anyone in need. Because Pigs are so generous they give willingly of their time and money to help those less fortunate than themselves. Sometimes people take advantage of their exceptionally good natures, but they seldom bear a grudge and always give others chance after chance to redeem themselves. More than anything, these people like harmony and detest discord, and will go to great lengths to overlook or excuse bad manners and crass behavior, or to smooth other people's ruffled feathers. However, if put upon too often, even this normally easygoing individual will draw the line and begin to get angry. A Pig in a rage is not a pretty sight!

Pig people can be taken advantage of, and certainly taken for granted, as they are so trustworthy and entirely dependable. By nature they are more at ease giving than receiving, and are always happy to share – although this works both ways, and they do not realize that some people are more possessive than they are and have no wish to share back.

LA DOLCE VITA

Yet despite their down-to-earth good cheer, Pig people are arch-sensualists at heart. They adore the good things in life and have a special fondness for an easy life. Creature comforts are essential to their well-being and, if the truth is told, it is a pampered life of luxury that these people truly crave. This is the one area in which a Pig can go wrong: for just as Pig people will put everything they have into their work, or into helping others, they can also sometimes be found giving themselves a bit too whole-heartedly to a life of pleasure.

YEARS OF THE PIG

Twelfth and last in the cycle, Pig Years follow on from Dog Years and recur every twelfth year thereafter. As the Chinese New Year starts on a different date each year, it is essential to check the calendar to find the exact day on which each Pig Year begins.

1911 ★ 1923 ★ 1935
1947 ★ 1959 ★ 1971
1983 ★ 1995 ★ 2007

FACTS ABOUT PIGS

People born in the Year of the Pig share specific characteristics that are common to all other Pigs. To say that someone is a Pig is simply a shorthand way of describing that individual's personality. Here are the salient features associated with this sign.

PIG FACTS
Twelfth in order ★ Chinese name – ZHU, sign of honesty
Hour – 9pm–10:59pm ★ Month – November
Western counterpart – Scorpio

CHARACTERISTICS
Sincerity ★ Gregariousness ★ Diligence ★ Generosity
Obligingness ★ Unpretentiousness

Naivety ✸ Materialism ✸ Superficiality
Pigheadedness ✸ Gullibility ✸ Laziness

IN YOUR ELEMENT

In addition to the Animal signs that recur once every 12 years, the 5 Chinese elements of Metal, Water, Wood, Fire, and Earth also play their part. This means that a 5-year cycle of characteristics is overlaid on the original 12-year cycle. The Pig birth year is the first guide to the personality as determined by the Chinese horoscope, but the characteristics of each generation of Pig are slightly modified by one of the elements, depending on the overlaying of the 5-year cycle.

THE METAL PIG 1911 AND 1971

Strong and assertive, the Metal Pig is a passionate creature who puts one hundred percent into everything he or she does – and especially into relationships with others. At work, the Metal Pig is cheerful and industrious, to a partner he or she is faithful and true, and to everyone with whom this elemental Pig comes in contact, this brand of Pig is worth his or her weight in gold. Not endowed with good judgement where others are concerned, Metal Pigs think everyone else is better than they actually are, but they are strong enough to cope with any difficulties that may sometimes arise as a result of this, and can be tough opponents to beat, should the situation ever arise.

THE WATER PIG 1923 AND 1983

The influence of Water makes the generous, kind Pig infinitely malleable and too trusting for his or her own good. Nevertheless, these elemental Pigs are adept at dealing with people and have a gift for divining what is going on in other people's minds. As a result, although they are easily influenced, they can also be highly persuasive with others. By nature helpful and kind, they like to be of service. A hard worker and often keen and successful in business, this is also a very sociable Animal who loves parties. Yet in fact, the Water Pig is happiest of all in the bosom of the family.

THE WOOD PIG 1935 AND 1995

Gifts of subtlety and diplomacy stand the Wood Pig in good stead when handling other people. Characteristically big-hearted and generous, these Pigs are unstinting in giving time and money to worthwhile and charitable causes. They are practical and hard-working, and know how to apply themselves in order to be successful in their aims and how to persuade others to support their causes. They also have generous and optimistic natures, coupled with a good sense of humor, which makes them very popular with everyone they come across. Understanding and cooperative, they work well with others and are especially good at dealing with people.

THE FIRE PIG 1947 AND 2007

Adventurous, bold, and dynamic, the Fire Pig is as generous and quick to support a worthy cause as all the Pigs. But these Pigs are capable of outstanding acts of heroism, for, once they have fixed on an objective, it is almost impossible to deflect them from their course. Fire adds an emotional intensity to the Pig's nature, and gives them great energy. The Pig person with Fire in the soul can act impulsively and will take bold risks, which sometimes pay off and sometimes don't. Normally generous, the Fire Pig will do everything to maintain his or her family in wealth and comfort and this kind of person also makes a good, magnanimous boss. Only if things go really wrong can the Fire Pig show an almost bullish intractability and aggressive streak. Deep down and underneath it all, this Pig is definitely an out-and-out pleasure-seeker.

THE EARTH PIG 1959 AND 2019

Easygoing and sensible, the solid Earth Pig is bound to be happy in his or her family, and with his or her circumstances – in fact, with life in general. Earth bestows upon this patient and reliable creature a strong practical bent, so that Earth Pigs take a methodical approach to organizing their affairs. This kind of Pig is successful at work without needing to be right at the top of the ladder – although he or she is not without ambition and can also be astute in financial matters. However, the Pig's love of a pleasant social life, with plenty of good food and drink, is still present in the Earth Pig's makeup, and some Earth Pigs need to battle with a tendency to overindulge.

Health and habitat

HEALTH AND CONSTITUTION

Although people born under the sign of the Pig are generally robust, their tendency toward self-indulgence and a life of sedentary habits can lead to health problems. The stomach and intestines are the Pig's vulnerable spots, and Pigs need to watch a tendency to put on weight, and should make a point of taking exercise. Like the Rabbit and the Sheep, Pigs love peace and harmony, and they are gregarious and love company. Loneliness or an unsettled lifestyle will play havoc with a Pig's health.

THE PIG AT HOME

Being a sensualist, the Pig's home is warm, deeply comfortable, and inviting. Impressing others is very important to Pig people, and this means getting the décor just so, but Pigs should guard against showiness. At their most creative in their own home, they can turn the smallest shack into a palace. But they can also be a paradox – sometimes working until they drop, sometimes so sedentary that an earthquake couldn't prise them off the sofa. So though Pig people create beautiful things, when it comes to housework they may not be quite so assiduous.

Career and wealth

THE PIG AT WORK

These adaptable and easygoing folk are suited to a wide range of occupations, although they particularly excel in the creative professions. They tackle jobs methodically and enthusiastically, without making a fuss about it, and are always willing to take on a good load and to help colleagues who are under pressure or in a jam. This earns them the liking of the people they work with and makes them good in a team. Pigs also have an attention to detail that earns them the reputation for fine workmanship.

FINANCE AND THE PIG

Pig people take real pleasure in spending money, both on themselves and on others, and they are giving and generous to a fault. They have extravagant tastes and tend to go for the deluxe model of whatever they are buying, although this is not for show, but just for the pure enjoyment. Yet despite such seeming profligacy, Pig people can be canny where money is concerned, knowing how to snuffle out a truffle on the forest floor, and they generally seem to know how to come by cash when they need it. However, some Pigs would be wise to think a little more about saving for a rainy day.

LEFT *The adaptable and easy-going Pig loves creature comforts and luxurious surroundings.*

All those who are born in the Year of the Pig share not only similar talents and inherent skills, but also the same kind of aims and ambitions in life. The occupations that best suit the Pig mentality and abilities are listed here.

PIGS MAKE EXCELLENT

Students ★ Teachers
Researchers ★ Designers
Artists ★ Window-dressers
Florists ★ Actors
Entertainers ★ Craftworkers
Nurses ★ Doctors ★ Vets
Dentists ★ Dieticians
Hoteliers ★ Farmers
Butchers
Gamekeepers
Caterers

COMPATIBLE BUSINESS PARTNERS

Whether Pigs benefit from or constantly conflict with their business partners depends, as in all relationships, on whether their Animal signs are harmonious or antagonistic to each other. Taking into consideration the compatibility of the elements between themselves and their working colleagues can also be very useful.

PIGS RULED BY	BENEFIT FROM	ARE ANTAGONISTIC TO
Metal	Earth Oxen	Fire Rats
Water	Metal Pigs	Earth Tigers
Wood	Water Dragons	Metal Roosters
Fire	Wood Rabbits	Water Horses
Earth	Fire Sheep	Wood Snakes

Leisure and pleasures

THE PIG ON VACATION

People born under the sign of the Pig are busy, hard-working individuals. True, they do have an inclination to a touch of self-indulgence, and nothing gives them greater pleasure than food. In fact, all Pigs have a love of the delights of cuisine, most having prodigious appetites and many being gastronomes in their own right. Taking a Cordon Bleu cookery course in France, then, or touring the great malt whiskey distilleries of Scotland would bring immense satisfaction to these gourmets. But in general, relaxing holidays are made for Pig-born individuals - especially expensive ones in five-star hotels. With their love of the easy life, lying back on a sandy beach or soaking up the sun while the waiter brings them a long, cold piña colada is just about the Pig's idea of heaven. A weekend at the Ritz would never go amiss.

FRIENDS AND FOE

People born in the Year of the Pig are naturally generous folk. There is always a warm welcome at their house and a place at their table, for these people cannot bear to see anyone go hungry or cold. Jovial *bon vivants*, all Pigs make brilliant cooks and excellent hosts and hostesses. Even the most casual invitation to dinner will turn out to be a memorable occasion crowned by a sumptuous feast. With their amicable, outgoing dispositions, a close social circle is important to Pig-born folk. These people truly cherish their friends, love any sort of get-together, are genuinely pleased when people drop in unexpectedly, and delight in going out and partying with a crowd until dawn. Few people could be more loyal or willing to lend a hand to a friend in need than a Pig-born native. Goodnatured and undemanding, they make many friends throughout their lives and find very few enemies .

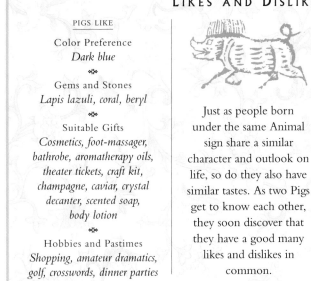

LIKES AND DISLIKES

PIGS LIKE

Color Preference
Dark blue

Gems and Stones
Lapis lazuli, coral, beryl

Suitable Gifts
Cosmetics, foot-massager, bathrobe, aromatherapy oils, theater tickets, craft kit, champagne, caviar, crystal decanter, scented soap, body lotion

Hobbies and Pastimes
Shopping, amateur dramatics, golf, crosswords, dinner parties

Just as people born under the same Animal sign share a similar character and outlook on life, so do they also have similar tastes. As two Pigs get to know each other, they soon discover that they have a good many likes and dislikes in common.

PIGS DISLIKE

Arguments

Not having money in their pockets

Unlawful behavior

An empty refridgerator

LEFT *People born under the sign of the Pig will work hard and cheerfully, as long as they can have a luxury holiday – preferably in a faraway place – at the end of it all.*

Pig parents and babies

To bask in the love of a close knit family is all that an individual born in the year of the Pig really asks of life. In China, the Year of the Pig symbolizes the home and family, so being born under this influence means that Pig natives are domestic creatures, at their happiest among the people they love. Pigs are devoted parents. In fact, the normally cool and mild-mannered adult Pig would turn into a vicious wild boar should anyone threaten to harm a hair on their infant's head. Pigs put their children first and care for their every need, even go without something themselves, if necessary, in order to provide for their young.

Since Pig-born individuals like a soft and easy life themselves, they are generous to a fault where their children are concerned, and tend to spoil their darlings. At home, Pig parents take a relaxed approach to life and they believe in providing their offspring with a calm and harmonious environment in which to grow and develop. But they do insist on politeness and good manners and, because culture and refinement are also high on the agenda of the Pig, they will instill in their Piglets an appreciation of the arts and make sure that they take their youngsters to theaters and museums almost from the moment their babies are born.

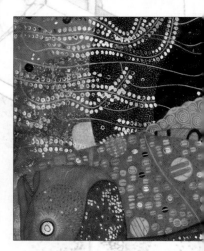

ABOVE *A love of luxury encourages Pig parents to make life easy for their offspring, too.*

BELOW LEFT *Little Pigs have an easy and cheerful disposition that makes them popular.*

THE PIG BABY AND CHILD

Easygoing and happy-go-lucky are the two principle characteristics with which a baby Pig is born and which he or she takes to the grave. Affectionate and friendly, young Piglets make cheerful and easy companions, popular with teachers and classmates alike. Indeed, with their sunny smiles and open, trusting ways, they are a delight to have around. They do, however, have considerable appetites, and need large quantities of food to keep them satisfied. But childhood holds few fears for those born under this sign, which produces well-balanced, self-confident children with laid-back dispositions that enable them to take life any way it comes.

PIG PARENT/CHILD RELATIONSHIPS

For some parents, their children's personalities harmonize perfectly with their own. Others find that no matter how much they may love their offspring, they are simply not on the same wavelength. Below are the compatibility ratings between Pig parents and their children.

PIGS WITH	UNDER THE SAME ROOF	COMPATIBILITY RATING
Rat	amicable	✓✓✓
Ox	solid affection	✓✓✓
Tiger	pulling in opposite directions	✓
Rabbit	joyous	✓✓✓
Dragon	fun and games	✓✓
Snake	relaxed	✓✓✓
Horse	needs own space	✓
Sheep	everything in common	✓✓✓✓
Monkey	shared humor	✓✓✓
Rooster	supportive	✓✓
Dog	warm ties	✓✓
Pig	so comfortable	✓✓✓✓

RATINGS ✓ uphill struggle ✓✓ some complications
✓✓✓ easy bonding ✓✓✓✓ on the same wavelength

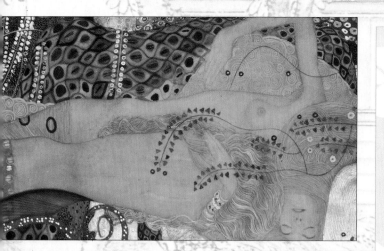

Lovers and spouses

THE PIG LOVER

In the Orient, the pig is regarded as a symbol of contentment and good fortune. And in general Pigs can be
described as happy, good-natured, and satisfied with their
lot. Of all the Animals in the Chinese horoscope, they
are perhaps the ones most suited to married life, and they
function at their best when attached to a doting partner.
Warm and loving, Pig-born people give their affection
generously, adoring the physical proximity of another
body to snuggle up to.

It is said that Pig-born folk possess healthy libidos,
that they revel in sex and can be physically demanding
between the sheets. Many are promiscuous in their
younger years and some can develop a rather earthy or
bawdy side to their natures, tending, if uncontrolled,
towards lasciviousness.

LOYAL PARTNER

It may not be the grand passion that drives the Pig into
marriage, but more the promise of companionship and
security. When Pigs decide to settle down they make a
loyal partner, caring and considerate of the one they love.
They seek harmony in a relationship and avoid
confrontations like the plague, preferring to go with the
flow. As they sink into a hot bath – all Pigs adore the
sensual luxury of bathing – they should take a deep
breath and count their blessings.

THE PIG LOVE PARTNER

Most people warm to those born in the year of the Pig,
and many suit them as a partner. But a few can't stand
that easy manner and love of luxury. The panel (right)
shows how the other signs are matched to the Pig.

PARTNERS IN LOVE

PIG ♥ RAT
*A rollercoaster of a relationship.
Terrific attraction and companionship between you, but watch
those bills!*

PIG ♥ OX
*Sexual attraction and some
shared attitudes can produce
harmony and contentment if
both try hard.*

PIG ♥ TIGER
*Friendship and shared interests
bode well for this union.*

PIG ♥ RABBIT
*Warm, comfortable, and close.
Tipped for enduring love.*

PIG ♥ DRAGON
*A caring, sharing, and deeply
loving partnership.*

PIG ♥ SNAKE
Alas, little common ground.

PIG ♥ HORSE
*A laid-back affair, but who
would remember to pay the
bills or stock the 'fridge?*

PIG ♥ SHEEP
*Plenty of understanding and
love make this a winning team.*

PIG ♥ MONKEY
*Occasional strife heightens the
sexual tension between you.*

PIG ♥ ROOSTER
*Despite your temperamental
differences, you two could really
make this work; it is worth it if
you do.*

PIG ♥ DOG
*A solid, amicable, but rather
unadventurous partnership.*

PIG ♥ PIG
*Early understanding between the
pair of you later palls.*

LOVE PARTNERS AT A GLANCE

PIGS WITH:	TIPS ON TOGETHERNESS	COMPATIBILITY
Rat	great happiness and good friends	♥♥♥
Ox	worth persisting at	♥♥
Tiger	good humor keeps you smiling	♥♥♥
Rabbit	shared togetherness	♥♥♥♥
Dragon	sooooo comfy!	♥♥♥
Snake	deep divisions	♥
Horse	nice but unrealistic	♥♥
Sheep	champagne and caviar	♥♥♥♥
Monkey	a colorful affair	♥♥♥
Rooster	worth persevering	♥♥♥
Dog	honest and sincere	♥♥♥
Pig	a prickly partnership	♥♥

COMPATIBILITY RATINGS: ♥ *conflict* ♥♥ *work at it*
♥♥♥ *strong sexual attraction* ♥♥♥♥ *heavenly!*

EAST MEETS WEST

ARIES PIG

Aries Pigs are energetic and full of *joie de vivre*. They make warm and affectionate friends and lusty lovers. They have huge appetites, both physically and mentally, and can take on any task that is thrown at them. They are open and trusting in life, enthusiastic, and optimistic.

TAUREAN PIG

Taurus gives the Pig extra sensuality and buckets of charm. These Pigs relish their security and adore luxury, but they are also realists with a good head for money. They are no strangers to hard work and they have their feet firmly planted on the ground.

GEMINI PIG

Gemini Pigs are hugely sociable, at their best presiding over a dinner party at a table laden with a feast fit for a king. Appearances are so important to them that they often fall in love for the wrong reasons.

CANCERIAN PIG

These are homely but creative creatures, with a love of family and idyllically happy sitting by their own hearth. Cooking or baking, potting jams or transplanting lettuces is heaven to Cancerian Pigs, who are generous and big-hearted, especially with loved ones.

LEONINE PIG

Leonine Pigs are larger than life. They put their all into everything they do, whether at work, at play, at home, at relationships, or even at sex. Open and generous, benevolent and big-hearted, they give freely to those they love, but they can let their appetites get the better of them.

VIRGO PIG

Virgo Pigs are loyal, faithful, and unwaveringly dedicated to those they love. They know how to tighten their belts in time of crisis and the Virgoan Pig parent would be the first to go without and make sacrifices for the good of the family. However, these Pigs will unleash their fury if these same loved ones let them down.

LIBRAN PIG

Libran Pigs seek beauty, creativity, and refinement in their lives, their homes, and their partners, and crave a life of ease. Genial, tolerant, and easy-going, these people make sociable and affable companions. Indecision, however, is the Libran Pig's greatest foible.

SCORPIO PIG

Scorpio Pigs are ambitious. They know from a very young age that success equals money and that money equals power. Come hell or high water, the Scorpio Pig makes it rich at some point in his or her life. Partners are advised never, ever to cross this Pig in love, because that Scorpionic sting in their tails can prove lethal.

SAGITTARIAN PIG

These are generous and genial personalities, who attract a large and faithful following. Sagittarian Pigs dispense largesse all around, scattering optimism and good cheer. No-one leaves their tables hungry or goes without when these Pigs are around. And for them all goes well.

CAPRICORN PIG

These are solid citizens, industrious, responsible, and realistic, and staunch upholders of values and tradition. They never shrink from their duty, especially when their family is involved. But they still know when enough is enough and will then down tools and put their feet up.

AQUARIAN PIG

These Pigs are bright and breezy, chatty and sociable, popular and sought-after. Communicating with people is what the Aquarian Pig does best. People listen to them, take their advice, copy their habits and their styles. They themselves quickly get bored and want to move on.

PISCEAN PIG

These are less indulgent Pigs, often with remarkable artistic talents. Being loved, being attached, and feeling secure are fundamental to their well-being and they will do anything in their power to keep a relationship alive.

Famous Pigs

Pigs love luxury and can be pretty messy. They are warm, generous, and loving, and adore their families. They give willingly and cheerfully of their wealth, energy, and time – to those they love and even to people they hardly know, and they never leave anyone in the lurch. Pigs are sincere and obliging, and a comfort and delight to others, and they have great sticking power when it comes to seeing anything through, even though they can occasionally be lazy.

◄ Albert Schweitzer

This Pig-born person had a great supply of the sign's love for music and talent for performing, and also showed the Pig's humanitarian desire to help the deprived or unfortunate. This multi-talented Frenchman funded his Nobel Peace Prize-winning work as a missionary surgeon by giving organ recitals. He was a theologian and writer on both theology and music, as well as a gentle, kind, and untiring worker for the people of Gabon, West Africa.

► Arnold Schwarzenegger

Another Pig-born entertainer, and hugely successful at it, Arnold Schwarzenegger has such presence and character that he was even able to draw a cinema audience in his first English-language films without really being able to speak English very well himself. Perhaps he is thick-skinned, as Pigs are supposed to be, because he has cheerfully survived many rude reviews. He also shows the Pig's humor in his occasional comic roles.

▲ Fred Astaire

Like many Pigs, he was not strictly good-looking, but oh so charming with his relaxed manner and boyish grin. But Fred Astaire worked hard at his talent. He started his dancing career as a child and stuck to it for over 40 years. He was an innovative choreographer as well as a dancer and singer, and later became a serious actor. Despite his altruistic concern for the rights of others he was a lover of champagne and luxury, too. His most famous partner, Ginger Rogers, was also a Pig-born person.

▼ Tennessee Williams

This playwright from Mississippi was a different kind of entertainer-Pig, successfully drawing audiences for his plays, which were mostly set in the Deep South and were written mainly in the 1940s and '50s. Some of them also became very successful films. He had the cheerful, easygoing look of the Pig-born person and that full glass spells enjoyment of luxury.

▲ Maria Callas

One aspect of the Pig-born person is a love of music, and particularly of opera. The operatic prima donna Maria Callas fits that description. Entertaining and pleasing others is something Pigs like to do, and Callas had this gift in abundance. With the Pig's gift for work and resilience she worked her way up from poverty and obscurity to become one of the best-known sopranos of all time. Many Pigs also manage to acquire wealth in their lives – they need it for their luxurious habits – Maria Callas did this in her own right and through her relationship with the millionaire Aristotle Onassis.

Part Three

THE ANIMAL YEARS

*Understanding how the Animal
influences of the years to come
can guide our fortunes*

The years in focus

The shifting patterns of the planets subtly change their influence on all things in the universe. From ancient times Chinese astrologers observing these patterns began to recognize recurring themes that can still be observed today. For example, Oxen years are times of steady growth, while Tiger years bring danger and political unrest. In Pig years the population booms, while under the tricky Monkey, though our plans may go awry, scientific advances and technological innovations take a quantum leap forward. By studying the specific influences of each Animal year, we can prepare in advance for the trends that will affect all global matters, politically, economically, and socially, and that, in so doing, touch upon our own lives.

THE YEAR OF THE RAT

This, the first year in a new cycle, is an excellent period for new beginnings and fresh starts. Rat years are a time of regeneration and renewal. Market economies are buoyant, spirits rise, and things are generally improving. This is the time to begin projects, lay foundations, announce new plans, launch new products, forge new links, get married, buy a house, start a family or, if necessary, turn over a new leaf. New ventures started this year do not, however, yield quick returns. This a not time for complacency. The Rat is constantly on the go, using his wits, with his eye always on the big prize. Opportunities will abound for quick, smart, and clever people to grab and turn them to their own advantage. But the influence of the Rat favors the careful investor. If plans are wisely laid, there will be returns in the fullness of time.

EVENTS AND INVENTIONS
ASSOCIATED WITH RAT YEARS

Many events in Rat Years are notable for their pioneering qualities. They include:
❖ *invention of the transistor* ❖ *introduction of CS gas, self-winding watch, stainless steel, communication satellites, lasers, long-playing records* ❖ *patenting of cellophane* ❖ *plans for the supersonic Concord* ❖ *introduction of British National Health Service* ❖ *WHO established in Geneva* ❖ *The U.N. Declaration of Human Rights* ❖ *the Organization for European Economic Co-Operation (OEEC) set up* ❖ *first public announcements about the greenhouse effect.*

THE YEAR OF THE OX

Ox years bring stability and measured growth, when patient, diligent work pays off. This is the Harvest year, when we reap what we have sown and harvest the fruits of past efforts. Harvest time is no time for idleness, and people need to keep an eye on their interests in an Ox Year. Putting decisions on hold in business or affairs of the heart may result in agreements and engagements being cut short or protracted indefinitely. Contracts must be signed, sealed, and delivered on the dot in this year. This conservative year favors traditional values and tastes, and is not a time for grandiose schemes or outrageous fashions. "Slowly but surely" and "Better the devil you know" are the mottoes of the Ox.

EVENTS AND INVENTIONS
ASSOCIATED WITH OX YEARS

Many events that occur during Ox years concern safety, medicine, and the earth including:
❖ *invention of Marconi's transatlantic wireless signal, Gillette's safety razor, Hunt's safety pin* ❖ *the diesel motor* ❖ *the use of radium treatment for cancer* ❖ *San Francisco's Golden Gate Bridge* ❖ *launching of Amnesty International* ❖ *Anglo-French agreement to construct the Channel Tunnel* ❖ *British miners on strike* ❖ *Oil embargo, leading to conservation of fuel.*

THE YEAR OF THE TIGER

Tiger Years announce themselves with a roar and bring conflict, devastation, international crises, and political upheavals. Incidents occur suddenly, giving little warning of their profound impact and unleashing trains of events whose consequences leave humankind reeling for years to come. The daring and the brave fare best in Tiger years. This is no time for the meek and the timid. Grand schemes and extravagant gestures are the order of the day. For the impulsive, risks may backfire, but those with nerves of steel will find that the thrill of danger sharpens their appetites and hones their claws. Emotionally, this is a year for passion and intrigue, but those tempted to embark on an illicit fling may experience devastating repercussions of any action taken in the Year of the Tiger.

EVENTS AND INVENTIONS
ASSOCIATED WITH TIGER YEARS

Many events occurring in Tiger years are startling, or make their presence felt. Linked with Tiger years are the discovery, invention, patenting, marketing or manufacturing of
❖ *dynamite* ❖ *television* ❖ *disc brakes* ❖ *the vacuum cleaner* ❖ *Edison's electric battery* ❖ *the photocopier*

THE YEAR OF THE RABBIT

Sandwiched between two of the most turbulent and unpredictable Animal signs, the Rabbit brings a year that may be likened to the eye of the storm. This is a time of recuperation, a year in which to soothe your nerves and catch your breath. This is certainly not a year in which to force issues, as all efforts will fall upon stony ground and melt in the heat of the sun. But it is a time for negotiation, for diplomatic relations, and for reaching settlements and mutual agreements. The year of the Rabbit focuses on women and their interests: children and the family, food and welfare, home and domestic security become salient issues. Medical advances will be made and the arts will be a prominent feature on the agenda.

EVENTS AND INVENTIONS
ASSOCIATED WITH RABBIT YEARS

Among the events, discoveries and inventions brought in Rabbit years are ❖ the first talking movie ❖ theory of relativity ❖ quasars ❖ nylon stockings ❖ DDT ❖ first woman to climb Mount Everest ❖ Entente Cordiale ❖ New York's World Fair ❖ the Festival of Britain

THE YEAR OF THE DRAGON

Drama characterizes the Dragon Year, both in lavish events and in unpredictability. The year is marked at its beginning and end by significant international developments. The bizarre and the unexpected are associated with this sign. The performing arts, fashion, and cultural events come under favorable auspices – the more original, the better. Magnificent projects and outlandish schemes are the order of the day. Financially the feel-good factor sweeps us along on a wave of elation; risks are taken, fortunes are made and lost. As the Dragon brings good fortune, this is an auspicious year in which to get married, and also to have a baby, since Dragon children bring luck to the household. Starting a business or initiating a major project in this year will all bring success.

EVENTS AND INVENTIONS
ASSOCIATED WITH DRAGON YEARS

Some world-changing inventions and "firsts" are linked to Dragon years, including: ❖ the thermos bottle ❖ scheduled television service ❖ electron microscope ❖ civil rights movements ❖ mechanical heart ❖ genetically altered mouse

THE YEAR OF THE SNAKE

After the dramas of the Year of the Dragon, Snake Years come as watershed periods, restoring order and bringing comparative peace. In these years we can quietly draw breath and slowly reassess our situation. It would be wise not to take anything on trust, however. Duplicity is in the air and it is advisable to read the small print carefully. Treachery, political machinations, and conspiracy will be rife, and international affairs are likely to be peppered with shady dealings. As the Snake is a symbol of fertility, issues of conception and morality will be aired and headlines will reveal sex scandals in high places. Snake years herald an economic upturn and money markets, the arts, and communications will be buoyant The fashion-conscious will favor sophistication.

EVENTS AND INVENTIONS
ASSOCIATED WITH SNAKE YEARS

The discoveries, inventions, and styles of Snake years are linked to the Snake's deep wisdom and almost extra-sensory perspicacity, and sinuous style ❖ IQ tests ❖ rings of Uranus discovered ❖ the Oscar awards ❖ Chanel fashions ❖ DNA discovered ❖ advances in psychology

THE YEAR OF THE SHEEP

The Year of the Sheep slows the pace and brings tranquillity. The focus is on domestic life: love, marriage, the family, and having babies all come under good auspices now. Politically, this is a period of reconciliation, a time for healing rifts, and for diplomatic moves. The signing of treaties and international trade agreements finds favor. Commercially, it is inadvisable to launch new products or strike out in different directions, but a time in which to reaffirm contacts, secure links with existing markets, and bring past efforts to fruition. Awareness about ecology and the needs of humanity will be raised. Charitable organizations, caring institutions, and medical advances will make the news. The fashion industry and the world of the arts will enjoy a bumper year.

EVENTS AND INVENTIONS ASSOCIATED WITH SHEEP YEARS

Associated with peace, the Year of the Sheep has marked the discovery or invention of ❖ color photography ❖ the steamroller ❖ the heart transplant ❖ Vitamin B12 ❖ It is the year of ❖ the first Montessori school ❖ Mother Teresa's Nobel prize

THE YEAR OF THE MONKEY

Nothing is straightforward in the Year of the Monkey. Try as we might to attend to every detail, somewhere along the line something will happen to make our plans come unstuck. We can expect the unexpected, and gremlins abound. Whether buying or selling, going on vacation, or simply organizing a party, check your insurance policies carefully and have alternative plans up your sleeve. A decided undercurrent of instability pervades the economy, undermining governments and unsettling international politics. Fast-talking and quick-witted people win the day. The Monkey year also has an upbeat, progressive swing to it. The world of communications will flourish and all the industries that depend on mental or manual dexterity will make progress under the influence of the Monkey's agile intelligence.

EVENTS AND INVENTIONS ASSOCIATED WITH MONKEY YEARS

New products, "firsts," and inventions associated with this year include: ❖ liquid helium ❖ Bakelite ❖ the sub-machine gun ❖ radio astronomy ❖ the Zippo lighter ❖ mobile phones ❖ neutrons ❖ astronauts orbiting the moon

THE YEAR OF THE HORSE

In Horse years there is a sense of hurtling headlong. Affairs are spirited, events erratic, trading brisk, and emotions volatile. Energy and action characterize the year; and, for some, acting on impulse and following instincts will bring success. Husbandry and good housekeeping are not the most salient of Horse attributes, so this is a year for keeping a tight hold on the purse strings. The economy is unstable; bad management, both personal and political, leads to wild fluctuations in fortunes, and there will be much spending and borrowing. Freedom is the buzz word: leisure, travel, and all outdoor pursuits are favored under the auspices of the Horse. In this year marriage is on the increase, but so too is divorce.

EVENTS AND INVENTIONS ASSOCIATED WITH HORSE YEARS

Some of the dynamic discoveries, inventions, and events associated with the Year of the Horse are ❖ the discovery of the planet Pluto ❖ atomic fission ❖ the structure of DNA ❖ the Big Bang theory ❖ flashbulbs ❖ magnetic tape

THE YEAR OF THE ROOSTER

This is a time for looking onward and upward. Politically and domestically, the downtrodden make their voices heard, the aggrieved or tyrannized will stand up for themselves, and bullies will now get their due comeuppance. Relationships are never well-starred in Rooster years, however, and for those having difficulties with their partners, reconciliation may not come so easily. The best thing is to steer clear of disagreements and to wait for more harmonious trends next year. We should all beware of nagging and being overly critical. In fashion, flaunting your image is all-important. In Rooster years clothes and jewelry hit the headlines.

EVENTS AND INVENTIONS
ASSOCIATED WITH ROOSTER YEARS

The Rooster is candid and outspoken. New products, "firsts," and inventions associated with Rooster years include: ❖ *newsreels* ❖ *insulin* ❖ *the IMF* ❖ *the United Nations* ❖ *interferon* ❖ *nuclear fusion* ❖ *manmade satellites*

THE YEAR OF THE DOG

Environmental issues and humanitarian schemes come to the forefront in Dog years. Idealism, a key Dog concept, opens the way for grand philanthropic gestures. Conservation, animal welfare, and civil liberties all come under the aegis of the Year of the Dog. Politically, governments should review their defence budgets and give greater priority to internal security. On the domestic front, the sign of the Dog is linked to property, and we are advised to look after our personal effects and to upgrade our burglar alarm systems. The focus in the year is on family life. Marriage in the Year of the Dog brings happiness and good fortune.

EVENTS AND INVENTIONS
ASSOCIATED WITH DOG YEARS

The Dog is quick-witted but full of anxiety. New products, "firsts," and inventions associated with Dog years include: ❖ *X-rays* ❖ *the atomic bomb* ❖ *the Iron Curtain* ❖ *first Cannes Film Festival* ❖ *discovery of Tutankhamen's tomb*

THE YEAR OF THE PIG

This year marks the end of the cycle and is a year in which to concentrate on endings rather than beginnings. Affairs should be put in order, ready for the new cycle. There will be a decided sense of optimism in the air, with the economy taking an upswing. There should be a feel-good factor, and the Pig year is a time for conspicuous consumption, having a good time, eating, drinking, and enjoying ourselves. The leisure industry and trade in luxury goods both do well, gambling flourishes, and records are broken in the world of sports. This year also favors domestic matters.

EVENTS AND INVENTIONS
ASSOCIATED WITH PIG YEARS

The Pig is associated with the family. New products, "firsts," and inventions associated with Pig years include: ❖ *vitamins* ❖ *plastic* ❖ *Kodachrome color film* ❖ *carbon 14* ❖ *the transistor* ❖ *the Rorschach inkblot test* ❖ *discovery of Australopithecus*

Animal fortunes

The Lunar Year which began on February 19, 1996 marked the beginning of a new 12-year cycle in the Chinese calendar. As the Animal Years run through their sequence in this cycle, people born under each sign will be subject to the influences of each new Animal Year. How your relationships, aspirations, and worldly prospects are likely to fare will be affected by the interaction between your own sign and each Animal ruler in turn. Being prepared for your changing fortunes helps you to deal with the helpful or hindering influences – remember, forewarned is forearmed!

ABOVE *Each year has its own fortunes in store.*

RAT FORTUNES FOR THE YEARS AHEAD

1996 YEAR OF THE RAT   *19 Feb. 1996 – 7 Feb. 1997*

This, their own year, is a busy year for Rat people and one that augurs well for their worldly aspirations. In their careers, Rats could be taking a quantum leap forward as promotion or a new job beckons. There will be new opportunities for both expanding their financial prospects and widening their social networks. This is a time for Rats to get out and have some fun. Any new friendships that Rats start now could blossom into long-term romance.

YEAR TREND: progressive

1997 YEAR OF THE OX   *8 Feb. 1997 – 27 Jan. 1998*

Following last year's career advancement, Rats will now perhaps begin to feel the pressure as they begin to take on more duties and responsibilities. But this is still an auspicious time for Rat people, and they should make steady progress in 1997. No major domestic upheavals are forecast now. In fact, family life is stable and a source of joy. Moreover, the emotional picture is sweet.

YEAR TREND: stable

1998 YEAR OF THE TIGER   *28 Jan. 1998 – 15 Feb. 1999*

Rats are famous for their rashness and for a tendency to take the odd gamble. As 1998 carries elements that are notoriously unpredictable and unstable, however, Rats are advised to curb impulsiveness and avoid taking unwise risks during this year. Travel for work and for personal pleasure could figure strongly. For some, this year may herald the parting of the ways.

YEAR TREND: fair

1999 YEAR OF THE RABBIT   *16 Feb. 1999 – 4 Feb. 2000*

The slower pace of the Rabbit Year is not especially suited to the Rat's go-getting, ambitious mentality, so Rats may find themselves champing at the bit through 1999. Their best advice is to take it easy, relax and let their hair down – but beware, because this doesn't mean they can afford to spend lavishly! Rats should concentrate on their families this year: some quality time spent with the people they love most will bring contentment.

YEAR TREND: frustrating

2000 YEAR OF THE DRAGON   *5 Feb. 2000 – 23 Jan. 2001*

This is more the Rat's kind of year: pacy, daring, exciting, and with just an edge of danger to spice it up. For Rat people, 2000 will be a year of lucky breaks and lucky escapes. Career prospects are exceedingly good, finances are buoyant, and love affairs will set the Rat's pulse racing and toes tingling. The only tiny proviso here is that Rat people should not allow others to exploit their generosity.

YEAR TREND: highly successful

2001 YEAR OF THE SNAKE   *24 Jan. 2001 – 11 Feb. 2002*

Things are never what they seem in the Year of the Snake. Rats should take care to read all the small print and study people's body language carefully. Otherwise, they could end up out-of-pocket or bruised – physically or emotionally. Prospects improve at the end of the year.

YEAR TREND: approach with caution

2002 YEAR OF THE HORSE   *12 Feb. 2002 – 31 Jan. 2003*

The erratic and impulsive elements of the Year of the Horse will only exacerbate the Rat's already rash and impetuous tendencies. Rats will be tempted to throw caution to the wind; circumstances will urge them to spend more than they can afford; relationships could become complicated and messy. Only discipline and self-control will save Rat people from the pitfalls.

YEAR TREND: volatile

2003 YEAR OF THE SHEEP *1 Feb. 2003 – 21 Jan. 2004*

After the turmoil of the last 12 months, the Year of the Sheep affords Rats gradual progress in which to redress the balance and regain lost ground. There will be opportunities for Rats to sort out their finances and increase their incomes. Career and occupation take on a renewed and welcomed impetus. Relations with loved ones can be mended and improved.

YEAR TREND: improvement and recovery

2004 YEAR OF THE MONKEY *22 Jan. 2004 – 8 Feb. 2005*

The inventive jollity of the Monkey influence is highly conducive to the Rat's sense of adventure. This is a year in which the fertile Rat mind can pay him or her dividends. The Rat's social life will be active and buoyant, so all Rats should take advantage of the auspices and have a good time. For those who are committed, domestic affairs should be harmonious. For others, romance brings lightness of heart.

YEAR TREND: a time for enjoyment

2005 YEAR OF THE ROOSTER *9 Feb. 2005 – 28 Jan. 2006*

This Rooster Year is a busy one for Rats. Important events are likely to happen thick and fast, keeping all Rats active and on their toes. What appear at first sight to be obstacles or challenges will, in the end, turn out to be nothing short of blessings in disguise. Disagreements between existing partners can now be resolved. Otherwise, those Rats seeking romance could find it this year.

YEAR TREND: setbacks but positive surprises

2006 YEAR OF THE DOG *29 Jan. 2006 – 17 Feb. 2007*

This year could be a demanding time for Rats if they take on more than they can realistically deal with, as projects can prove to be unexpectedly fraught with worry and anxiety. Happily, there will be people ready to reach out to help, but Rats should also be careful not to take them for granted. In general, 2006 is not a particularly auspicious year for relationships, but meeting others halfway would certainly help to ease the tension.

YEAR TREND: unsettling

2007 YEAR OF THE PIG *18 Feb. 2007 – 6 Feb. 2008*

If relationships have taken a hammering lately, they should now start to improve. Warmth and understanding between Rats and their partners could slowly return. If, however, they have gone their separate ways, this is the year for Rats to get out and think about making a fresh start. Socially, the tempo will increase, with opportunities to link up with the person of their dreams.

YEAR TREND: preparation for the new

OX FORTUNES FOR THE YEARS AHEAD

1996 YEAR OF THE RAT *19 Feb. 1996 – 7 Feb. 1997*

In business and financial matters, Oxen can expect to do very well in a Rat Year. There could be promotion at work, or expansion for the Ox boss. The Ox could rise to a position of authority as a reward for previous efforts. In matters of the heart, however, things are different – love and relationships go awry.

YEAR TREND: beware relationships

1997 YEAR OF THE OX *8 Feb. 1997 – 27 Jan. 1998*

This is the Ox's year, and Oxen will be quite at home with the steady pace of 1997. The Year of the Ox spells delays for everyone, but Oxen are happy to work away in the background making gradual progress. Ox emotions are heightened, with family life and romance destined for success.

YEAR TREND: satisfying

1998 YEAR OF THE TIGER *28 Jan. 1998 – 15 Feb. 1999*

The Tiger Year is never an easy time for stability-loving Oxen, with so much drama and tension always in the air. Somehow, friction at home and at work will have them locking horns frequently with others. Luckily, Oxen are able to keep their heads, and their natural perseverance will see them through.

YEAR TREND: a time for keeping your cool

1999 YEAR OF THE RABBIT *16 Feb. 1999 – 4 Feb. 2000*

After the dramatic storms of the Tiger Year, 1999 comes as balm to soothe the Ox's nerves. A few wrinkles may have to be ironed out this year, but Oxen can expect more success all around, especially in their emotional lives. The Rabbit favors peace and home, and fortune will smile on Ox people's relationships.

YEAR TREND: lucky in love

2000 YEAR OF THE DRAGON *5 Feb. 2000 – 23 Jan. 2001*

Dragon Years favor the daring and the flamboyant – not qualities of the Ox – so this is likely to be a frustrating time for Oxen. The Ox's efforts will fail to receive the merit they deserve, but Oxen will be kept busy with the rapid changes that bring in the new millennium. Friends will lend a helping hand.

YEAR TREND: unpromising

2001 YEAR OF THE SNAKE *24 Jan. 2001 – 11 Feb. 2002*

Chickens come home to roost this year – which is only fair, given the disappointment of the last 12 months. Past efforts pay off handsomely and Oxen can take major strides forward. This is the time for Ox people to grab the opportunities offered to them, including invitations that will widen their social network. Romance will blossom for the Ox this year.

YEAR TREND: deeply rewarding

2002 YEAR OF THE HORSE *12 Feb. 2002 – 31 Jan. 2003*

Events this year are likely to be volatile – which is not designed to suit the Ox's temperament. There may be disappointments as life throws some unexpected curveballs in the Ox's quiet path and affairs of the heart will be just as fickle and unsatisfactory.

YEAR TREND: unsettling

2003 YEAR OF THE SHEEP *1 Feb. 2003 – 21 Jan. 2004*

This will be a year of ups and downs; what the Ox loses in terms of work and money, he or she will gain in love and romance. Oxen should not take any risks, especially with their finances, and should focus their attention rather than scattering their energies. Family, friends and lovers all bring welcome emotional support.

YEAR TREND: emotionally uplifting

2004 YEAR OF THE MONKEY *22 Jan. 2004 – 8 Feb. 2005*

Nothing should be taken for granted in a Monkey Year, and Ox folk might find this year trying. Yet honors and recognition could await the Ox as the more wayward aspects of the year defer to the Ox's common sense and practical expertise. Romance ticks over.

YEAR TREND: unexpected opportunities

2005 YEAR OF THE ROOSTER *9 Feb. 2005 – 28 Jan. 2006*

If life has been in the doldrums over the last few years, Ox people can now take heart. The influence of the Rooster Year offers opportunities for turning over a new leaf. This may involve a new relationship, a change of job, or a major move, and the only proviso is: read the small print carefully.

YEAR TREND: upwardly mobile

2006 YEAR OF THE DOG *29 Jan. 2006 – 17 Feb. 2007*

Other Animals may find Dog Years, stressful but Oxen just bulldoze their way through all the obstacles in their paths. Looking back, they will wonder what all the fuss was about. For Ox people, this is an excellent year in which to get married and to be getting out more.

YEAR TREND: a pleasing outcome

2007 YEAR OF THE PIG *18 Feb. 2007 – 6 Feb. 2008*

The good auspices of 2007 favor those born in the Year of the Ox. They may not make great progress, and financially they should expect only modest gains, but the benefits are that life will be stable, with the emphasis on revitalization. Intimate relationships and family ties bring amusement as well as joy.

YEAR TREND: favors hearth and home

TIGER FORTUNES FOR THE YEARS AHEAD

1996 YEAR OF THE RAT *19 Feb. 1996 – 7 Feb. 1997*

The pacy nature of the Rat Year may incline Tigers to take undue risks or to overstretch themselves and their resources. This is not a particularly lucky year for Tigers and they should watch their finances. Social and emotional life, however, fare a good deal better.

YEAR TREND: control your spending

1997 YEAR OF THE OX *8 Feb. 1997 – 27 Jan. 1998*

The slower pace and need for restraint required in an Ox Year are not well suited to the Tiger's fiery needs, so 1997 is likely to be frustrating. Emotionally and at work, this will be a year for overcoming obstacles to personal progress.

YEAR TREND: maintain a low profile

1998 YEAR OF THE TIGER *28 Jan. 1998 – 15 Feb. 1999*

Most Tigers will be relieved to see the back of the Year of the Ox and give a cheer for 1998. Tigers will be more active this year and their prospects will improve dramatically, but Tigers should beware of throwing all caution to the wind and should remember to put something away for a rainy day.

YEAR TREND: a time to spread your wings

1999 YEAR OF THE RABBIT *16 Feb. 1999 – 4 Feb. 2000*

Last year's activity will continue to pay dividends for Tigers now, so they will feel lighter at heart and inclined to have some fun. Their emotional lives and love affairs bring Tigers much satisfaction.

YEAR TREND: take things easy

2000 YEAR OF THE DRAGON *5 Feb. 2000 – 23 Jan. 2001*

Tigers get high on the electrically charged atmosphere of Dragon Years, so the first year of the new millennium promises to bring Tiger people excitement and a positive sense of challenge in which to push their objectives forward. Love will seek the Tiger out this year.

YEAR TREND: heady

2001 YEAR OF THE SNAKE *24 Jan. 2001 – 11 Feb. 2002*

If there is one area of the Tiger's life above all others that could give rise to problems this year, it is that of relationships. Dealings with relatives, colleagues, and lovers may not be quite as straightforward as the Tiger would like, and emotional entanglements could cost him or her dearly.

YEAR TREND: beware dangerous undercurrents

2002 YEAR OF THE HORSE *12 Feb. 2002 – 31 Jan. 2003*

This year the Tiger's worldly aspirations take a quantum leap forward. Past efforts will be recognized and rewarded and a step up the ladder could result in a nice boost to income. Meanwhile, passion is the name of the dating game among Tiger lovers.

YEAR TREND: upbeat

2003 YEAR OF THE SHEEP *1 Feb. 2003 – 21 Jan. 2004*

Although 2003 will lack a certain pizzazz for the Tiger, they can still make slow and steady progress. For the best outcome, though, they should use this year as a sabbatical from their normal pressures.

YEAR TREND: learn the meaning of tranquillity

2004 YEAR OF THE MONKEY *22 Jan. 2004 – 8 Feb. 2005*

Despite some financial problems and the occasional unexpected hurdle, there will be plenty of scope and opportunities for Tigers to make decent progress this year. Emotionally, it is a time for compromises, since people and events will sorely try the Tiger's patience.

YEAR TREND: watch out for gremlins

2005 YEAR OF THE ROOSTER *9 Feb. 2005 – 28 Jan. 2006*

The Rooster promises a buoyant and stimulating year. Tiger finances will be especially pleasing and their careers should go well. Tigers could achieve at least one of their major ambitions in 2005. Social life, too, will be busy, with lots of happy comings and goings.

YEAR TREND: a time of prosperity and well-being

2006 YEAR OF THE DOG *29 Jan. 2006 – 17 Feb. 2007*

Domestically stable and romantically uplifting, 2006 will be a year when friends, colleagues, and relatives will bend over backwards to smooth the Tiger's path to success. Prospects are excellent for those Tigers seeking romance or putting down roots.

YEAR TREND: a very satisfying year

2007 YEAR OF THE PIG *18 Feb. 2007 – 6 Feb. 2008*

This is the year in which Tigers should keep their eyes open for any opportunities that come their way and make sure they are in a position to grab them. This is not a year in which to be shy and retiring; Tigers must promote themselves and their interests if they want to succeed. Romance is steady.

YEAR TREND: go for it

RABBIT FORTUNES FOR THE YEARS AHEAD

1996 YEAR OF THE RAT *19 Feb. 1996 – 7 Feb. 1997*

The high-octane pulse of the Rat Year is not conducive to the Rabbit person's need for a calm existence, so 1996 may be unsettling for Rabbit folk. On the whole this year is an uphill struggle, especially financially, though some progress is made.

YEAR TREND: give new projects the go-ahead

1997 YEAR OF THE OX *8 Feb. 1997 – 27 Jan. 1998*

Matters domestic, rather than occupational, are noted for Rabbits during an Ox Year. The even pace of 1997 will be much more to the Rabbit's liking and will encourage Rabbits to spend time with friends and loved ones.

YEAR TREND: buy, sell, or improve your home

1998 YEAR OF THE TIGER *28 Jan. 1998 – 15 Feb. 1999*

Despite the dramatic turn of events so characteristic of Tiger Years, Rabbits should find themselves prospering now. This is an excellent time to put plans and projects into operation, as long as care is taken to read the small print carefully.

YEAR TREND: lay down future foundations

1999 YEAR OF THE RABBIT *16 Feb. 1999 – 4 Feb. 2000*

Each Animal's own birth year is a favorable time for people born under that guiding sign. In this high-profile year for Rabbits, everything they touch seems to turn to gold. Physically, the Rabbit feels excellent, work is successful, and past efforts are rewarded. Romance blossoms and love ties bring happiness.

YEAR TREND: reviving, restoring, and reuniting

2000 YEAR OF THE DRAGON *5 Feb. 2000 – 23 Jan. 2001*

After all the benefits of the previous year, this year may seem less smooth. Dragon Years can be tricky for Rabbits, and they may find that a few hurdles need to be negotiated during 2000. They will need to put in considerable overtime in all spheres of their lives in order to make any progress now.

YEAR TREND: beware of get-rich-quick schemes

2001 YEAR OF THE SNAKE *24 Jan. 2001 – 11 Feb. 2002*

Snake Years are generally auspicious for Rabbits, and the trends in 2001 could well be in their favor. However, new romantic liaisons that may promise a lot could leave the Rabbit in a very embarrassing situation.

YEAR TREND: don't judge a book by its cover!

2002 YEAR OF THE HORSE *12 Feb. 2002 – 31 Jan. 2003*

Socially, 2002 is likely to be a busy year in which Rabbits will extend their network of contacts. In the long run, new acquaintances could prove fortunate in helping the Rabbit to achieve his or her aims. Encounters lead to romance.

YEAR TREND: love is bittersweet

2003 YEAR OF THE SHEEP *1 Feb. 2003 – 21 Jan. 2004*

The Year of the Sheep is calming and settling, and suits the Rabbit's gentle temperament. Domestically and emotionally, 2003 will prove very satisfying for Rabbit folk. Existing relationships are harmonious, while single Rabbits are likely to find true love now. Their social lives are buzzing and occupational matters are rewarding.

YEAR TREND: go for a new image

2004 YEAR OF THE MONKEY *22 Jan. 2004 – 8 Feb. 2005*

This is a year of mixed blessings for Rabbits, when fortune smiles on their love lives but hinders their progress at work. In particular, finances could be strained, and Rabbits are advised to be especially prudent this year over spending.

YEAR TREND: don't exceed your limits

2005 YEAR OF THE ROOSTER *9 Feb. 2005 – 28 Jan. 2006*

Somehow or other, the Year of the Rooster can always throw up difficulties for Rabbit folk. Keeping a low profile throughout 2005 is the best way for Rabbits to avoid the pitfalls and frustrations they usually encounter in a Rooster Year. They are advised to concentrate on domestic pleasures and quality time with loved ones.

YEAR TREND: keep aspirations modest

2006 YEAR OF THE DOG *29 Jan. 2006 – 17 Feb. 2007*

Dog Years are times in which Rabbits can make up lost ground. With no major hurdles either at work or in romance, Rabbits should make steady progress now. Intimate and business partners alike are supportive to their aims.

YEAR TREND: set your sights high

2007 YEAR OF THE PIG *18 Feb. 2007 – 6 Feb. 2008*

Rabbits can relax and let their hair down this year. They should join a club, take up a new hobby, accept all invitations, travel, and expand their horizons. Progress at work is moderate, but love makes up for everything. Marriage now is highly auspicious.

YEAR TREND: romance is in the air

DRAGON FORTUNES FOR THE YEARS AHEAD

1996 YEAR OF THE RAT *19 Feb. 1996 – 7 Feb. 1997*

Dragons are at their best when the pace is lively and exciting, and this year promises to be just that. Dragon people should corner the market with their lateral thinking and come up with something new that will capture the spirit of the moment. The course of love runs smoothly for Dragons this year.

YEAR TREND: show your guts

1997 YEAR OF THE OX
8 Feb. 1997 – 27 Jan. 1998

Probity should be the Dragon's watchword this year, in business and in romance – particularly for single Dragons embarking on new love affairs. Success comes to those who keep their heads down and make steady progress. Heart's ease is found in established relationships.

YEAR TREND: slow but sure

1998 YEAR OF THE TIGER
28 Jan. 1998 – 15 Feb. 1999

Relationships may not be all they appear on the surface during the Year of the Tiger, so Dragons who dislike any form of commitment need to beware. This applies just as much to romantic ties as it does to business associates.

YEAR TREND: you can't please everybody

ABOVE *For Dragons, love will prosper in the Year of the Rat.*

1999 YEAR OF THE RABBIT *16 Feb. 1999 – 4 Feb. 2000*

Dragons can expect a calmer year with less volcanic activity than of late. A good time to reap the fruits of past endeavors. Wise Dragons will use this year to gather their energies for the galvanic events of 2000, which kick-start the new millennium.

YEAR TREND: a time for recuperation

2000 YEAR OF THE DRAGON *5 Feb. 2000 – 23 Jan. 2001*

The frenetic beat that accompanies the Dragon's own year will come as sweet music to Dragon people. Their efforts will be recognized and rewarded, and success will follow effortlessly. Romantic interludes quicken the Dragon's pulse.

YEAR TREND: love is high on the agenda

2001 YEAR OF THE SNAKE *24 Jan. 2001 – 11 Feb. 2002*

Friends and associates will hear the Dragon say, "I told you so!" repeatedly this year, and Dragons will be rubbing their hands with glee as their chickens come home to roost. Dragon people will rake in the profits of past endeavors, but their lovers will feel ignored.

YEAR TREND: show loved ones you care

2002 YEAR OF THE HORSE *12 Feb. 2002 – 31 Jan. 2003*

This year has an unpredictable quality about it that Dragons will not find displeasing, as they like thinking on their feet and are adaptable enough to capitalize handsomely on its vagaries. The diary will be full and the Dragon love life turns on the heat.

YEAR TREND: it's party time!

2003 YEAR OF THE SHEEP
1 Feb. 2003 – 21 Jan. 2004

After the relentless onslaught of the Horse Year, 2003 will come as a relief and give Dragons time to draw breath. Dragon people should take every opportunity to rest and recuperate. For those who can get away, romance beckons in distant places.

YEAR TREND: a time for tying up loose ends

2004 YEAR OF THE MONKEY
22 Jan. 2004 – 8 Feb. 2005

Events happen thick and fast this year and many opportunities come the Dragon's way. However, they should not leave too much to chance, nor overstretch resources. A bit of give and take will help to smooth relationships.

YEAR TREND: put loved ones first

2005 YEAR OF THE ROOSTER *9 Feb. 2005 – 28 Jan. 2006*

In Rooster years Dragons make meteoric advances in their lives. Whether it's fame and fortune, position and power, status and prestige, or love and romance they seek, with Lady Luck positively smiling on them throughout 2005, how can they fail to succeed?

YEAR TREND: a time of superlative achievement

2006 YEAR OF THE DOG
29 Jan. 2006 – 17 Feb. 2007

A tricky year, when Dragons must practice patience and learn to count to ten before they speak hastily. Any hitches and setbacks at work are more than offset by a settled and contented home life.

YEAR TREND: keep a low profile

2007 YEAR OF THE PIG
18 Feb. 2007 – 6 Feb. 2008

A highly productive and progressive year, in which Dragons can make up any ground they might have lost last year. Chances are they could come into some money. Socially, the scene is exciting, with plenty of invitations and parties to keep Dragons amused.

YEAR TREND: the unexpected comes up trumps!

ABOVE *The Year of the Pig will be party year for Dragon people.*

SNAKE FORTUNES FOR THE YEARS AHEAD

1996 YEAR OF THE RAT *19 Feb. 1996 – 7 Feb. 1997*
Though not fast-paced creatures, Snakes will find the lively scenario presented by this year invigorating, as it inspires them to spark off new ideas. If they want to pursue different avenues, this is a good time to seize the opportunities that the year has in store.

YEAR TREND: a busy year

1997 YEAR OF THE OX *8 Feb. 1997 – 27 Jan. 1998*
This will be an auspicious year for Snakes, with a steady pace that is highly conducive to the Snake nature. Snakes will get results at work and in their personal lives by allowing the Snake's innate intuitive faculties free rein and by acting on their hunches.

YEAR TREND: strike while the iron is hot

1998 YEAR OF THE TIGER *28 Jan. 1998 – 15 Feb. 1999*
Tiger Years are often fraught with furious activity and hidden dangers, which is inimical to Snakes. So 1998 will not be an easy time for Snake people and they should stay on the sidelines until the stampede is over. Emotions, too, are volatile.

YEAR TREND: keep a low profile

1999 YEAR OF THE RABBIT *16 Feb. 1999 – 4 Feb. 2000*
This is a time for Snakes to shake out their glad rags and head for the bright lights. Socializing and attending cultural events will take up a lot of their time, especially if they are connected with the beauty business. Snakes should beware entanglements or sexual intrigue, as indiscretion could cost them dearly.

YEAR TREND: a time for prudence and circumspection

2000 YEAR OF THE DRAGON *5 Feb. 2000 – 23 Jan. 2001*
Last year's rumors rumble on and add fuel to the rollercoaster of events of this dramatic year. Snakes, who thrive on tranquillity, will find the atmosphere unsettling, but they should take heart, conserve strength and money, and wait for the hubbub to blow over.

YEAR TREND: watch and wait

2001 YEAR OF THE SNAKE *24 Jan. 2001 – 11 Feb. 2002*
This is the Snake's own year – a time when major advances can be made and Snake people's efforts come to fruition. Ambitions can be realized now and talents rewarded. Snakes should acknowledge those who love and support them as they rise up the ladder.

YEAR TREND: personally satisfying

2002 YEAR OF THE HORSE *12 Feb. 2002 – 31 Jan. 2003*
This year, occupational matters are likely to fare much better than affairs of the heart. At work Snakes can make good progress, but need to curb those Machiavellian tactics that they are so fond of. Love affairs may cause the Snake grief.

YEAR TREND: keep all your dealings above board

2003 YEAR OF THE SHEEP *1 Feb. 2003 – 21 Jan. 2004*
Sticking to the tried and tested this year will yield results. Snake people should put major new plans aside for another year, when they will enjoy a more favorable reception. They need to maintain a high profile, though, because contacts they make now, both personally and professionally, will prove beneficial in the long run.

YEAR TREND: glamor brings success

2004 YEAR OF THE MONKEY *22 Jan. 2004 – 8 Feb. 2005*
Appearances can be deceptive in the Year of the Monkey. Snakes should check their facts and never underestimate colleagues, lovers, or opponents. Taking sides will only compound issues and compromise their integrity, but love ties will be strengthened and intimate relationships bring joy.

YEAR TREND: a time for sitting on the fence

2005 YEAR OF THE ROOSTER *9 Feb. 2005 – 28 Jan. 2006*
There may be early setbacks, but Snake people should not be demoralized; their prospects will improve as the year progresses. At work, their efforts will be rewarded. At home, harmony reigns and time spent with partners and loved ones will compensate for any upsets to worldly aspirations.

YEAR TREND: financially expensive but emotionally satisfying

2006 YEAR OF THE DOG *29 Jan. 2006 – 17 Feb. 2007*
This should be a year full of activity. Putting into practice ideas that have been on the back burner will bring results for Snakes now, and fresh initiatives will snowball and attract financial rewards, seemingly with little effort. A relaxation programme would be beneficial.

YEAR TREND: being security-minded pays off

2007 YEAR OF THE PIG *18 Feb. 2007 – 6 Feb. 2008*

For Snakes, 2007 could be a difficult year when for every three steps they take forward, they are compelled to take two back. However, any impulsive action to make up lost ground will only backfire. Romantically, occupationally, and financially, the best advice is simply to bide their time.

YEAR TREND: frustrating

HORSE FORTUNES FOR THE YEARS AHEAD

1996 YEAR OF THE RAT *19 Feb. 1996 – 7 Feb. 1997*

As this is their opposite sign, the Rat Year is likely to be a difficult year for the Horse. Problems and obstacles will dog the Horse's steps and slow down progress in almost every area. Romance is unsatisfactory and relationships cause conflict.

YEAR TREND: keep a low profile

1997 YEAR OF THE OX *8 Feb. 1997 – 27 Jan. 1998*

Last year's difficulties have the Horse champing at the bit and raring to go, but the Oxen trends still urge caution and Horses must consolidate their position rather than striking out in new directions.

YEAR TREND: love brings comfort

1998 YEAR OF THE TIGER *28 Jan. 1998 – 15 Feb. 1999*

At last you get the green light to forge ahead as the vibrant undercurrent to this year is highly conducive to the Horse's nature. Horse people will be partying through 1998, but, while the socializing brings useful contacts, it also cuts deep into the wallet.

YEAR TREND: take care of finances

1999 YEAR OF THE RABBIT *16 Feb. 1999 – 4 Feb. 2000*

For single Horses seeking a soul mate, romance is likely to be a bugbear this year. New relationships are mismatched, unfulfilling, or short-lived. Committed Horses fare a good deal better, and find contentment within the family.

YEAR TREND: take things easy

2000 YEAR OF THE DRAGON *5 Feb. 2000 – 23 Jan. 2001*

Unpredictable Dragon Years give plenty of scope to the Horse's inventive genius. Horses must be prepared to grab unexpected opportunities, to travel at the drop of a hat, and to cultivate people in high places. In love, Horses will find temptation is all around them.

YEAR TREND: stimulating

2001 YEAR OF THE SNAKE *24 Jan. 2001 – 11 Feb. 2002*

Clandestine romantic entanglements could well upset the applecart this year, with their consequent emotional scenes disturbing the Horse's peace of mind. Relationships in general could prove a minefield, and Horses must be circumspect in dealings with others.

YEAR TREND: beware interpersonal involvements

2002 YEAR OF THE HORSE *12 Feb. 2002 – 31 Jan. 2003*

This is the Horse's own year, when Horse people can confidently expand in all areas. New plans put into motion now will flourish and meet with approval. Horse folk should follow their instincts but avoid upsetting the status quo in their relationships.

YEAR TREND: a prosperous year

2003 YEAR OF THE SHEEP *1 Feb. 2003 – 21 Jan. 2004*

For the Horse, this is a year in which to stick to tried and tested ideas at work and put ambitious plans on the back burner. The Sheep's calming influence can help the Horse to cultivate peace and harmony with his or her loved ones.

YEAR TREND: steady progress

2004 YEAR OF THE MONKEY *22 Jan. 2004 – 8 Feb. 2005*

The lively pace of this Monkey year will suit the Horse's adventurous nature, so the Horse is likely to make great progress. Now is the time for Horses to push forward with those ambitious schemes – the more inventive and unusual, the better. True love beckons.

YEAR TREND: keep busy and stay confident

2005 YEAR OF THE ROOSTER *9 Feb. 2005 – 28 Jan. 2006*

Though the overall trends for 2005 are progressive, at work Horse people may not achieve as much as they wish. The secret is to maintain a steady pace and to advance slowly but surely. Social life, friendships, and romance make it all worthwhile.

YEAR TREND: short breaks bring much joy

2006 YEAR OF THE DOG *29 Jan. 2006 – 17 Feb. 2007*

An auspicious year for Horse people, when they can forge ahead and make excellent progress. Work, academic studies, and sporting activities all bring their rewards and recognition. Stabilizing new relationships, getting married, or moving home bring success.

YEAR TREND: optimism rules

2007 YEAR OF THE PIG *18 Feb. 2007 – 6 Feb. 2008*

Money matters come to the forefront this year because finances are positively buoyant. But what comes in goes out just as easily as domestic expenses prove a drain on resources. In love matters, the Horse should make his or her feelings known.

YEAR TREND: financially, keep one step ahead

SHEEP FORTUNES FOR THE YEARS AHEAD

1996 YEAR OF THE RAT *19 Feb. 1996 – 7 Feb. 1997*

In Rat years, Sheep can make good headway both professionally and personally. The trends are very much in the Sheep's favor and there will be openings and opportunities for advancement. Meeting new people this year could lead to the blossoming of true love.

YEAR TREND: steady progress

1997 YEAR OF THE OX   8 Feb. 1997 – 27 Jan. 1998

Antagonistic elements are likely to thwart the Sheep's progress in 1997. The Ox is the opposite sign, so Sheep can expect challenge on all fronts. It would be a good idea to maintain a low profile and shelve ambitious plans.

YEAR TREND: uncongenial

1998 YEAR OF THE TIGER   28 Jan. 1998 – 15 Feb. 1999

It will be tough for Sheep to keep up with events in 1998, but at least the trends are not negative. Sheep will be kept busy interweaving all the various strands in their lives but, though at times bewildering, the year will certainly be interesting.

YEAR TREND: somewhat bemusing

1999 YEAR OF THE RABBIT   16 Feb. 1999 – 4 Feb. 2000

This promises to be a pleasing year, with both the pace and atmosphere congenial to the Sheep's nature. Now Sheep can make easy progress, and their achievements will bring satisfaction. Romance is highlighted this year.

YEAR TREND: excellent prospects

2000 YEAR OF THE DRAGON   5 Feb. 2000 – 23 Jan. 2001

Fasten your seatbelt, Sheep people, because this is going to be a bumpy ride – not that events will necessarily be unpleasant, but Sheep will be expected to sustain the pressure just to keep their heads above water. Intimate relationships, however, bring solace and support.

YEAR TREND: mixed blessings

2001 YEAR OF THE SNAKE   24 Jan. 2001 – 11 Feb. 2002

The excellent auspices of the Snake will present Sheep with many opportunities in which to spread their wings. At work, past efforts will be recognized and rewarded. Progress will seem effortless, and socially, Sheep will be popular.

YEAR TREND: extremely satisfying

2002 YEAR OF THE HORSE   12 Feb. 2002 – 31 Jan. 2003

This year brings highs and lows in affairs of the heart. The trends are in the Sheep's favor, so Sheep should be able to negotiate any pitfalls in their path.

YEAR TREND: leisure pursuits pay dividends

2003 YEAR OF THE SHEEP   1 Feb. 2003 – 21 Jan. 2004

Although this, their own year, is an auspicious one all around for Sheep, it is their social life that will keep them especially busy and buoyant throughout 2003. The emphasis during this year will be on domestic affairs and personal relationships. For single Sheep, romance is definitely on the cards.

YEAR TREND: be practical

2004 YEAR OF THE MONKEY   22 Jan. 2004 – 8 Feb. 2005

Monkey years, notorious for their racy turn of events, are not compatible with the Sheep's nature, which prefers a slower tempo. Consequently, the shifting sands of 2004 will present Sheep people with many minor but irksome difficulties, and gremlins will undermine their relationships.

YEAR TREND: frustrating misunderstandings

2005 YEAR OF THE ROOSTER   9 Feb. 2005 – 28 Jan. 2006

If last year tied Sheep in knots, this year gives them the opportunity to unravel all the tangles and make a fresh start. Responsibilities that have weighed heavily, or burdens that the Sheep has been carrying at work, may now be shed successfully. Leisure and pleasure beckon the Sheep onward.

YEAR TREND: a time of new beginnings

2006 YEAR OF THE DOG   29 Jan. 2006 – 17 Feb. 2007

Dog years are generally difficult for Sheep, so they are likely to find 2006 a challenging time. Sheep need to keep a low profile, but should not bow out of the fray altogether. Success comes, as always, by getting the balance right.

YEAR TREND: acknowledge lovers and supporters

2007 YEAR OF THE PIG   18 Feb. 2007 – 6 Feb. 2008

A much happier and more satisfying time than of late is on the cards for Sheep this year. At work, forward planning brings results, and a windfall could come the Sheep's way. This will be an excellent year for getting married or starting a family.

YEAR TREND: brighter prospects in store

MONKEY FORTUNES FOR THE YEARS AHEAD

1996 YEAR OF THE RAT   19 Feb. 1996 – 7 Feb. 1997

Monkeys can use the good auspices of the Rat year to expand their ideas, to promote ambitions and projects that are close to their hearts. This is a lucky time for them and gives Monkeys every opportunity to succeed in almost anything they attempt.

YEAR TREND: go for it!

1997 YEAR OF THE OX   8 Feb. 1997 – 27 Jan. 1998

Consolidation is the name of the game this year; the tempo at work will slow down, giving Monkeys more time to concentrate on their personal lives. Future plans and worldly aspirations should be put on hold while the Monkey spends quality time with loved ones.

YEAR TREND: moderate progress

1998 YEAR OF THE TIGER   28 Jan. 1998 – 15 Feb. 1999

Tiger years are never easy times for Monkeys, and pushing themselves or their plans forward now will only attract hostility. Under such unfavorable conditions, their best bet is just to work as steadily and calmly as they can.

YEAR TREND: keep a low profile

1999 YEAR OF THE RABBIT *16 Feb. 1999 – 4 Feb. 2000*

A brighter year than last, and Monkeys will feel the forces are with them rather than against them. New ideas will be favorably received and opportunities arise unexpectedly. There are excellent auguries for moving or refurbishing the Monkey home.

YEAR TREND: creativity brings success

2000 YEAR OF THE DRAGON *5 Feb. 2000 – 23 Jan. 2001*

Everything about the Dragon year is suited to the Monkey's mentality and ambitions. Monkeys put their ideas across confidently and their efforts meet with success. Recognition and career advancement are assured. A romantic meeting promises enduring love.

YEAR TREND: thrilling

2001 YEAR OF THE SNAKE *24 Jan. 2001 – 11 Feb. 2002*

Although Monkeys will undoubtedly make headway, behind-the-scenes activity may well undermine progress in their careers. They need to be aware or else they could find themselves beaten at the very last minute. Relationships are equally unsettled, but friends see the Monkey through.

YEAR TREND: disappointing

2002 YEAR OF THE HORSE *12 Feb. 2002 – 31 Jan. 2003*

This will be a fortunate year for Monkeys, with some lucky opportunities and perhaps a windfall landing in their laps. Monkeys will enjoy the fast tempo of events, but are warned to moderate over-confidence and impulsive action.

YEAR TREND: generally happy and lucky

ABOVE *In love and in friendships, Monkeys should think before they speak.*

2003 YEAR OF THE SHEEP *1 Feb. 2003 – 21 Jan. 2004*

Occupationally, this year will bring plenty of opportunity for Monkeys to make money, and for traveling and widening their network of contacts. The down side of the year is that relationships could prove problematic unless Monkeys think before they speak.

YEAR TREND: let sleeping dogs lie

2004 YEAR OF THE MONKEY *22 Jan. 2004 – 8 Feb. 2005*

In this, the Monkey's own year, Monkey people will be popular with friends and acquaintances seeking out their company. If a Monkey is looking for that special person with whom to spend the rest of his or her life, this could be a good year.

YEAR TREND: a time of real progress

2005 YEAR OF THE ROOSTER *9 Feb. 2005 – 28 Jan. 2006*

If Monkeys put in the work, they can be sure that their efforts will be repaid handsomely this year. They need to mix pleasure with business to relieve the hectic schedule that 2005 has in store. Love, relationships, and emotions are stable.

YEAR TREND: busy and constructive

2006 YEAR OF THE DOG *29 Jan. 2006 – 17 Feb. 2007*

The pace continues relentlessly, and though luck is on the Monkey's side, Monkeys are advised to scrutinize the small print in any business dealings as fraud and trickery are about this year. Otherwise, this is an auspicious time for those contemplating marriage.

YEAR TREND: If in doubt, leave it out

2007 YEAR OF THE PIG *18 Feb. 2007 – 6 Feb. 2008*

Carelessness and impatience are the Monkey's bugbears this year, but application and an astute sense of timing will ensure success. Relationships warm their hearts.

YEAR TREND: care and attention bring results

ROOSTER FORTUNES FOR THE YEARS AHEAD

1996 YEAR OF THE RAT *19 Feb. 1996 – 7 Feb. 1997*

Rat years are never easy for Roosters, so 1996 is likely to present them with a few hurdles. Career progress is slow and patchy, and heavy expenses may have Roosters dipping into their hard-earned savings. Relationships, too, create difficulties.

YEAR TREND: keep a low profile

1997 YEAR OF THE OX *8 Feb. 1997 – 27 Jan. 1998*

In this auspicious period for Roosters they can recoup last year's losses. At work they make progress by leaps and bounds, their endeavors reaping rewards. The Rooster's prestige and reputation increase. Emotional ties bring joy.

YEAR TREND: expect openings and opportunities

LEFT *The Year of the Dragon
could be the year of a crucial love
affair for Roosters.*

2003 YEAR OF THE SHEEP *1 Feb. 2003 – 21 Jan. 2004*
A promising year in which Roosters can bring many projects to
fruition, advance their worldly expectations, and see some very satisfying results for their endeavors. Roosters should relax with their
loved ones but also get out and about to extend their social networks.
YEAR TREND: pleasing developments

2004 YEAR OF THE MONKEY *22 Jan. 2004 – 8 Feb. 2005*
Though opportunities abound for career advancement, problems on
the home front will need careful handling this year. Single Rooster-
born folk will fare a good deal better than their married counterparts as personal relationships blossom.
YEAR TREND: keep an eye behind the scenes

2005 YEAR OF THE ROOSTER *9 Feb. 2005 – 28 Jan. 2006*
This is the Rooster's own year. Roosters will feel confident and
relaxed under their own Rooster auspices. Now they can promote
existing plans and projects at work, although new ventures should be
put on hold. Domestic affairs bring rewards.
YEAR TREND: believe in yourself

2006 YEAR OF THE DOG
29 Jan. 2006 – 17 Feb. 2007
For Roosters, this is a year for getting their
shoulders to the wheel to ensure success.
Unprofessional conduct, poor workmanship,
or taking short-cuts is likely to backfire.
Talking through problems could save
a Rooster's relationship.
YEAR TREND: don't take risks

2007 YEAR OF THE PIG
18 Feb. 2007 – 6 Feb. 2008
After last year's frustrating grind,
the Year of the Pig brings
distinct improvement to both
career matters and domestic
affairs. With romantic ties
strengthening and relationships flourishing, the
prospects bode well for
weddings and births.
YEAR TREND: financial
pressures ease

ABOVE *The last year in the
cycle will be a happy one at
work and at home.*

1998 YEAR OF THE TIGER *28 Jan. 1998 – 15 Feb. 1999*
Events happen thick and fast in Tiger years, requiring quick wits and
lightning decisions. As long as Roosters keep on top of the action,
they will come out winning in 1998. Now is the time to set plans in
motion and consider long-term ambitions.
YEAR TREND: commitment brings satisfaction

1999 YEAR OF THE RABBIT *16 Feb. 1999 – 4 Feb. 2000*
Rabbit years encourage Roosters to overspend, so that by the end of
the decade they could find themselves seriously broke. Moderating
their outlook and expectations minimizes disappointment financially,
occupationally, and romantically.
YEAR TREND: teamwork brings results

2000 YEAR OF THE DRAGON *5 Feb. 2000 –
23 Jan. 2001*
This is a high spot in the 12-year cycle, when Roosters are
given the opportunity to shine. Favorable aspects now
encourage the Rooster to make great advances, which bring
prosperity and recognition. Intimate partnerships blossom.
YEAR TREND: let your hair down

2001 YEAR OF THE SNAKE *24 Jan. 2001 –
11 Feb. 2002*
Last year's favorable auspices sweep the Rooster along
through the Year of the Snake, too. Good fortune smiles
on those Roosters involved in the arts, the world of music,
fashion, or anything to do with the beauty industry.
YEAR TREND: progressive

2002 YEAR OF THE HORSE *12 Feb. 2002 – 31 Jan. 2003*
Typical of the erratic nature of the Horse, this will be a year of ups
and downs for the Rooster, although the pluses will balance out the
minuses. Romantic liaisons and family life all suffer from the same
volatile influences.
YEAR TREND: mixed fortunes

DOG FORTUNES FOR THE YEARS AHEAD

1996 YEAR OF THE RAT   *19 Feb. 1996 – 7 Feb. 1997*

An all-around prosperous and auspicious year for Dogs in which they can make good progress and advance their worldly aspirations. Though Dogs are conservative and not known to be lovers of change, this is a time for something different. Any new schemes the Dog person initiates or new directions he or she takes now will find favor and bring success.

YEAR TREND: expansion holds the key

1997 YEAR OF THE OX   *8 Feb. 1997 – 27 Jan. 1998*

Dogs should leave new plans to bubble away on the back burner this year, since pushing themselves forwards in Oxen Years will only attract ill-will. They should concentrate on matters closer to home instead, and spend quality time with their nearest and dearest. Simple pleasures bring happiness.

YEAR TREND: cultivate your garden

1998 YEAR OF THE TIGER   *28 Jan. 1998 – 15 Feb. 1999*

Now is the time for Dogs to give those new ideas an airing if they want them to reap rewards. Past efforts and hard work will be recognized by superiors who will support the Dog's aims and facilitate his or her progress. If looking for romance, Dogs could meet their soulmate this year.

YEAR TREND: a busy time

1999 YEAR OF THE RABBIT   *16 Feb. 1999 – 4 Feb. 2000*

Despite the Dog's preference for the status quo, any fresh starts that Dog people decide to make in the Year of the Rabbit will ultimately prove successful. Now is the time to consider making changes or changing courses. Whether it is changing jobs, starting a business, moving home, getting married or having a baby, Dogs will find that luck and good fortune are on their side.

YEAR TREND: ambitions are fulfilled

2000 YEAR OF THE DRAGON   *5 Feb. 2000 – 23 Jan. 2001*

Dragon Years are never the easiest of times for Dog folk. The dramatic nature of the year presents them with several hurdles that have to be negotiated, and the atmosphere of high tension brings out their anxieties. It's best for Dogs to keep their heads down and follow the pack this year.

YEAR TREND: watch your finances

2001 YEAR OF THE SNAKE   *24 Jan. 2001 – 11 Feb. 2002*

After the turmoil of last year, Dogs will find this a much more favorable period and one that offers plenty of opportunities to stabilize their position. There will be success at work and the Dog's efforts will be recognized, but spending time at home with family and loved ones will bring deep contentment.

YEAR TREND: satisfying

2002 YEAR OF THE HORSE   *12 Feb. 2002 – 31 Jan. 2003*

This will be another favourable and busy year. With so much to do and so many places to visit, a Dog's feet will hardly have time to touch the ground. Socially, too, Dogs are in for a whirlwind of a time, and whether they are at work or at play, the emphasis will be on expanding their horizons and having fun.

YEAR TREND: auspicious and progressive

2003 YEAR OF THE SHEEP   *1 Feb. 2003 – 21 Jan. 2004*

In Sheep years the emphasis falls on home and family. Domestically, Dogs are likely to encounter difficulties, because repairs to their house may cost a lot. A move is on the cards, and this will prove beneficial retrospectively. Loved ones are supportive.

YEAR TREND: difficult but heart-warming

2004 YEAR OF THE MONKEY   *22 Jan. 2004 – 8 Feb. 2005*

Last year's domestic problems rumble on, and a change of residence becomes imminent. Nevertheless, Dogs will make better progress now, and by the end of 2004 they should find themselves in stronger positions both materially and occupationally. The Monkey influence means that the Dog's social life is buzzing.

YEAR TREND: keep a high profile

2005 YEAR OF THE ROOSTER   *9 Feb. 2005 – 28 Jan. 2006*

Events occur thick and fast throughout 2005, and no sooner has the Dog dealt with one crisis than another problem lands in his or her lap. But Dogs also have some remarkably lucky breaks this year to even the score. So, if you are a Dog, accentuate the positive with those golden opportunities that will highlight the year.

YEAR TREND: ups and downs

2006 YEAR OF THE DOG   *29 Jan. 2006 – 17 Feb. 2007*

The Dog's own year promises to be an auspicious time when Dogs can recoup many of the losses they have incurred in recent times. Whatever their ambitions, they will find plenty of scope for making rapid progress and attaining the recognition they deserve.

YEAR TREND: a time of steady increase

2007 YEAR OF THE PIG   *18 Feb. 2007 – 6 Feb. 2008*

The Year of the Pig promises welcome ease and contentment. A legal, financial, or health problem that has been hanging over many a Dog is soon resolved, giving way to a sense of peace and well-being. Dogs will feel that they have now turned the corner, and that the future is looking rosy. Relationships bring joy.

YEAR TREND: a time to relax

PIG FORTUNES FOR THE YEARS AHEAD

1996 YEAR OF THE RAT *19 Feb. 1996 – 7 Feb. 1997*

Rat years herald a fresh start and new opportunities, and this has a destabilizing effect on the Pig. Pigs prefer a settled atmosphere, so the sense of shifting sands may disturb their peace of mind. Take heart, though, it isn't all bleak, and you will win through.

YEAR TREND: think positive

1997 YEAR OF THE OX *8 Feb. 1997 – 27 Jan. 1998*

A bright and hopeful year in which the Pig's innate talents come to the fore. Pigs should now listen to their intuition and, though they should avoid financial risks, they should begin laying foundations for the future. Family life is happy but romance could prove unstable.

YEAR TREND: follow your instincts

1998 YEAR OF THE TIGER *28 Jan. 1998 – 15 Feb. 1999*

The quickening pulse of the Tiger Year is not well suited to the Pig's laid-back nature, so Pigs could be confronted with many situations that will try their patience. Money and personal relationships are particularly problematic. People may not be trustworthy this year.

YEAR TREND: keep your head down

1999 YEAR OF THE RABBIT *16 Feb. 1999 – 4 Feb. 2000*

This year comes as balm to soothe a Pig's wounds. At work, progress is made by leaps and bounds; at home, the Pig person feels much more settled and happier than of late. It's a time to celebrate and to enjoy life.

YEAR TREND: things are looking up

2000 YEAR OF THE DRAGON *5 Feb. 2000 – 23 Jan. 2001*

One or two unusual events are likely to punctuate the year, bringing highlights to an otherwise steady and settled 12-month period. Socializing, attending cultural functions, and maintaining a high profile will not only extend the Pig's network of contacts, but will also attract valuable allies.

YEAR TREND: pleasing prospects

2001 YEAR OF THE SNAKE *24 Jan. 2001 – 11 Feb. 2002*

Snake years are notorious for producing an atmosphere of uneasiness and disquiet that affects everyone in one form or another. For the Pig, the focus falls on family affairs, where scandal or loss may disturb the pattern of life. Expenditure needs to be controlled.

YEAR TREND: a time for taking stock

2002 YEAR OF THE HORSE *12 Feb. 2002 – 31 Jan. 2003*

A busy year in which the Pig can recoup any past losses and make steady headway. At work, earlier efforts will now be rewarded, giving Pigs a well-deserved sense of optimism and well-being. Family life will be pleasant and prosperous.

YEAR TREND: pleasing results

2003 YEAR OF THE SHEEP *1 Feb. 2003 – 21 Jan. 2004*

Although at work progress is generally slow at the moment, Sheep years are auspicious times for the Pig in love and marriage. Since Pigs thrive in an atmosphere of domestic tranquillity and contentment, they should find that, emotionally, 2003 will be an immensely fulfilling and satisfying time for them.

YEAR TREND: relationships bring happiness

2004 YEAR OF THE MONKEY *22 Jan. 2004 – 8 Feb. 2005*

Not the easiest of years for Pigs, mainly because they will find it hard to make ends meet. A lack of support from those around them adds to the feeling of life being an uphill struggle. Romance, however, lightens the load considerably, especially for new lovers.

YEAR TREND: modest gains

2005 YEAR OF THE ROOSTER *9 Feb. 2005 – 28 Jan. 2006*

It looks as if the Pig's money problems should iron themselves out this year, but Pigs are warned not to take any financial risks. In business, progress could be erratic and there will be hurdles to be jumped that require careful negotiation. Relationships, too, will be prone to suffer from underlying tensions.

YEAR TREND: an uphill struggle

2006 YEAR OF THE DOG *29 Jan. 2006 – 17 Feb. 2007*

This year improves as it advances; early difficulties give way to later triumphs. Now is a good time to review your aims and objectives if you are a Pig, and to start making plans for the future. This is a particularly auspicious time for Pig people to consider marriage, moving, or starting a family.

YEAR TREND: improved circumstances

2007 YEAR OF THE PIG *18 Feb. 2007 – 6 Feb. 2008*

This is the year in which the Pig can make excellent progress in many areas of life. Plans put into motion last year come to fruition now and any residual domestic or relationship problems can be ironed out. The good auspices favor marriage or moving home.

YEAR TREND: happy times

Index